HOW TO MANAGE A SUCCESSFUL CATERING BUSINESS

MANFRED KETTERER

HAYDEN BOOK COMPANY, INC.
Rochelle Park, New Jersey

To Krista and Robert

Library of Congress Cataloging in Publication Data

Ketterer, Manfred.
  How to manage a successful catering business.

  Includes index.
  1. Caterers and catering—Management. I. Title.
TX911.3.M27K47   642.4
ISBN 0-8104-9482-5

Printed in the United States of America

1	2	3	4	5	6	7	8	9	PRINTING

82 83 84 85 86 87 88 89 90   YEAR

ACKNOWLEDGMENTS

No career or book can be successful without the assistance of others. The number of my business associates and teachers through the years is too extensive to list, but I would like to thank each of them for their time and patience. Through this book their teaching continues. I thank my wife, Grace, for her encouragement throughout and her long and tedious hours of typing; Henry Woods, who helped me prepare this work for publishing; Louise Danielenko for her rare talent and attention in organizing the material; Rabbi Simon for his review and suggestions pertaining to kosher matters; and Mr. Dale Dunivan of King Arthur, Inc., for his review of the chapter on function room furniture.

CONTENTS

Introduction

A caterer performs a variety of tasks ranging from preparing and delivering a simple tray of hors d'oeuvres to organizing a banquet for thousands of people complete with a nine course menu, bar and table beverages, and appropriate service. Whatever the size of the function, the caterer must manage it flawlessly. To orchestrate a successful event, the caterer must draw upon his training, experience, and talents. This book will discuss the many factors involved in organizing functions and try to shed some light on the procedures and problems that become part of the daily life of every caterer.

The primary concern of all caterers is to provide customers with excellent food, beverages, service, and equipment. By doing this consistently the caterer will build and maintain a solid reputation and ensure a successful business. Simultaneously, the caterer owes it to himself and the people in his employ to make the maximum profit while providing the customer with full value for his dollar.

To obtain the necessary training before one enters the catering business it is recommended that he first attend a culinary school to acquire the basic knowledge and techniques of proper food preparation, service, and management, and second that he work for at least one year with one or more reputable caterers in the area in which he intends to start a business.

Adequate schooling and practical experience will save the potential caterer countless hours of trial and error, and, by avoiding mistakes, it will save him a great deal of money. Time spent in school and on the job will also allow him to build confidence in constructing and preparing proper menus. In addition, he will be able to make the necessary contacts with purveyors, enabling him to later buy the appropriate merchandise at the best price and quality. Work experience as a supervisor will give him the necessary composure and skill to manage a complete affair from start to finish. By working, the prospective caterer will be able to evaluate the area in which he intends to start his business, test the existing demand for services, and estimate the volume of business needed for success.

Catering is a profitable business that has grown at a steady pace since World War II. This growth is attributed to increased individual incomes as well as the entrance of both husbands and wives into the labor market. As the demand by individuals and corporations for catering services increased, more and more on- and off-premise catering operations entered this high-profit business. Newly constructed hotels and catering establishments began to include adequate banquet facilities, enabling them to capitalize on the growing demand and high profit margins.

Catering is still expanding and growing. This book analyzes why catering is so popular and shows the reader how to make it profitable.

SECTION I

Overview

You've made the decision to go into the catering business. What precisely is involved?

This section answers that question in general terms and discusses the primary considerations in setting up a catering operation. Since the success of any catering establishment depends on careful planning and efficient design, the better part of this initial section concentrates on these important points. But first, let's consider why catering is a viable business venture in today's economy.

Chapter 1

Advantages of the Catering Business

Catering is one of the simplest ways of making money in the foodservice industry. Why? Primarily because it is a volume business in which food is sold, and to a certain degree paid for, *before* it is prepared. Thus, a catered affair is a known and consequently controllable business transaction that generates a sizable profit.

Many clear-cut advantages over other branches of the foodservice industry stem from this condition. Among these advantages are:

1. Deposits
2. Controllable food costs
3. Controllable labor costs
4. Controllable energy costs
5. Limited inventories
6. Additional revenues
7. Accurate forecasting
8. Low initial investment
9. Business by contract
10. Direct-payment system
11. "Free" advertising

Deposits

Caterers can solicit a deposit from a customer as a binder to the contract or agreement. The policy of most caterers is to request an initial deposit or down payment ranging from 10 to 25% of the total estimated cost of a function, or an initial per-person down payment, for example, $2.00 for each prospective guest. Most caterers require additional deposits at intervals from the signing of the initial contract to the date of the function. In instances in which a caterer has earned a superior reputation or there is an exceptional demand for his facilities, he may require payment of the entire amount prior to the affair. Some caterers feel that asking for prepayment of the entire amount is an excessive and unfair demand and usually require no more than 50% advance payment. Without question, though, all caterers do require some form of deposit to defray the food, equipment, and labor expenses incurred prior to the date of the function.

The collection of deposits creates certain benefits for the caterer: (1) It provides working capital and a constant cash flow. (2) Because of the fear of losing a deposit, customers are less apt to cancel an affair without a serious reason. (3) In the event of cancellation, the caterer's loss is reduced.

Certain circumstances dictate waiving the customary deposit. For example, a customer or firm that has generated a substantial amount of repeat business may only be required to sign a letter to confirm the arrangements.

Controllable Food Costs

Because the number of guests for an affair is known in advance, the exact amount of food can be ordered. Adherence to strict portion control procedures can eliminate waste. Food costs are thus manageable.

The high-volume nature of catering establishes buying power at the market. With advance planning, purchases can be made at the lowest price for the highest quality. Many caterers save additional money by buying and transporting their own purchases directly from the market. This eliminates the expense of dealing through purveyors.

Controllable Labor Costs

Low and controllable labor costs can be established by hiring only those service personnel who will be needed for a function. The exact working hours and schedules of these workers can be determined in advance. Only "key" personnel need be hired on a full-time basis. Additional labor is employed only if there is business to warrant it. Because much of the catering is done on weekends or in seasonally peak periods, a readily available part-time labor market is vital. People such as teachers, housewives, and students often supplement their regular incomes by working functions on a per diem basis, providing the caterer with an inexpensive source of labor. These part-time, on-call workers customarily command lower wages, fewer raises, and less fringe benefits than regular, full-time employees.

No great skill is needed to work on a catered affair. A well-planned yet simple training program can easily provide inexperienced but willing employees with all the proficiency they will need to build confidence and composure. Of course, close supervision is essential. Dividing the staff into partnerships or teams can help distribute inexperienced personnel among the more seasoned veterans.

Controllable Energy Costs

Energy costs from lighting, heat, air-conditioning, ventilation, etc., can be cut or controlled because function rooms will be closed when there are no bookings. Energy costs in the kitchen can be curtailed by establishing efficient preparation and production schedules.

Limited Inventories

Since only food and equipment for each scheduled occasion need be available, low inventories can be carried. Of course, certain staple food items should always be on hand, but only those perishable food items that will be immediately used ought to be purchased. Ideally, inventories on many products will be zero immediately after an affair takes place. This zero level can be maintained until another party is catered.

Additional Revenues

Caterers often receive additional revenues by contracting outside professional services for the client, such as photographers, florists, or musicians. The caterer is usually paid a commission or a flat fee for arranging these ancillary or auxiliary services.

A secondary business such as a restaurant or bar may be connected to a catering facility. These side enterprises will often increase sales from exposure to the large number of guests present at most catered functions.

Accurate Forecasting

Accurate forecasting of sales and profits is available through predetermined business scheduled weeks and months in advance. This information will be especially important when expansion, physical improvement, or capital expenditure is planned.

Catered affairs generally take place on schedule. Since the cancellation of a catered function creates a hardship for the organization and guests as well as the caterer (tickets sold, invitations sent, etc.), a cancellation due to inclement weather and the like seldom occurs unless extreme conditions prevail.

Low Initial Investment

It is common for a catering business to start small and grow as the demand for services increases. Thus, limited capital is required to get started on a small scale. Early investment can be kept low by obtaining needed equipment on a rental basis. Payrolls can be minimized through owner participation in kitchen or service activities. Limiting the initial investment also limits the risk in the event the business fails.

Business by Contract

Signed contracts are used for all catered functions. Contracts guarantee in advance a specific number of guests. Charges and plans can be made accordingly. Conditions can be included in the contract to protect the caterer against such problems as negligence by the patron or cancellation of the affair. Also, contracts for guaranteed future bookings can be used as collateral when business loans are negotiated.

Direct-Payment System

Deposits and final payments at the completion of a function are generally made in lump sums by check or money order directly to the owner or his salesman. By eliminating numerous cash transactions, the handling of payments becomes manageable and complex control systems become unnecessary.

"Free" Advertising

A great deal of "free" advertising is provided to the caterer by the client who announces and promotes his own function in the media. Celebrities, politicians, and other influential guests are often invited to all types of business, religious, social, and charitable functions. These affairs frequently receive attention from the press and help imprint the caterer's name on the mind of the public. Finally, what could be better advertising than the plaudits of satisfied guests being repeated over and over again to friends and acquaintances.

Chapter 2

Financial and Legal Considerations

There is more to the catering business than just offering fine food and impeccable service and making a profit. The professional caterer, like any other businessman, must also concern himself with a myriad of financial and legal matters, such as the kinds of taxes he will have to pay, the types of insurances he must carry to adequately protect his employees and his business, and the federal, state, and local laws that apply to his operation.

Even the most astute caterer, however, may find his business in jeopardy because of legal or financial oversights. A skillful attorney and an expert accountant are essential to counsel and assist with these matters. It is advisable that both these professionals have prior restaurant experience and show an active interest in the success of your operation by being readily available when needed.

Financial Considerations

A capable accountant will unquestionably save your operation money through his knowledge of accounting, controls, and sound fiscal management; by initiating legal tax benefits and business deductions; and by keeping accurate business records. An accountant will set up your business books as well as perform all the necessary accounting procedures. He will know what, to whom, and when reports must be made, in addition to what notices must be posted on your premises.

Caterers should be familiar with the Fair Labor Standards Act which establishes standards for minimum wage, overtime pay, equal pay, and child labor provisions. Caterers are also required by law to maintain current and accurate records of all transacted business. Federal, state, and local taxes must also be reported, collected, and paid on schedule. A system of recording payroll and sales information should be initiated and periodically analyzed by your accountant to determine the relationship (percentage) between payroll costs and total sales revenue.

An accountant will be able to prepare a budget to lend direction to your operation so that it can plan its future growth. A budget is used as a projection of estimated or expected income, expenses, and profit for a given period of time. It is usually prepared on an annual basis and can then be broken down on a quarterly, monthly, or even weekly basis. Realistic figures must be used to ensure accuracy; no guesswork should ever be used. If done properly, a budget will enable management to wisely make decisions as to how to spend its money to get the best results. For example, caterers often must determine whether it is better to buy prepared or fresh foods. With an accurate, current budget based on present conditions, it is possible to evaluate all the hidden costs of both alternatives, and to come to a conclusion as to the best return on your investment.

Operating costs must be constantly analyzed to determine if profits are high or low in relationship to the volume of sales incurred. Expense and sales records should be kept and compared to discover how your business is progressing on a daily, weekly, and monthly basis. Detailed information concerning amounts and percentages on food, beverage, labor, inventory, and overhead costs should be accurately compiled by your accountant.

By preparing a profit and loss statement and a balance sheet, a caterer will know how business is currently performing and what its financial condition is as of the last entry into the books. The profit and loss statement will list your income and deduct your expenses and as a result reveal your net profit or loss. A balance sheet will show your financial strength and also give an indication of the health of your business in relation to your assets, liabilities, and net worth. Both these forms are measurements of your business and should be studied closely to determine how, why, and where your finances are being apportioned. Your accountant should be able to intelligently compare one period of time to another and advise where weaknesses and strengths are evolving and to pinpoint any trends developing so that corrective action can be taken if needed.

The accountant will apply for a business identification number for sales and income taxes. Should a tax audit be conducted by any government agency, you should advise your accountant to be available for assistance.

There are many hints and suggestions your accountant will offer as time and business progresses. Questions and problems will arise and a close relationship and free exchange of information between you and your accountant is required to assure success.

Insurance

While an accountant can lend assistance concerning controllable financial circumstances, further safeguards must be taken to protect your business and its employees from uncontrollable, unforeseen occurrences. Whether you are conducting an on- or off-premise catering operation, adequate insurance coverage is imperative against all risks and hazards that may occur at your facility.

To find out how much and what types of insurance your business needs, seek the counsel of several insurance agents, brokers, or advisors. Do not be concerned only with the best price, but more important, opt for the best or maximum comprehensive coverage available for your particular needs. As a general rule, adequate insurance coverage should cost approximately 1 or 2% of your total sales. Be certain that you have all the necessary insurance coverage needed to protect yourself as well as what is required by law.

Various state and federal laws will mandate that your business be covered with several types and amounts of insurance. The following paragraphs describe the types of insurances that may pertain to your business. Each should be discussed with both your insurance agent and accountant to determine what specific requirements are needed for the best protection of your particular business.

For employee coverage the following insurances should be investigated in detail.

Worker's compensation is a type of insurance that an employer must fully pay to protect the employees from medical costs and loss of income, which may arise due to a work-related accident. Rates or premiums are based on the level of risk involved with the job. The employer pays a premium determined by total amount of payroll dollars and the number of employees, considering a past loss experience rate over a year's period. A reduction in premiums will be made for a low amount of claims attributable to safe working conditions. An increase will be made with a high number of claims due to hazardous conditions. Several states have different laws pertaining to the benefits of workman's compensation. Laws and rates pertaining to your state can be acquired by writing to the Superintendent of Documents, U.S. Government Printing Office, Washington, D.C. 20402. Some states will offer a choice of being insured through a private insurance company or through a state insurance fund. All employers should carry this injury insurance since the cost is relatively inexpensive in relation to the protection it offers. Be warned that where no coverage exists, employees who become injured on the job could sue heavily for damages.

Social security insurance (FICA) is retirement insurance paid by both employer and employee. A percentage of a salary (6.65% of the first $29,700 in 1981) is withheld from each worker's wage via payroll deduction. Congress can change the percentate and may extend coverage by initiating programs like Medicare. There are many benefits provided by this social insurance, some of which include guaranteed income for persons reaching the required retirement age (62 or 65); benefits to families in which death or disability of a breadwinner occurs; health insurance for the aged, etc.

State disability insurance is required by certain states and is similar in effect to workman's compensation in that it protects an employee by providing him with a percentage of his weekly wage in the event of an injury incurred off the job. There may be a maximum ceiling on the amount receivable per week, and the benefits usually last for a duration of 26 weeks, effectively starting about 8 days after terminating employment.

Unemployment insurance is carried in some states and provides an employee with a guaranteed income for loss of employment for just cause. This benefit lasts for a specific amount of time but may be extended at certain times by the federal government when the state employment benefits lapse. The employer pays the total amount of this insurance, in the form of a percentage of payroll taxes, with a maximum ceiling, which varies from state to state. The premium depends on the rate of former employees applying for and receiving unemployment insurance benefits. The more former employees receiving unemployment benefits, the higher the employer's rate.

For additional employee benefits, an employer may consider the following "fringe" insurances that may be paid partially or fully by the employer on an individual or group basis. Due to a lower risk factor when dealing in numbers, group plans may be purchased cheaper than the individual plans. By providing these insurance inducements, an employer will get the best and most qualified help available, help reduce expensive and costly turnover and training programs, and through the betterment of morale, help increase productivity and profit.

Life insurance is a policy that pays benefits to those named as beneficiaries upon the death of a policyholder. This insurance can also be purchased to protect against loss of a partner or owner in case of death.

Accident and health insurance covers employees against injuries or illness that occur off the job and are not related to the job. It will cover the loss of income and the expenses incurred due to an inability to work. This type of insurance when provided by an employer usually exceeds the benefits an employee may receive under a workman's compensation policy. It can offer protection from hospitalization and surgical costs, loss of income either on a set-dollar or on a percentage-of-salary basis, family medical expenses, accidental death, loss of limb, or other circumstances stated on the policy.

Pension and retirement insurance provides retirement income after a certain number of years with an employer or upon reaching a specified retirement age. Pension plans and funds vary as to coverage and terms and can be paid totally or partially by the employer and employee through payroll deduction.

Union welfare plan is usually negotiated with a contract for unionized workers and is paid by the employer. It usually provides coverage for hospitalization, group life insurance, pensions, welfare plans, and other fringes determined through labor–management negotiations.

To protect a caterer against claims by a customer, loss of business, or property damage, the following insurances should be carried:

General business insurance (carried by all businesses) will protect the caterer against most physical property losses from fire, lightening, smoke, theft, burglary, robbery, sprinkler leakage, water damage, boiler break-downs, bad debts, and other perils.

Building insurance can be carried if the caterer owns the building. It is protection against damage occurring to any permanent fixture belonging to or constituting a part of the building, and also to the machinery used in the service of the building such as air-conditioning and heating units, plumbing, or elevators. This policy usually pays for the present or used value of the damaged property, not its original value. If improvements are made on a building, a clause to cover them in the event of loss should be included in the policy.

Contents insurance covers all losses of the contents of the building that are not covered or insured under a building insurance policy.

Business interruption insurance reimburses a business for loss of income resulting from the operator's inability to conduct business in a normal fashion because of disruption caused by an accident to the boiler or other machinery listed in the policy. Coverage may include such items as rent, taxes, salaries, reopening costs, and interest or profits lost as a result of the business disruption.

Comprehensive general liability insurance covers a claim a customer may have against a caterer for personal or bodily injury incurred on or near the premise due to neglect. Claims may be due to bodily injury as a result of the following: falling on a wet floor; tripping on steps that are inadequately lit, or tripping on torn or defective carpeting.

Product liability insurance usually falls under the comprehensive general liability insurance coverage and protects a caterer against any claim due to contaminated or unsanitary foods and beverages due to employee neglect; for example, foreign objects or particles found in food or a ptomaine poisoning outbreak. This insurance also covers third-party liability, such as when convenience foods purchased for a function prove to be defective and a customer suit results.

To protect off-premise caterers, the following additional insurances should be considered:

Equipment insurance (floater policy) protects against damages to equipment when transported from job to job. To be fully covered, all items insured must be listed on the policy in order to make a claim.

Commercial truck accident insurance covers any suit due to liability of operator involving bodily injury or property damage to members of the public. There is also cargo insurance available that covers food supplies lost while in transit or when being loaded or unloaded from an insured truck. Comprehensive coverage will insure a vehicle against loss by fire, theft, or other physical damage such as broken windshields.

An accident report should be made out immediately after an accident occurs and submitted to the insurance carrier as quickly as possible for further investigation of claims.

To protect a caterer against employee wrongdoing or outside burglary, the following insurance can be purchased:

Fidelity bond insurance protects against loss of money, securities, or other property due to employee embezzlement or obstruction of funds or by outside burglary. It also covers against the disappearance or destruction of property by employees.

Depositor's forgery bond insurance protects a caterer against loss resulting from forgery or alteration of checks, bank deposits, notes, promises, or orders to pay issued by him. It also protects against any loss through the acceptance of these instruments from others.

To insure quick processing of all claims, the proper claim forms should be filled out completely and accurately with all requested information before being submitted to the insurance company. It is also advisable to contact your insurance agent or broker as soon as any serious accident or claim arises. Remember! It is your responsibility to prove financial loss when collection becomes necessary.

It is also advisable to discuss with your insurance agent ways to combine or reduce insurance rates by perhaps reviewing the overlapping coverage of policies or by installing or adding health and safety features to your establishment that will reduce the possibility of accidents or loss and should result in lower insurance costs.

Legal Considerations

A competent attorney is necessary to start and develop your business. It may be advisable to hire a local attorney familiar with all local zoning ordinances and laws. Leases, titles, contracts, property liens, licenses, permits, agreements, legal suits, and other legal matters do require the services of a knowledgable attorney and cannot be undertaken by the inexperienced without severe repercussions. Most attorneys are hired on a regular basis, since they are needed from time to time, but if they are frequently called for it may be advisable to employ an attorney on a retainer or set fee basis. Again, it becomes vital for any legal problem that an open dialogue be established to assure prompt solution.

Zoning Laws

Local zoning laws or ordinances should be investigated, studied, and strictly observed by the caterer at all times. Before any violations occur, there should be a three-way communication between the caterer, his attorney, and the local authorities responsible for zoning regulations. Each area or locality will vary as to the rigidity of enforcing its zoning laws, but violations can be costly, resulting in fines or temporary or permanent loss of business.

Some residential areas are extremely critical of large catering establishments with their high-volume business, since they create heavy traffic patterns and tend to disrupt the rural tone of a quiet neighborhood. A caterer may find that local residents or citizen groups will sign petitions of protest to try and block establishment or operation of your catering business in their area because they fear littering, noise, and reckless driving due to the late hours of operation and the serving of drinks.

Zoning variances may become impossible to obtain in some areas. If zoning is permitted, then local regulations may be enforced rigidly as to licensing and standards of operation. Some points worthy of investigation concerning zoning laws are as follows:

1. Type, size, and location of the business
2. Necessary licenses required to operate
3. Necessary building and fire codes, inspections, certificates, or permits required
4. Restrictions as to hours and days of operation
5. Restrictions as to noise and loitering of patrons
6. Storage restrictions
7. Size, type, and location of signs
8. Health and sanitation regulations
9. Parking restrictions
10. Commercial vehicle restrictions
11. Illumination of the premises

It is always advisable and advantageous to hire a local attorney well versed in the local zoning laws, rules, and regulations. Knowing the local government and its personnel and procedures can be a valuable asset for your business. In all cases, it is essential that a caterer make every effort to conform with all the local zoning laws, to avoid any ill will or adverse community relations.

Health Laws

Since he is dealing with the public selling of food, every caterer must have a Board of Health license. It is advisable that you visit your local health department to become acquainted with the officers, inspectors, and health regulations of your area. Inquiries should be made regarding the necessary applications for permits or licenses required to operate. Permits, licenses, and fees may vary according to type, size, classification, and location of your establishment. If all requirements are met, then a permit and license are issued.

Inspectors will then visit and issue sanitation inspection reports periodically. If a violation exists, it must be corrected immediately. The inspector will return to check if the violation has been rectified. If the violation continues, a warning, temporary suspension, or revocation of license will occur. In some cases, a hearing will be scheduled, which will mean additional legal expense. Bad publicity and temporary or permanent business loss may result from recurring violations.

It is the moral responsibility of all caterers to provide sanitary and safe facilities for their patrons and employees. Besides meeting the requirements of the Board of Health, operating a clean establishment is good business. Customers prize a clean establishment. Cleanliness increases employee morale and helps increase business, since employees will promote their place of employment to potential patrons by "word of mouth" advertising—your most effective tool!

Liquor Laws

A liquor license is required by law for any caterer who sells liquor whether on or off the premises. Laws, fees, and requirements vary from state to state.

Many states are guided by Alcoholic Beverage Control (ABC) laws, which were established to control and protect the public against liquor abuse. State and local liquor authorities are in charge of issuing licenses and permits and thoroughly and closely investigate the background of each applicant. Revocation, suspension, and cancellation of licenses may result from any violation of these laws.

Besides having to submit a thorough personal questionnaire, an applicant may be required by state law to submit the following information and pay the following fees.

1. A statement of personal finances including all lenders of money
2. Fingerprints (for certain types of liquor licenses)
3. Bonding
4. A filing fee for license application
5. A license fee usually paid annually or on a flat sum basis according to population or market value of the area
6. A transfer fee required in some states where licenses can be passed on to a new owner
7. Photographs of premise
8. Diagrams and sketches of physical facilities and outside elevation
9. Conditions of sale
10. Name of landlord and terms of lease arrangement
11. Approval of all licenses and permits (health, building, fire, etc.) necessary to conduct business

A license may be revoked, cancelled, or disapproved in some states for the following reasons:

1. False information given on an application
2. Suppression or omission of required information
3. Serious arrest, indictment, summons, or conviction
4. Violation of the minimum age requirement
5. Not being a citizen of the United States (with the exception of certain countries where reciprocal trade agreements exist)
6. Certain law enforcement officials where conflict of interest may occur
7. Previous suspension or revocation of license

It would be advisable to request a copy of all the liquor laws of your particular state and locality so that you may become familiar with all the rules and regulations pertaining to your area. In states where liquor licenses are issued, the approximate length of time it normally takes to process or transfer a license will be specified. There are stipulations that may be required, such as posting signs in windows or advertisements in newspapers so that the public has a right to lodge a protest against issuance of a license. The owing of back taxes, minimum distance requirements from your licensed premise to a place of worship or school, conformity with all necessary health, sanitation, fire and building requirements may be a few of the laws that, if not examined, could cause a delay or refusal of issuance of a license. It may not be necessary to employ an attorney to assist you in filing and procuring a liquor license, but it may be advisable to employ one if you have any doubts as to procedure. An attorney who has past experience in the area of liquor-licensing laws may expedite issuance. Error in filing or a wrong application form where there are several may cause unnecessary delay and undue expense.

If an alteration or extension to your physical plant is to be made prior to or during license issuance, then it is always advisable to first get approval from the state and local liquor authorities. Such notification is required, and failure to do so could be a violation.

Specific liquor licenses may be obtained in certain areas for catering establishments that hold only catered affairs in one or more ballrooms, reception, or banquet facilities. Some states require, in addition to a regular license, a special liquor permit for catered parties that offer off-premise liquor consumption for sale. Each function requires a separate permit, and the fee varies from state to state.

Since the liquor laws vary from state to state, it is recommended that you investigate the laws of your area by contacting your local or state liquor authority. If for any reason you are cited for violation for any infraction, do not hesitate to employ an attorney immediately to protect yourself against possible loss of license.

If for any reason an accountant, attorney, or other professional does not prove satisfactory because he is not knowledgeable, helpful, or available, it is suggested that you look elsewhere for these vital services. It may be inconvenient and embarrassing, but nevertheless your survival depends on it! If you run into a roadblock as to getting competent professional assistance, it may be advisable to contact your local restaurant association or several local restaurant owners to ask them for references. There are local professional legal and accounting associations that may know of or recommend several competent individuals who specialize in the restaurant or catering field.

Chapter 3

The On-Premise Catering Operation

A client often selects a catering establishment because of its physical attractiveness. Basically, the selection is made to impress the invited guests. For this reason, caterers should be aware of the importance of the appearance of the entire facility and must constantly consider investing to improve both the property and building in order to increase sales.

Since every catering operation is basically a showplace where customers come to be entertained and live out their fantasies, to achieve maximum effect it is advisable to hire experienced architects, designers, consultants, decorators, landscape artists, lighting technicians, etc. The very early stages of both exterior and interior design and development are the most practical times to seek such guidance. Often, caterers make the error of doing their own planning, designing, and constructing only to find that better results could have been achieved by hiring skilled professionals. Often, the saving a professional can realize in materials and labor will more than offset fees or service charges. More importantly, more professional and effective results will be achieved!

The Exterior

Due to ever-rising construction costs, rather than construct new buildings many caterers now convert existing vacant facilities such as theaters, car dealerships, and supermarkets, which have many built-in, high-costing features like parking facilities, air-conditioning, heating, sprinkler systems, kitchens, refrigeration facilities, etc. The exterior of such structures, which may be unattractive, can be made more appealing by just about any relatively inexpensive resurfacing material such as aluminum siding or other weather-resistant material, and with the addition of effective lighting any building can be transformed into an attractive structure.

The client will begin to formulate an opinion or judge a catering establishment immediately upon arriving at the location. The sale must begin to be triggered even before the client has set foot inside. To obtain maximum results, the following points should be considered when designing the exterior of an operation.

Signs should be attractive and adequately illuminated. Details and requirements should be discussed with the sign company engaged. Do not overdo it. Blend the sign with the character and tone of the establishment. Costs can range from several hundred to thousands of dollars depending on the size, colors, and how intricate or complicated the design. Signs may be bought or leased but, whichever arrangement is made, maintenance contracts and insurance coverage should be investigated to cover costly repairs and protect against damage. Signs in the immediate vicinity leading to your establishment should also be considered for additional advertising and to serve as directions for customers. Investigate zoning laws to insure no violations or restrictions will occur when or where the sign is installed.

Attractive borders surrounding or accenting the property line may add a touch of charm, enhance signs, and provide privacy. Consider adding ornate iron gates or fencing, stone or brick walls, decorated pillars or columns, hedging, or other borders to enhance the property.

Outdoor lighting such as decorative lamplights, lanterns, or torch lighting can be installed along the entire approach and around the building. The placement of lighting in areas where there are gardens and benches will add charm, romance, and excitement to the grounds. The placement of hundreds of tiny decorated lights in the shrubbery along the approach will create a fairyland effect, especially effective during the holiday seasons. Direct and indirect lighting can transform landscaping into effective settings at night. It can illuminate, accent, highlight, reflect, and add subtle tones and colors to the building, water displays or cascades, steps, patios, terraces, walkways or paths, retaining walls, planters, fencing, driveways, parking areas, statues, and other displays on your property to bring out the maximum dimension and effect desired. Besides being decorative, lighting prevents accidents and protects against vandalism.

Professional landscaping will achieve a tasteful layout with a balanced selection of gardens, lawns, shrubbery or hedges, plants, trees, and flowers. A gardener may be required to maintain the grounds. Flowers grown on the property can be utilized for decorating the interior or for table flowers.

Water displays can add a pleasing effect to any scene when arranged properly. Spurting and flowing fountains, rushing waterfalls or multitiered cascades, winding and gurgling streams, and reflecting ponds or pools are natural attractions during daylight and become transformed into a wonderful sight with the proper placement of light and color at night. Such additions as bridges or crossovers, water mills, floating plants, swans, ducks, etc., will add additional conversation pieces to your establishment.

Outdoor art displays, positioned and lighted properly, such as statues, sculptures, designs, antiques, etc., will add formality, grandeur, and charm to your grounds.

Outdoor settings and structures such as level or raised patios and terraces constructed of stone, brick, or slate with umbrella tables and chairs are conducive to outside parties or functions on seasonable days. Consider outdoor gazebos and large permanent tent structures or pavillions from which additional revenue can be derived during warmer months. The installation of a permanent canopy for outdoor wedding ceremonies should also be considered if the demand exists.

Canopies, overhangs, or awnings extending from the building offer the twofold advantage of protecting against inclement weather and giving a touch of formality to the operation. A carpet can be placed under the canopy leading into the establishment for the same reasons.

Adequate parking facilities with wide and easily accessible entrances and exits are a selling factor and should be made available for the convenience of the guests. One parking space should be allocated for every two to four seats of the operation's seating capacity and be within easy walking distance of the entrance to the building. Investigate various price ranges and request estimates from several road-constructing firms as to the cost of concrete, asphalt, and gravel work needed. These firms may offer many ideas and suggestions as to types of materials to get the maximum result for your investment.

The parking area should be well lighted for safety, convenience, and protection against vandalism. Signs should be arranged to direct the flow of traffic into and out of the desired parking locations without difficulty and traffic congestion. When valet parking is initiated, the installation of a parking shed or hut near the main entrance is advisable so that the parking attendants can observe the traffic, store all the necessary parking and directional signs, tickets, flashlights, first aid and emergency car kits, umbrellas, weather mats, uniforms, and other items.

A garbage and refuse area should be completely screened, hidden from public view, and be protected against rodent and vermin infestation. Garbage bins, compactors, and other refuse containers should be within easy access of the kitchen and the pickup point of the sanitation truck. This area should be constructed so that it can be cleaned and hosed down periodically. If feasible, separate refrigerated rooms for garbage and delivery drop-offs should be considered to insure the highest standards of health and sanitation protection.

The Interior

In planning or designing the interior of your establishment, the following points should be discussed with your professional consultants to achieve the maximum results.

Sufficient width and height for entrances to all rooms are necessary to assure smooth traffic flow for large functions and for the delivery of large items, e.g., for trade shows where automobiles, boats, etc., will be on display. Ramps should be installed for ease of delivery and for the convenience of the handicapped.

An enclosed vestibule or entrance area, preferably heated and air conditioned, should be adequate in size to comfortably accommodate customers who are arriving or waiting to leave. This should be a double-doored area used as a buffer zone between the outside entrance and the lobby to conserve energy. Rubber or other weatherized matting or carpeting should cover this area.

A main lobby or separate lobbies adequate in size to accommodate the total number of guests arriving for one function. This area should be functional as well as comfortable and decorated professionally with furniture, carpeting, accessories, and fixtures to give the customer a pleasurable first impression of the establishment's interior. It should be designed to expedite the flow of guests to their prospective rooms.

Within or near the lobby the following facilities should be easily accessible.

Checkroom facilities should be large enough to accomodate one checking space for each attending guest. Enough room should be provided for racks and aisles so that garments can be easily reached. Since most guests usually arrive at one time, it is essential that coatrooms be designed to give the quickest possible service to avoid excessive waiting and customer complaints. To solve this situation, automated checking systems, additional facilities, or extra help for peak checking times should be utilized. Slots or racks should be constructed to keep hats checked separately. Lighting should be installed so that all items checked, checking tickets, and numbers can be easily read by the checking attendants. If tipping or a checkroom gratuity is required or requested by management, then a locked, tamper-proof box should be permanently installed to prevent vandalism or pilferage.

Men's and ladies' lounges should be adequate in size and number to accommodate large numbers of guests at one time and be easily accessible from all areas. Special attention should be placed on these facilities, since many potential clients will often request to see these areas or in some cases will check them without management's awareness. Since these customers will correlate the cleanliness of the rest rooms with that of the entire catering operation, every step should be taken to keep these facilities in an immaculate condition and also to keep them fully stocked.

Men's and ladies' room attendants should be employed or at least be made available for a customer who may request this service and to make certain that these facilities are properly serviced during a function.

The banquet or catering office is the sales center of the catering operation where a prospective customer discusses all the details of a particular function with a salesman or the owner himself. This office should be strategically situated so that inquiring customers can locate it easily. (See Chapter 4 for a more detailed description of the banquet office.)

The business office handles the accounting, correspondence, filing, etc. It should be separate from, but close to, the banquet office, since they perform interrelated functions.

Bridal or dressing rooms are needed for wedding receptions or for other functions where privacy is needed. Ideally, there should be one bridal or dressing room constructed for each function room. Champagne or cocktails and hors d'oeuvres can be served privately to members of a bridal party or other small party before they join a reception or other function. These rooms can also be used as changing rooms for fashion shows, theater presentations, or other functions where a change of clothing is needed. They can also be used for small groups or gatherings, meetings, as a rest or sick area, for private phone conversations, etc.

Each one of these rooms should be professionally decorated and ideally include rest room facilities, closets, dressing tables, sofas, chairs, writing desk, lamps, cocktail tables, or other furniture. Carpeting on walls, mirrored ceilings, piped-in music, or other different or imaginative touches are also effective. Attention should be given to the decor of these rooms because it may be a deciding factor in the selection of a catering establishment.

Public telephones should be installed in the lobby area for convenience and accessibility. A sufficient number should be made available with complete privacy. Telephone jacks should be installed so telephone calls can be transferred to the various rooms. A paging system should also be installed in all rooms so that a customer can be informed of any incoming calls. A telephone consultant should be consulted for advice on placement, newest equipment available, rates, accessories available, or for any other information or problem that may arise in the placement or use of telephone communications.

Cigarette vending machines should be placed in a convenient location in or near the lobby area. These machines will prove to be an additional source of revenue. They can be bought outright, operated, stocked, and serviced by management or can be contracted from a vending company who will offer financial terms or pay commissions for the location of the machine usually based on a percentage of gross sales. Where vending machines may not be desirable or suitable to the decor of the establishment, tobacco products can be dispensed separately from the checkroom or another convenient area.

Private reception rooms or cocktail areas ajoining and leading into each banquet or function room can be used for the sale of food and beverage, especially liquor, principally in the form of cocktail hours, prior and in addition to an affair. Since the sale of liquor is extremely profitable, these facilities should receive vital consideration. This reception area should be approximately one-third of the total size of its adjacent banquet facility, large enough to accommodate the total number of guests attending the function as well as a complete cocktail reception setup which may include buffet tables, cocktail tables and chairs, and portable bars. When this area is not being used for food and beverage sales as part of a function, then it can be used for a separate function for additional revenue.

Banquet or function rooms are the main rooms of a catering operation. These rooms should range in size to accommodate the many different types and sizes of affairs, but basically the larger the capacity the higher the potential for profit. Certain locations will need larger facilities for such functions as political affairs, trade shows, conventions, dances, etc. These larger rooms should be subdivided by soundproof folding doors, so that they can be sold as individual smaller units, which should have separate entrances and exits. Also, any problems with traffic flow or noise from the adjoining rooms must be solved to prevent complaints and to insure privacy. As banquet rooms are subdivided, so too should the cocktail areas be subdivided, so that these smaller units can be sold jointly for smaller functions. The more versatility built into an operation the higher the possibility of profit. Keep in mind that these divisions will also affect the operation and design of the kitchen.

There are many companies that specialize in folding doors, which are constantly being improved as to design, materials, and soundproofing ability. These doors can be permanently installed when placed on tracks and can be easily folded and stored in "closets" and be completely hidden from public view when not in use. These folding doors can also be purchased as portable units and can be moved and positioned where needed. The advantage to these portable units is that they need no special installation and can be moved and divide any area as needed; the disadvantage is that they are hard to move and handle and need more personnel and time to set up.

When constructing or expanding a catering establishment, consider having at least three rooms that will accommodate approximately 150, 250, and 500 or more. All three should lead into a kitchen to cut costs and achieve central control. The larger-sized rooms can be divided into smaller units as previously mentioned. Potential or future expansion of the operation should also be considered, especially in the early stages of planning and construction, and allowances be made to compensate should it become necessary.

For any large room, consideration should be given to constructing a raised permanent or portable, centrally located stage area for shows, bands, speeches, or other presentations. A portable stage is more adaptable, although the permanent stage can be made to appear more professional. To conserve space when a permanent stage is constructed, a pullout dance floor on rollers can be installed under the stage area for easy storage and increased seating capacity when not in use. If there is an existing dance floor, the area under the stage can be used for storage.

Special stage lighting and sound equipment monitored through a control room should be considered for professional results if a large permanent theatrical stage is constructed. A sound technician should be hired to install the proper audio system.

Dressing rooms, furnished basically with chairs, mirrors, coatracks, washing facilities, and dressing tables, leading from the stage for make-up and clothing changes are worthwhile additions for events needing shows.

Entrances and exits to the stage should be sufficiently long and wide and, if possible, easily accessible to accommodate band or show equipment, displays for various exhibitions or trade shows, etc. For easy mobility and access, ramps should be installed up to the stage area. For safety reasons, carpeted stairs and protective rails should be installed leading to any elevated area.

Since motion pictures or other video presentations are often used, each room should have a screen of sufficient size located in such a way that all persons can view it.

Public address and sound systems are required for most functions and should be constantly checked for peak performance. Ceiling speakers should be installed to give a balanced sound throughout the entire establishment. Since many audio problems occur constantly, it would be wise to investigate a repair and service contract and have additional emergency equipment available when sound problems arise. Public address systems, tapes, and recordings should be able to be played through your sound system for each room as needed.

A reasonable amount of audio equipment should be offered to any customer at no additional charge, e.g., a microphone with an accompanying lectern or podium. When an additional or unusual amount of audiovisual equipment is required, then it becomes the responsibility of the customer to rent it from the caterer or an audiovisual firm.

Lighting should be installed by a lighting technician to obtain maximum effect. When placed correctly, lighting can add tremendously to the atmosphere, mood, or special effects needed for the room. By the proper positioning of the various lighting fixtures, such as high-hats, sconces, pin or spotlights, chandeliers, and other decorative lighting fixtures, effective results can be obtained at a reasonable cost.

All rooms should have dimmer or rheostat switches so that any level of lighting can be achieved. Perhaps additional electrical lines may have to be installed to produce the required bright lighting. Special lighting effects should be installed where dramatic or theatrical results are to be achieved, such as spotlights on specially decorated tables, dance or stage areas, or other points of interest.

Electrical outlets and microphone jacks should be installed conveniently around all rooms. Take into consideration the position and location of special tables and areas such as a dais, band areas, or other locations where special placement of outlets and mike jacks may be required. Floor plans and setups change for each function, so keep these possible changes in mind when installing these outlets so as to cover all possible situations. The placement of floor plugs and mike jacks may be feasible to eliminate the problem of using long and dangerous extension cords. If extension cords are needed, they should be covered by tape, carpet, or metal covers to eliminate the possibility of an accident. To prevent microphones from being stolen or lost, mike locks should be installed.

It is always wiser to install extra electrical outlets for each room because there are always those functions or shows that will require their use. It is also advisable to have an illustrated floor plan drawn for each room indicating where all electrical outlets and microphone jacks are located for easy identification by a customer.

An adequate-sized dance floor is essential for each banquet room, since many customers attach a great deal of importance to this. Approximately one-sixth of the total room or about four square feet per person should be allocated for a dance floor.

Since a small dance floor may lead to criticism and the possible loss of a function, serious consideration should be given to enlargement of this area. Many customers have a misconception about dancing space. It should be pointed out to them that at an average function only one-third to one-half of the total number of guests will dance at one time.

When laying carpet in a room, it is advisable to have your carpet installer cut an extra piece to cover the dance area, which can be secured with snaps or fasteners when the dance area is not needed.

Where a dance floor is needed and none exists, such as in a cocktail area where a customer has requested dancing or when more dance space is needed, a portable dance floor may be used. Portable dance floors can be bought, rented, or made. A roll-out floor is a one-piece portable surface made by gluing one-inch-wide shellacked slats of hard wood onto canvas backing and cut to any desired size such as 10 x 10 feet or 10 x 20 feet. These floors are now also made in lightweight plastic.

Another type of portable dance floor is a sectional dance floor, which is made up of many small square or rectangular sections, e.g., 4 x 4 feet or 3 x 6 feet. The sections can be attached to each other by grooves, screws, slips, or other fastening devices. A sectional dance floor can be constructed to any size or to cover any desired area. For safety and strength, they also have wedge-shaped inclining metal or wood strips, which surround the dance floor so that a guest will not trip over the exposed blunt, raised edges of the floor.

Sufficient heating and air-conditioning are needed to keep rooms comfortable under maximum occupancy. Body heat will quickly raise room temperature, especially when large numbers of guests arrive at one time. Therefore, it is important to adjust the room's temperature to compensate for this rise in body heat. Customers may briefly complain about a room being too cool, especially if they are the first to enter, but must be assured that as soon as the room fills with guests it will be very comfortable. A room becomes difficult to cool, unless it has tremendous cooling power or air-conditioning output, once it is filled to capacity.

Besides having the proper or additional amount of air-conditioning and heating units to adequately handle each room, consider installing many individual units, versus a central system, for emergencies when malfunctions occur. Individual units can be replaced and there will never be a situation in which the whole system will be shut down.

Exhaust systems should be installed to extract smoke and stale air and to recirculate fresh air. If this exhaust system is not installed or does not function properly, it will result in irritation and uncomfortable conditions, which will result in customer complaints.

The decor of the catering operation should be handled by a designer or architect who has the training and experience. Basically, the caterer should provide the architect with the practical concerns of the operation such as the different table sizes and designs used, the various selections of colored linens offered, the various types of functions to be held, the menu selections, and all other important information about the operation including the problems and your preferences. The professional will then design and decorate the rooms for maximum effect using this information.

Redecoration, primarily in drapery, carpeting, and decor, should be considered approximately every 5 years, especially when repeat business is established and change of decor will improve business. Commercial grades of decorating materials should be used for the best maintenance, wear, and durability. It is advised that carpeting should carry a design or pattern to hide the many ills, such as discarded papers or other noticable objects especially when cleanup is not immediately available. Light-colored carpeting should be avoided, since it will readily show and hold any spills, stains, or burns. Dark-colored carpeting should also be avoided because lighter objects such as cigarettes or papers are highly noticable against the dark background. Carpeting with neutral tones with dark designs or patterns is the best type one can buy to achieve the best appearance considering the numerous unpreventable abuses the carpeting will sustain.

Chapel facilities are an important consideration to increase sales. Often customers will request to have ceremonies on the premises to save time, expense, and planning. If a catering operation is in an area where ceremonies are marketable, evidenced by customer inquiry or demand, then it may be feasible to construct or at least be able to convert an existing room or facility into a chapel to fill this need.

If construction of a permanent chapel facility is feasible, then some of the following points should be incorporated into its planning. It should be an interfaith chapel for adaptablility purposes, and most fixtures should be portable and easy to store. By incorporating stained glass windows, raised platforms or altars, podium and microphones, portable canopies, chairs, dimmer or rheostat switches, candle holders, and other chapel materials, a chapel can be arranged to conduct the services for any religious denomination without any difficulty.

If a permanent chapel is not feasible due to lack of space, capital, or demand, then a temporary facility can be improvised from any available room large enough to accommodate a ceremony. This room can be made into a chapel by simply arranging the accoutrements of the particular religious ceremony in such a way as to simulate the chapel setting. When the lights are dimmed, an ordinary room becomes transformed into an adequate chapel facility.

An area outside the chapel should be available to organize the introduction of the processional and for a receiving line after the recessional. ————

If weather permits and an attractive outdoor area is available, then this same chapel arrangement for indoors could be used effectively for a pleasant outdoor ceremony.

Storage areas should be constructed to house all the existing equipment of the establishment that may have to be removed from the function rooms, such as portable platforms, podiums, and lecterns. This area should be conveniently located for easy access from all rooms and should be locked or secured when not in use. Responsibility for the equipment should be delegated and an inventory taken periodically to keep stock records current.

A workshop or repair area should be equipped with the proper tools and equipment for a handyman to repair, maintain, or construct the necessary equipment needed to continue an operation.

Locker or employee areas should be installed so that employees can change their clothing and store personal items. Washroom and toilet facilities with good lighting and ventilation should be decorated cheerfully to build morale. Hampers for soiled uniforms and laundry, receptacles for refuse, and signs reminding employees to wash hands after using restroom facilities should be included in this changing area. This area should also include the time clock, a bulletin board, and lockers and should be furnished with cots and dining facilities.

Linen room facilities should have sufficient shelving and space to store the various linens, skirting, uniforms, cleaning cloths, and other laundry items needed. A question may arise as to which is more profitable, to operate a self-sufficient on-premise laundry or to use an outside laundry service. The answer lies in how much volume the catering operation produces and how much can be saved taking into account installation of commercial washers, dryers, presses, and the additional operational expenses such as labor, cleaning materials, and overhead attached to operating such a laundry system.

The liquor room should have sufficient shelving and bins to store the maximum amount of liquors, wines, beers, and bar equipment needed.

This area must be dry and cool to keep the alcoholic beverages at the desired temperature. It should also be clean and well lit. This room should be adequately locked with only *one* key person responsible for handling the distribution and inventory.

Safety and fire protection devices must be available for all areas of the building to comply with fire and building codes in your area. Fire and building inspectors will visit your premises to check and issue a written report on any hazardous condition or violation of the codes.

The following paragraphs describe some of the safety and fire devices that, when installed properly, will prevent potential hazards and accidents and also reduce insurance rates.

Exit lights should be installed over all exit doors and be easily visible from all parts of every room. Exit lights must be kept lit at all times when the building is occupied.

An emergency lighting system should be installed in all rooms in the event that electrical power failures arise. Adequate lighting will be made available through this battery-operated emergency system, which works automatically when the electrical supply is interrupted. These batteries must be checked periodically, usually through a light indicator, to insure that sufficient battery power will be available under emergency conditions.

Smoke and heat detectors or water sprinkler systems should be installed in all areas to signal or extinguish a fire.

Fire extinguishers should be installed in sufficient numbers and be accessible and must be checked periodically. Tags should be attached to each extinguisher for the inspector to mark on each visit. Inquiry should be made as to the various types of chemicals available for extinguishers to be most effective for the different types of fires.

Fire-resistant drapes and carpeting and other decorative materials are mandatory for all public establishments to prevent fires from occurring and spreading.

Emergency crash or handle bars should be installed on all exit doors leading to the outside of the building. All exit and emergency doors should be free of obstructions to allow the free flow of traffic in case of any emergency.

Occupancy signs may be required by law to be posted in all rooms to indicate the maximum number of persons allowed in each room for safety reasons. No function should be contracted or held for more than this maximum number.

Prevention through safety training programs and inspections under government-supervised agencies such as OSHA are effective ways to make all employees aware of the hazardous safety conditions surrounding them. These programs will prevent accidents. Through participation in these programs, insurance rates will be lowered and most important potential accidents and human suffering will be avoided.

SECTION II

Sales

The thrust of any catering operation is derived from sales and the people responsible for this segment of the business. In this section, the banquet office, the center of all sales activity, is described, and what you should expect from your sales staff is delineated. In addition, a system for booking functions is offered, as well as strategies for soliciting business and augmenting sales. Finally, weekly sales meetings are recommended as a means of monitoring all sales-related activities.

Chapter 4

The Banquet Office

The banquet office is the information and sales center of a catering operation. Inquiring customers enter the banquet office seeking such information as menus, prices, available facilities, dates, times, and other details associated with an affair. Hence, the banquet office must be conducive to business and equipped with the necessary materials to assist in facilitating a sale.

Some of the amenities that will help promote sales and that should be kept in mind when designing the banquet office include:

1. A comfortable reception area with ample seating
2. A receptionist to screen and schedule arriving customers
3. Refreshments and reading materials in the event customers must be detained
4. Visual presentations of previous functions held at the establishment in the form of videotapes or slides

Complete privacy must be insured inside the banquet office, which should be decorated tastefully, keeping in mind the business nature of the locale. Furnish the room with office furniture, business machines, telephones, and other equipment needed to conduct business in a professional manner. An adding machine or calculator must be handy, since it will be needed to make all the required estimates and other computations.

Since committees and groups of inquirers often visit and gather information for a function, there should be comfortable seating for six to eight persons. The banquet office should be designed to give the impression that the function will be well organized and thoroughly supervised from beginning to end. The banquet office should reflect a positive, professional image.

Staff the office so information is available not only during office hours but also during evenings and weekends. Try to accommodate customers making inquiries on their free time. Conspicuously post office hours so a customer will know when best to obtain information. Carefully arrange and space appointments so each and every inquirer has sufficient time to obtain needed information without interruption. Try to avoid "backing up" customers. This creates ill will, can lead to a client being given hasty and incomplete information, and ultimately will result in lost sales.

33

Printed forms and promotional material should be readily available for a clear, orderly, and concise sales presentation. The following is a list of the required printed material:

1. Banquet and package plan menus constructed for various functions
2. All forms needed to conduct and organize business—estimates, contracts, floor plans, bills, purchase orders, work orders, etc.
3. Advertising and promotional materials used to display and describe your facilities and services—color brochures, postcards, pamphlets, and reprints of complimentary reviews and articles from magazines and newspapers
4. Printed price lists and descriptions of services rendered by bands, entertainers, photographers, florists, limousine services, travel agents, bridal and tuxedo shops, printers, and other related outside services (see Chapter 22 for a detailed discussion of these services)
5. Checklists to assist the customer in arranging a successful affair, "helpful hint" booklets for the various social functions, place cards or seating cards, direction cards, diagrams and schematic drawings of rooms, or other instructive material

Every customer should be given a presentation folder containing all the above-mentioned printed materials. This folder and its contents must be skillfully designed because it will be critically analyzed and compared to those of your competitors. It is the professionalism of the salesman and his presentation that will sell the party! These folders should be made of glossy paper and include the name, address, telephone number, and logo of your catering operation. "Especially Made For You," "Custom Made For You," or a similar phrase should be printed on the outside cover to give the customer the impression that the presentation was specifically prepared for him.

Photographs are an effective method of explaining and selling food, services, and other items to potential customers and should be prominently displayed. Photographs can prove to be a concise, ready answer to the often asked question, "How does this look?" They can also save valuable time by showing what would otherwise be vaguely described verbally. A slide projector with a remote control switch can also be an effective sales tool. The customer can be shown, at the flick of a switch, how a room is decorated or what a particular food item looks like.

Ask the photographer working on your premises to display his best work, enlarged and strategically placed throughout the banquet office. The photographer benefits by having his name or studio on all photographic material. All inquiring customers will, of course, be directed to his services.

Photographic material should be available for easy reference. Photo albums, enlargements, transparencies, or other audiovisual material needed for your presentation should also be provided by the photographer. A complete wedding album showing important scenes and highlights of an affair can be used to stress food, decorations, and arrangements. Incorporate all key points of the affair from beginning to end, such as pictures of the chapel arrangements or wedding ceremony, the cocktail reception, the dinner or buffet setup, wedding cake, floral arrangements, and table configurations.

A complete bar mitzvah album, similar to a wedding album, can show all the important arrangements, decor, and special effects used to produce this type of affair.

Photos of all the social, business, and political events that are held on your premises will arouse interest and incite conversation, particularly if photos of celebrities and popular public figures attending these affairs are taken.

Photos of artistic showpieces and decorated foods such as ice carvings, butter sculptures, fruit and vegetable displays, hors d'oeuvres platters, aspic work, galantines, pâtés, and chaud froid pieces can highlight different food presentations and special serving equipment available for buffets and smorgasbords.

Photos of cakes decorated for different occasions can show the customer the available styles, number of tiers, ornaments, borders, flowers, fillings, frostings, and inscriptions. Color photos of dessert displays such as Viennese tables and pastry carts give the customer examples of the available presentations and selection of cakes, pies, pastries, danish, petit fours, cookies, and other dessert specialties.

Photos of various floral arrangements will exhibit the available colors, sizes, and forms used for table settings. Additional floral items that can be ordered to enhance an affair might also be shown; for example, flat table ferns, similax, potted plants, floral canopies, aisle baskets, and pedestals.

Photos of seating arrangements and table formations and shapes show a customer the setups available for his particular function or meeting; for example, a double-tiered dais, "U"-shaped tables, classroom style meetings, or the many other seating and buffet table setups available.

Photos of specialty or novelty items and promotional or theatrical innovations can show a customer some ways your catering operation can add appeal or a touch of "show biz" to any affair. These imaginative approaches generate additional profits. Some examples for children's parties and bar or bas mitzvahs are: sport or rock themes where color posters of football, baseball, hockey, or rock stars are displayed; ice cream and candy wagons; magic shows; balloons and streamers for table decorations; punch fountains; juke boxes; pinball and popcorn machines; and other ideas that will make a children's party more entertaining. For adults, a caterer may be able to put on a Hawaiian luau, an Old English feast, or a specific nationality night where the foods, beverages, costumes, and decor of a particular country or nation are featured.

A linen chart with sample swatches in the various colors of table-cloths and napkins should be available for the customer to select from. If lace overlays for individual tables or special skirting for decorating the dais, bridal table, buffet table, or other special table are offered, then samples should be readily available for inspection.

A small glass case, display cabinet, or area should exhibit a sample of the silver or goldware offered. This would include the pattern and style of silver or goldware and a silver- or gold-rimmed dinner plate and piece of glassware available for service. Some caterers offer goldware at an additional expense, while others, as a selling feature, include it with their more expensive affairs at no additional charge.

Set up a display case showing the novelty or specialty items that a customer may want to purchase as favors and from which a caterer can make additional revenue. These items would include printed menus, matches, cocktail napkins, drink stirrers, ashtrays, etc.

Letters of appreciation or thanks should be posted prominently around the banquet office so that a customer can read them at his leisure. These letters are a very effective means of "word-of-mouth" advertising, since they usually carry a sincere tone in praising your food, service, and facilities.

A miniature-scale model or visual presentation of the entire layout of your operation should be conveniently available to show and explain quickly and clearly to an inquiring customer the location and seating arrangements of the particular room to be booked for his function.

Having all of these materials in the banquet office will allow the salesman to give a complete sales presentation. Other components of the sales presentation are discussed in the next chapter.

Chapter 5

Selling and Booking Affairs

The high-volume catering operation will be successful only if it builds a reliable business and a steady clientele. To win over potential customers, every effort must be made to satisfy their every request, no matter how unusual. It is the sales personnel who must convince potential clients that their every wish and whim will be fulfilled. Therefore, it is the sales personnel who are primarily responsible for the revenue an operation generates.

Whether an operation is just starting out or has been in business for years, the steps involved in booking functions are identical. However, smaller operations generally have fewer personnel who share the responsibilities for booking functions, while high-volume caterers usually employ a large staff, with each employee being responsible for only one segment of the overall operation. Thus, the procedures and number of forms are proportional to the complexity of the operation.

While attracting new business is important to any operation, repeat business is essential to assure success. Since the need to "sell" your facilities and service is eliminated for repeat business, these customers may be handled differently from new clients. Therefore, we will consider repeat business separately later in this chapter.

New Business

The first step leading to a booking is the customer inquiry. To increase the probability of actually booking an affair, the salesman should schedule an appointment at the banquet facility rather than handle the inquiry over the telephone. By meeting with the potential customer, the salesman can evaluate his reactions and give a complete and effective sales presentation. Often, when business is conducted over the telephone, the caller can get an inaccurate impression, and the whole transaction may seem hurried and impersonal. More importantly, no sales presentation is complete without a tour of the facilities.

When meeting with a customer, the salesman should first find out what type of function or party the customer is planning, the number (minimum or maximum) of guests, and the date(s) and time(s) he has in mind. Before discussing further details, the salesman should check the

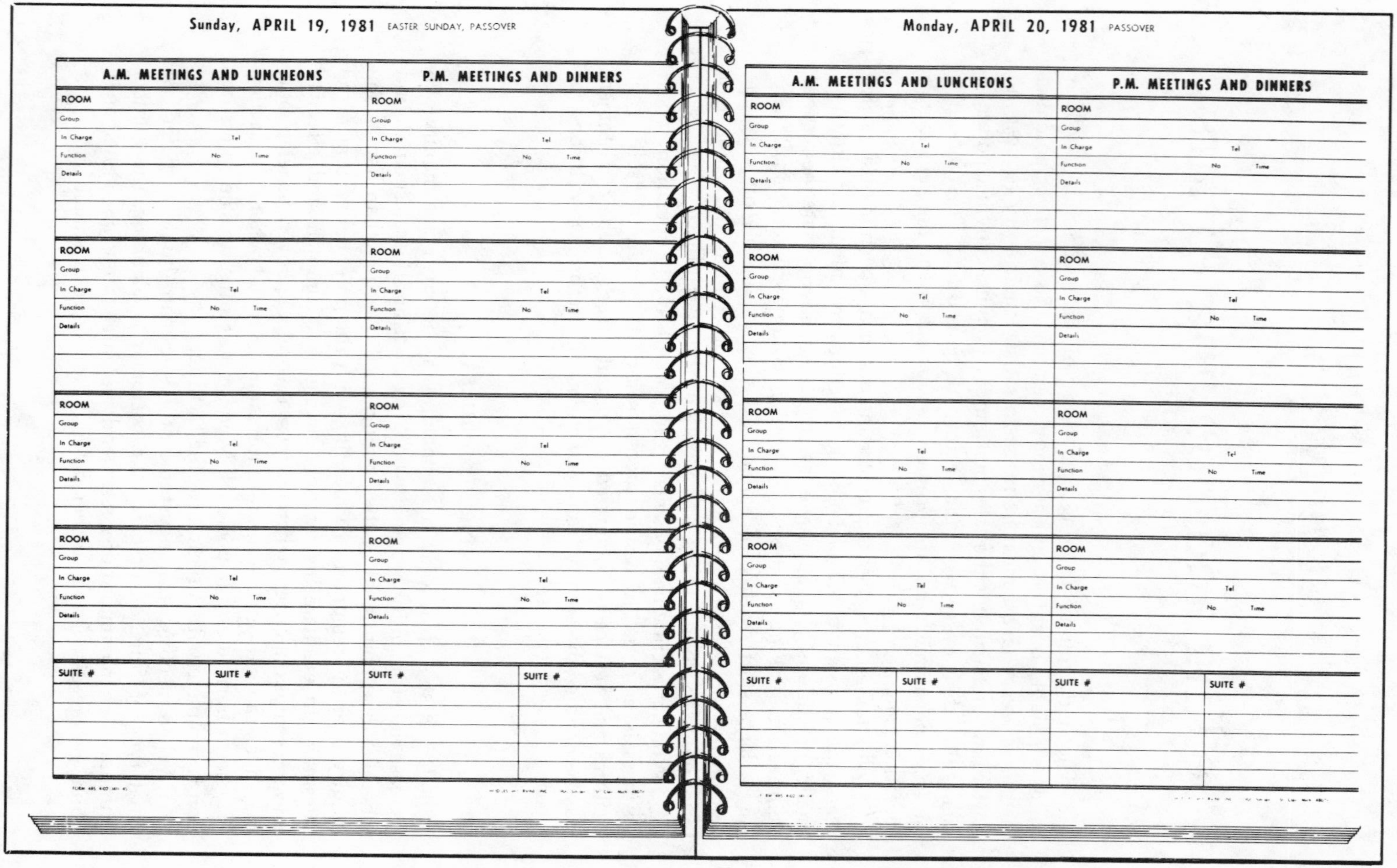

Fig. 5-1. Sample page from a function reservation book.

function reservation book (see Fig. 5-1) to see if there is an opening. The function reservation book is used to coordinate the assignment of all rooms to avoid conflicts such as double bookings, i.e., two parties scheduled for the same date, time, and function room. All function reservation books cover a one-year period, and, since they are custom made, they can be individualized to meet the requirements of a particular catering operation. For example, if your operation handles only afternoon and evening affairs, then each date in the book will be divided into these two periods. To insure control of bookings and to avoid conflicts, one person should be in charge of making entries into the reservation book. In very large operations, one person should be employed solely for this purpose.

If it is not possible to accommodate the customer's wishes regarding date, time, or room needed for his party, the salesman should offer alternatives according to what he does have available. In order to sell less desirable dates, management may offer incentives such as price reductions or an added dinner course. A caterer who has more than one location should refer business to the sister operation when he has no openings. All possibilities should be explored before letting the customer get away.

Once it has been determined that the customer can be accommodated, the salesman may ask how the inquirer came to learn of the establishment in order to ascertain what sources of advertising are proving successful. If the establishment was recommended to the customer by someone else, then a letter of appreciation should be sent to that party.

The astute salesman will also inquire whether the customer encountered any problems, such as careless service, at another catering operation. If any problems were encountered, the salesman should make a notation in the client's file so that special attention can be given to that aspect of the affair if he does book with him.

It should also be ascertained at this time whether there will be any special requirements. Will any of the guests be adhering to a special diet (salt-free, diabetic, vegetarian, kosher)? Will there be any special physical requirements (space left at a table for a guest in a wheelchair)?

With these questions out of the way, the salesman can now proceed to the next step—the estimate. An estimate is a price quote of the complete cost of the function. Every estimate will be different in format and price depending on the individual requirements and demands of each function. It is important to note that most customers will have visited or will be visiting several other caterers to obtain estimates. Care should be exercised in quoting prices and services, being sure they fall in line with your competitors. A complete set of pricing guidelines is offered in Chapter 8.

To illustrate how an estimate is given, let's take a look at two different functions. Case A is a retirement dinner/dance, and Case B a wedding reception package plan.

Case A. Mr. Patrick Cahill wishes to hold a retirement dinner for Mr. Stephen McConnell of the New York Telephone Company on Friday evening, January 23, 19XX, from 8 PM to 1 AM, for approximately 300 guests. After discussing the arrangements and prices for a banquet dinner and cocktail hour, Mr. Cahill indicates he would like to have the following: a butler style cocktail hour with unlimited liquor; a complete roast prime top sirloin of beef dinner; fifths[1] of rye and scotch placed on each table of ten; coat checking; and two lounge attendants, one each for the ladies' and men's rooms. Signs will be posted both at the checkroom and in the lounges stating that all gratuities have been paid by the host, informing the guests that tipping is not required. For the dais, he would like a large (long) floral centerpiece to be placed in front of the lectern; a regular (round) floral centerpiece for each table; and finally the five-piece house band for four hours starting at dinner time. See Fig. 5-2 for how the estimate for this function was derived.

Case B. Miss Jane Smith and Mr. John Peterson would like to first hold a wedding ceremony and then a cocktail reception and dinner on Saturday evening, May 4, 19XX, from 7 PM to 1 AM, for approximately 150 guests. The format for the evening is to be as follows:

> Wedding (chapel) ceremony from 7 to 8 PM
> Cocktail reception from 8 to 9 PM
> Dinner/dance from 9 PM to 1 AM

The arrangements include the following. For the ceremony: room rental for use and setup of the chapel; four floral aisle baskets to decorate the chapel; two floral pedestals or sprays; a runner for the bridal processional; and an organist to play during the ceremony. For the cocktail reception and dinner/dance: a buffet style cocktail hour; rock cornish game hen dinner; two lounge attendants; and a four-piece band for four hours. No checking facilities would be required for the month of May, with the exception of inclement weather. See Fig. 5-3 for the estimate that would be drawn up for this function.

If a customer requests a price per person, then simply divide the total amount of the estimate by the number of guests, e.g., in Case A, divide $11,855 by 300. This equals $39.52 per person, or $39.50 rounded off, which some caterers will do.

The estimate is made out in triplicate: one for the customer, one for the customer's file, and one for the department head to review. After the estimate has been explained, it is given to the customer in a presentation folder, which also contains the brochures, menus, and other promotional material. The salesman should then show the facilities to the customer. While showing the facilities, the salesman should discuss the affair and

---

[1]All bottles of liquor for banquets are sold in fifths (750 ml) rather than quarts (liters) because they are easier to sell due to their lower price. If a customer requests quarts (liters), the adjusted higher price would be charged. All setups, mixers, sodas, and ice are included in the price of bottles.

ABC Catering
120 Main Street
New City, N.Y. 10956

☐ Customer copy
☐ File copy
☐ Department head

Follow-up date_____

Estimate

Contact's name Mr. Patrick Cahill
Name of organization New York Telephone Company
Nature of function Retirement Dinner for Mr. Stephen McConnell
Address 230 West 23rd Street
City New York   State New York   Zip 10011
Phone Office: (212) 354-2000   Home: (516) 765-3311

	Time	Room
Day/date of function: Friday, 1-23-XX	8 PM to 1 AM	Blue Room & Foyer

SCHEDULE

No. of persons 300	Butler Style	8 to 9 PM	Blue Room
	Cocktail Hour		Foyer
	Dinner/Dance	9 PM to 1 AM	Blue Room

Number	Item	PP Price	Total
300	Cocktail Hour X Butler __ Buffet____	$ 8.00	$ 2,400.00
300	Dinner (Roast Prime Top Sirloin		
	of Beef)	14.00	4,200.00
	EXTRAS:		
30	Bottles of Rye (Seagrams 7)	28.00 ea.	840.00
30	Bottles of Scotch (Dewars)	30.00 ea.	900.00
	Total Food & Beverage		$ 8,340.00
	17% Gratuity on above		1,417.00
	8% City and State Tax on above		667.20
300	Coatroom Checking @	.50 PP	150.00
2	Lounge Attendants @	35.00 each	70.00
5	Piece Band for 4 hours @	600.00	600.00
	Piece Band for Ceremony @		
1	Large Floral Centerpieces @	30.00 each	30.00
29	Regular Floral Centerpieces @	20.00 each	580.00
	Floral Pedestals/Sprays @		
	Floral Aisle Baskets @		
	Floral Canopy @		
	Aisle Runner @		
	Rental (Chapel) @		
	Rental (Room) @		

Estimated by John Smith
Date 4-15-XX

TOTAL $11,855.00

The above prices are current prices that are subject to change by management due to increased costs of operation, food, beverage, labor, taxes, or other unforeseen reasons.

Fig. 5-2. Estimate drawn up for Case A.

answer any questions the customer may have. This is an excellent time for the salesman to promote the establishment by pointing out all the advantages and extra benefits if offers.

At this point, one of three things will occur: the customer will

ABC Catering
120 Main Street
New City, N.Y. 10956

☐ Customer copy
☐ File copy
☐ Department head

Follow-up date _____

Estimate

Contact's name __Miss Jane Smith_____

Name of organization _Jane Smith – John Peterson_____

Nature of function _Wedding Ceremony, Reception and Dinner/Dance_

Address _30 Red Hill Road_____

City _Pomona_____ State _New York_____ Zip ___10960___

Phone Office: _(212) 471-0450_____ Home: _(914) 751-0291_____

	Time	Room
Day/date of function: Saturday, 5-4-XX	7 PM to 1 AM	Chapel, Crystal Room & Foyer

SCHEDULE

No. of persons _150_			
	Wedding Ceremony	7 to 8 PM	Chapel
	Buffet Style		
	Cocktail Hour	8 to 9 PM	Crystal Foyer
	Dinner/Dance	9 PM to 1 AM	Crystal Room

Number	Item	PP Price	Total
_150_	Cocktail Hour __ Butler _X_ Buffet___	$10.00	$1,500.00
_150_	Dinner ___ Rock Cornish Hen		
	(Package Plan)	30.00	4,500.00

EXTRAS:

		Total Food & Beverage	$6,000.00
		17% Gratuity on above	n/a*
		8% City and State Tax on above	480.00
_____	Coatroom Checking	@ _____	n/a
_2_	Lounge Attendants	@ _____ 35.00 ea.	70.00
_4_	Piece Band for _4_ hours	@ _____ 500.00	500.00
_1_	Piece Band for Ceremony	@ _____ 100.00	100.00
_____	Large Floral Centerpieces	@ _____	
_____	Regular Floral Centerpieces	@ _____	
_2_	Floral Pedestals/Sprays	@ _____ 60.00	120.00
_4_	Floral Aisle Baskets	@ _____ 40.00	160.00
_____	Floral Canopy	@ _____	
_1_	Aisle Runner	@ _____ 30.00	30.00
_1_	Rental (Chapel)	@ _____ 100.00	100.00
_____	Rental (Room)	@ _____	

Estimated by _John Smith_____

Date __6-10-XX_____

TOTAL _$7,560.00_

The above prices are current prices that are subject to change by management due to increased costs of operation, food, beverage, labor, taxes, or other unforeseen reasons.

---

*17% gratuity is included in price of package plan.

Cocktail hour liquor is included in dinner package plan price.

Fig. 5-3. Estimate drawn up for Case B.

definitely book his function with the salesman; he will *tentatively* book the function; or he will choose *not* to book at this time. In the last case, if the salesman cannot convince the customer to at least tentatively book his affair, he should remind the customer that his preferred date may be taken if he does decide to book later. The salesman should also try to ascertain why the customer feels that the operation is not suitable for his function. It might turn out that the salesman may be able to overcome whatever the customer perceives as obstacles to land the account.

The customer who wants to definitely book a function is ready to confirm a date, time, and room. He probably has visited all the catering operations that interested him and he has chosen yours in which to hold his affair, or he may be so impressed by your establishment that he feels no need to look elsewhere. Whatever the reason, he commits himself to holding the function at your establishment. In this case, the definite booking request form (Fig. 5–4) is filled out and signed by the customer, and a deposit is secured. This form is also made out in triplicate: one for the customer, one for the customer's file, and one for the department head. The function is entered in the function reservation book in pen, indicating that it is a definite booking. Deposits received should be recorded in a deposit ledger and the customer given a receipt. The booking request form should also note that a deposit has been received. The customer should be informed at this time what the house policy is regarding deposit refunds: some caterers will refund a deposit only under certain conditions, while others maintain a policy of not refunding deposits for any reason.

A tentative booking is a "maybe" booking: the customer is definitely interested but not absolutely certain about booking with you. Although he may be impressed by your operation, there might be other caterers he is interested in visiting before making a final decision, or he may need to bring another party into the decision. At any rate, a tentative booking means that the customer's preferred date will be held for him for a specified amount of time (usually five to seven days). No deposit is required until the customer definitely books as discussed above.

For this type of booking, the tentative booking request form is filled out, and the function is entered in the reservation book in pencil. The tentative booking request form is similar to the one used for definite bookings with the exceptions that a "hold until" date is listed and the deposit required when the booking becomes definite is noted. The customer is asked to contact the salesman by the date given on the form, and if he doesn't, the salesman should contact him. If the customer has decided not to definitely book the function, the salesman again should try to determine why the customer has come to this decision. It is important that the salesman avoid being pushy while at the same time making the effort to accommodate the customer.

Again, the form is made out in triplicate: one for the customer, one

ABC Catering
120 Main Street
New City, N.Y. 10956

☐ Customer copy
☐ File copy
☐ Department head

Salesman _John Smith_
Follow-up date _4-27-XX_

Name of group _New York Telephone Company_
Type of function _Retirement Dinner for Mr. Stephen McConnell_
Person in charge _Mr. Patrick Cahill_ Phone Office: _(212) 354-2000_
Address _230 West 23 Street_ Home: _(516) 765-3311_
City _New York_ State _N.Y._ Zip _10018_

Day of week	Date	Attendance	Schedule	Function room assigned	Start	End	Rental charges
Friday	1-23-XX	300	Retirement Dinner	Blue Rm.	8 PM	1 AM	n/a
		300	Butler Style Cocktail Hour	Blue Rm. Foyer	8 PM	9 PM	n/a
		300	Dinner/ Dance	Blue Rm.	9 PM	1 AM	n/a

I understand that this serves as confirmation of the above affair for the number of guests given. Prices have been detailed in a written estimate.

A deposit of $_____ has been paid. I understand that 50% of the estimated balance will be required halfway between this date and the date of the affair, and that the remainder is to be paid on the date of the affair.

_____ (signature of engager)

_____ (signature of salesperson)

_____ (date)

Fig. 5-4. Definite booking request form.

for the customer's file, and one for the secretary, who maintains a list of all tentative dates and distributes it to all salesmen. The list includes the name of the organization or account; the date, time, and type of function; the date by which a decision must be made; the room(s) reserved; the number of expected guests; and the salesman's name. This list should be updated on a weekly basis as tentative dates are definitely booked or released. This list puts at the salesman's fingertips all dates that are temporarily being held but that may open up later.

All tentative dates should either become definite bookings or be cleared as soon as possible, since other customers may be making inquiries about these same dates. If another group wants to definitely book a date that is being held on a tentative basis by someone else, then the tentative party should be contacted immediately and asked to take the date or release it. If a person or group holds more than one date on a tentative basis, these should be cross-referenced in the reservation book, and the salesman should try to get a decision as soon as feasible. A date may also be tentatively held by a second group, but they should be told that someone else is already holding the date and will get first priority if they decide to definitely book. Then the salesman should contact the original party to expedite turning one of these into a definite booking.

When a group that has tentatively booked a function decides to make it definite, a letter of confirmation (Fig. 5-5) is then sent to the person in charge of the function. The customer signs and returns all copies but one, which he retains for himself, and forwards the required deposit.

Usually, there is no other contact with the client until the contract is signed. Prior to this, however, the client may request to change some aspect of the affair, such as the date or time. When such a change can be made, it should be confirmed in writing for everyone's protection. The change should also be recorded in the function reservation book and the appropriate personnel notified.

If a customer requests to be released from a definite booking, this should also be confirmed in writing (see Fig. 5-6), and the cancellation report (Fig. 5-7) should be completed and distributed. Naturally, releasing a customer from a definite booking is subject to certain stipulations, such as the customer reimbursing the caterer for any expenses incurred on his behalf up to the point of release.

Repeat Business

While soliciting new business is vital, it is repeat business that remains the backbone of any successful caterer. Repeat business is proof positive that your clients are satisfied with your facilities, food, and service. A repeat customer is not only a direct source of income but also a caterer's most reliable source of new business. A satisfied customer will eagerly recommend your services to others.

A caterer should make every effort to reserve and protect future dates for repeat clients, especially for those regular customers who have proven to generate substantial profits. If it is impossible to hold preferred dates due to previous bookings, then alternate dates should be offered and held to prevent the loss of these valuable repeat functions.

To increase the chances of getting repeat business, the salesman should try to reach the customer first. If you wait for the customer to come to you, he may be going elsewhere. Salesmen should contact the person in charge of a function immediately after it is held; the salesman can either call the customer directly and inquire if everything was satis-

ABC Catering
120 Main Street
New City, N.Y. 10956

June 13, 19XX

Mr. Patrick Cahill
New York Telephone Company
230 West 23rd Street
New York, N.Y. 10017

Dear Mr. Cahill:

In reference to our telephone conversation of June 11th, 19XX, it gives me great pleasure to confirm the following definite reservation:

Retirement Dinner for	
Mr. Stephen McConnell	Friday, January 23, 19XX
(Type of function, guest(s) of honor)	(Day and date of function)
Reception/Dinner/Dance	8 PM to 1 AM
(Schedule of function)	(Time of function)
Blue Room and Foyer	300
(Room(s) reserved)	(Approximate number of guests)

Prices and details for the above affair have been delineated in a written estimate.

Please sign all (3) copies and return (2), retaining one for yourself, along with your deposit of $1,000. Fifty percent of the estimated balance will be required halfway between the date of this letter and the date of the affair. The remainder is to be paid on the date of the affair.

About one month prior to the affair, we will contact you with regard to the signing of the contract. At this time, we will also make the final arrangements for your affair.

Please do not hesitate to call on us at any time for additional information or assistance.

We appreciate your patronage and look forward to serving you and your guests.

Cordially yours,

John Smith
Sales Representative

. . . .

I hereby confirm the above reservation and enclose a deposit of $_____ .

_____   _____
(Signature of engager)   (Date)

Fig. 5-5. Letter confirming definite booking.

**ABC Catering
120 Main Street
New City, N.Y. 10956**

ABC CATERING hereby releases (name of client or organization) from

any further contractual obligations for use of (room name) on

(date). It is understood that the amount of $_____ is to

be paid to ABC Catering for liquidated damages. Upon payment, the

caterer herewith releases the above-named party from any and all

claims either now or in the future. The leasee whose name appears

above agrees to do the same.

_____   _____
Signature of Leasee   Signature for ABC Catering

_____
Date

Fig. 5-6. Form used to release customer from definite booking.

factory, or he can send a thank-you letter in the form of a questionnaire (Fig. 5-8). The person or committee responsible for arranging an organization's function periodically changes, so it is important for the banquet salesman to contact the person currently in charge of the arrangements.

Since the repeat customer is already familiar with your operation, many times sales personnel will handle inquiries about another function over the telephone. It is advisable, however, to fill out a banquet inquiry report (Fig 5-9) for each telephone inquiry. Salesman can follow up on these informal inquiries and perhaps convert them into bookings. Also, by keeping a record of information imparted over the telephone, your salesmen will know what the customer was quoted when he comes in to discuss a function in greater detail at a later date.

Although dealings with repeat customers are more informal than with new customers, this does not preclude getting everything down in writing. All of the forms discussed under new business apply to the repeat customer as well, although much of the time the signing of booking request forms, confirmation letters, and contracts may be handled through the mail.

ABC Catering
120 Main Street
New City, N.Y. 10956

☐ General manager
☐ Director of catering
☐ File copy

Name of function _____

Type of function _____

Person in charge _____

Day and date of function _____

Number of persons _____

Room assigned _____

Time _____

Phone Office: _____ Home: _____

Amount of deposit on hand _____

Reason for cancellation _____

_____

_____

Has written confirmation of cancellation been received? _____

Has cancelled date been rescheduled?   ☐ Yes   ☐ No

If yes, what is new date? _____

Has action been taken on refund of deposit? _____

_____

Has a report of lost business been prepared? _____

Have all departments been notified of cancellation? _____

Has cancellation been entered in function reservation book? _____

Date _____   Salesperson _____

Fig. 5-7. Cancellation report.

ABC Catering
120 Main Street
New City, N.Y. 10956

Name of Person in Charge
Organization or Company
Address
City, State, Zip

We would like to take this opportunity to thank you for your recent
and most appreciated patronage.

In order that we may continue to improve our food, service, and
arrangements, we would appreciate it if you would take a moment to
fill out the following brief questionnaire:

Was the service satisfactory?	_____Yes	_____No
Were our employees courteous?	_____Yes	_____No
Was our food good?	_____Yes	_____No
Was it served hot?	_____Yes	_____No
Were our facilities clean?	_____Yes	_____No
Were your arrangements handled properly?	_____Yes	_____No
Would you recommend us to other potential customers?	_____Yes	_____No
Were you satisfied with the outside services we recommended? (photographer, musicians, limousine, etc.)	_____Yes	_____No

Other comments you wish to make_____

_____

_____

Thank you for your comments. May we again take this opportunity to
express our sincere appreciation for your past patronage. We are
looking forward to helping you arrange your next successful party.

Enclosed please find a stamped, self-addressed envelope for your
convenience.

                                        Sincerely yours,

                                        Name
                                        Title

Fig. 5-8. Follow-up letter including questionnaire.

ABC Catering
120 Main Street
New City, N.Y. 10956

☐ General manager
☐ Director of catering
☐ File copy

Date of inquiry_____

Name of organization_____

Function _____

Name of caller _____

Address _____

_____

Phone   Office: _____   Home: _____

Date requested _____

No. of persons _____   Time _____

Information required _____

_____

_____

_____

Details and prices quoted _____

_____

_____

_____
(Name of Salesperson)

Follow-up date _____

Action taken by caller (if caller does *not* book, state reason why and name of com-

petitor chosen by client) _____

_____

_____

_____

Fig. 5-9. Banquet inquiry report.

Contracts

The final formality in arranging an affair is the signing of the contract. This usually takes place about one month prior to the date of the affair, as insurance against rising prices. Contracts protect both the caterer and client by detailing all arrangements and stipulations. Nothing should be left to assumption. Figure 5-10 shows the contract that was drawn up for the retirement dinner presented as Case A earlier in this chapter.

Contracts should be prepared carefully so that all the details, arrangements, and prices are entered correctly. Some caterers may require additional deposits from their clients at the time the contract is signed. At this time, the salesman should stress the importance of the final guarantee (number of guests). The specific number of guests the client must pay for whether or not they actually attend the function must be pinpointed. Most caterers require customers to give a five- to seven-day notice on their final guarantees. Some caterers will allow as little as 48 hours' notice, which means that the caterer must act quickly to order, receive, and prepare his merchandise on time. Most caterers will stress that the amount of guests given on their final guarantee is not subject to change. Some caterers, perhaps to be more liberal or competitive, will give a leeway of approximately 5%, i.e., the client can have and not pay for 5% fewer guests in the event of sickness, cancellation, or other problems.

In an attempt to possibly increase revenue from an affair, additional suggestions or lists of other services available should be presented to the customer at this time. Since customers "soften" as the affair draws near, they may be receptive to adding to or enhancing the affair. All of the details already decided on should be reviewed at this time, as well as the total monies received to date and the balance due.

As with the other forms discussed so far in this chapter, contracts are made out in triplicate: one for the customer, one for the customer's file, and one for the employee in charge of the function. Later, as the date of the affair draws near, the details on the contract will be placed on the work order and referred to for ordering and requisitioning purposes.

To ensure the caterer complete protection, all stipulations should be reviewed by the caterer's attorney and printed on the reverse side of the contract. The following are sample "conditions of contract," or stipulations, that may be included.

1. Patron grants the right to the caterer to raise the prices quoted herein at the time of performance, or to make reasonable substitutions on the menu or for other items listed on the contract to meet increased costs for food, beverage, labor, taxes, currency values, or other operational costs.

2. A minimum deposit of ten percent (10%) of the estimated total bill is required at the time of the initial signing or confirmation for the facilities. Fifty percent (50%) of the balance is due no later than one

ABC Catering
120 Main Street
New City, N.Y. 10956

Banquet Contract

Name of engager Mr. Patrick Cahill   Type of function Retirement Dinner for
                                                           Mr. Stephen McConnell

Name of organization New York
                     Telephone Co.   Day and date Friday, 1-23-XX

Address. 230 West 23rd Street   Time From: 8 PM   To: 1 AM

         New York, N.Y. 10011   Room Blue

Phone Office: (212) 354-2000   Ceremony From: N/A To: _____

       Home: (516) 765-3311   Cocktail hour From: 8 PM To: 9 PM

                                           Room Blue Room Foyer

Approx. number of guests 300   Minimum guarantee 270   Final guarantee 278

Deposit $1,000   Receipt No. 342

COCKTAIL HOUR

Food	Liquor

Food

I. Butler style   Price: $8.00
   hors d'oeuvres   per person
   (see menu for selection)
II. Buffet style   Price: _____
    hors d'oeuvres   per person
    (see menu for selection)

A. Chafing dishes (choice of 5)

    1. _____
    2. _____
    3. _____
    4. _____
    5. _____

B. Cold platters (choice of 4)

    1. _____
    2. _____
    3. _____
    4. _____

C. Salads (choice of 3)

    1. _____
    2. _____
    3. _____

Liquor

From 2 open bars (unlimited)
  liquor for 1 hour from
  8 to 9 PM
Including:
  Manhattans
  Martinis
  Whisky Sours
  Scotch Sours
  Canadian Club Rye
  Dewars White Label Scotch
  Smirnoff Vodka
  Beefeater Gin
  Jack Daniels Bourbon
  Bacardi Rum
  White Wine

  (Includes all sodas,
  mixers, and juices)

Cheese platters, assorted breads, and fresh fruit arrangements

Fig. 5-10. Completed contract.

DINNER

Toast: <u>N/A</u>

Beverage with meal: <u>N/A</u>

Service time: <u>9 PM</u>

Price: <u>$14.00</u>   per person

Menu

Celery/Radishes/Olives/Carrot
  Spears
Melon in Port
Fresh Garden Vegetable Soup
Caesar Salad
Roast Prime Top Sirloin of Beef
Rissole Potatoes
Bouquetierre of Vegetables
Assorted French Pastries
Coffee-Tea-Milk
Mints and Nuts

Liquor

1 Bottle of Rye (Seagram 7) at
28.00 ea. and 1 Bottle of
Scotch (Dewars White Label) at
30.00 ea. for each table of 10
with setups

CEREMONY

Type <u>N/A</u>   Room_____ Time_____

Flowers _____ Colors_____

Music _____

Room rental_____

Other equipment _____

Rehearsal _____ Date _____ Time _____ Room _____

MISCELLANY

French Service <u>N/A</u>

Linens: Tablecloths <u>Light blue</u>   Lace cloths <u>N/A</u>

         Napkins <u>Royal blue</u>   Candles <u>Blue</u>

Flowers <u>1 large centerpiece; 29 regular centerpieces</u>   Colors <u>Light blue, dark blue, and white</u>

Fig. 5-10. Completed contract (*continued*).

Cake: Type N/A   No. of tiers_____

    Filling_____   Cut and serve _____

Viennese Table N/A _____

Music: Name Don Smith Orchestra   Price $600

    No. of pieces 5   Time: From 9 PM To 1 AM

    Preheat ____ to ____   Continuous ____ to ____

    Feed band Yes ____ No X

Photography Name N/A   Price_____

    Feed photographer Yes ____ No ____

Room rental N/A

Dressing room N/A

Checkroom .50 per person

Lounges 2 attendants @ 35.00 ea.

Cigarettes N/A   Cigars N/A

Printing (state amount, color, and inscriptions):

    Menus N/A

    Matches N/A

    Cocktail napkins N/A

    Stirrers N/A

    Other N/A

Audiovisual equipment _____

Remarks: Post "No Tipping" signs in checkroom and lounges

17% Gratuities on total food and beverage served   8% State and City Tax

Patrick Cahill   12-23-XX   *John Smith*
Engager   Date   ABC Catering

This Contract Is Subject to the Terms and Conditions Printed on the Reverse Side.

Fig. 5-10. Completed contract (*continued*).

month prior to the date of the function, and full payment of the remaining balance of the account is due at the end of the affair on the day of the function. Only cash, money order, or bank or certified check will be accepted. Credit cards are not accepted.

3. Deposits are not refundable.

4. No outside liquor or food is permitted on the premises without the consent of management, in which case a corkage fee will be charged for each bottle.

5. The hours herewith stipulated on the contract shall be strictly observed. The Patron agrees to pay the caterer for any overtime payments or expenses incurred by the caterer when permission is granted by management for the extension of time.

6. The person or organization assumes responsibility to reimburse the caterer for all damage to the establishment's property, including fixtures, furnishings, and other appurtenances and will surrender the rooms in the same order and condition as they were at the beginning of the function.

7. Patron and/or guests will confine themselves to the specific rooms rented and use such entrances and exits designated by the caterer.

8. When a situation arises beyond the control of the management, the establishment reserves the right to assign a similar facility and that all other stipulations and arrangements will apply as set forth in this contract.

9. Performance of this agreement is contingent upon the ability of the caterer to complete same and is not liable for the failure to complete this contract due to strikes, labor disputes, accidents, or any other causes beyond control of management preventing or interfering with performance.

10. Management reserves the right to cancel this agreement without notice and without liability when in the event of breach of this contract by the Patron or where the rules were not observed or where functions are of a nature not acceptable to this establishment.

11. Patron assumes responsibility for any and all damages, losses, and bodily injury caused by them or any of their guests or any other persons attending the function.

12. Patron agrees not to place or put up any displays, signs, banners, or other materials within the establishment without written permission of the caterer.

13. Management reserves the right to remove persons from leased premises that management deems objectionable without any responsibility therefore to leasee.

14. Management will not be responsible for articles of clothing lost, stolen, or left in the premises.

15. Management is not liable for any damage or loss to parked cars.

16. If affair is cancelled, management will demand damages including rental of premises.

17. Patron agrees to pay separately all federal, state, and municipal taxes which may be applicable and imposed by this agreement and on services rendered by the caterer in addition to the prices herein agreed upon.

18. Final arrangements pertaining to menu and other contract details and arrangements must be completed in full one (1) month prior to date of function.

19. Final guarantee as the number of persons must be given not later than seven (7) days before function. No reduction will be made from the final number guaranteed and charges will be made accordingly, nor will extra places be set for more than 5% over the preset guarantee.

20. This agreement is not assignable.

While it is important for the salesman to be sure that the customer understands all of the stipulations put forth in a contract, there are two points that the salesman should explain fully to every client: overtime and cancellations.

Overtime

Overtime services, and consequently charges, are usually an option at all functions, but especially for weddings, bar mitzvahs, and anniversaries—affairs that often extend beyond the time limit stated in the contract. Most caterers permit five hours for the whole function (one hour for the cocktail reception and four hours for the function). The client should be told that if it is possible for his function to run over the time contracted for (i.e., the room is not needed for another affair), the function will be allowed to continue and overtime charges will be levied. Usually the banquet representative or headwaiter will approach the host when the time limit expires and ask if he wishes to prolong the function for an additional hour. If he does not wish to do so, the music, if engaged, is stopped, and the service personnel begin to clear their tables. The charges should be explained to the customer before the day of the affair, though, to avoid misunderstanding later when the bill is to be paid. The customer may be charged for overtime in the following ways.

1. A charge may be levied for each attending guest, for example, $3.50 per person. This extra charge entitles the host to continued service and any additional liquor required (where unlimited liquor is offered) for one additional hour. For example, if there are 100 guests at a function and the overtime charge is $3.50 per person, an additional $350.00 would be added to the final bill.

2. Another method is to charge for service and liquor separately. A set amount, e.g., $10.00 per hour, is charged for every employee needed to

service the function (waiters, bartenders, check room and parking attendants, etc.). Another charge is applied for any additional bottles of liquor consumed during the hour. For example, if 15 employees are needed at $10.00 each ($150.00) and five bottles of liquor are consumed at $30.00 each ($150.00), then a charge of $300.00 would be applied to the final bill.

Most caterers prefer to use the first method because it guarantees a fixed liquor charge for what usually turns out to be a small amount of liquor consumed. Since most liquor is consumed during the early hours of an affair, very little will be needed during the last hour.

Overtime charges offer several advantages to a caterer.

1. They represent additional revenue to the caterer that was not anticipated.

2. These revenues are highly profitable, since generally the overtime does not require additional overtime payment to the employees because it falls within their regularly scheduled working hours. Management usually anticipates overtime by bringing in half the service crew an hour later than the early crew to cover any overtime possibility.

3. The overtime charge is based on the total number of guests even though many guests may have already left the premises or will be leaving prior to the completion of the overtime. Some caterers will give an allowance to a client when it becomes obvious to the host that many of his guests have already left. Other caterers will charge for the full number of guests regardless of the number remaining.

Keep in mind that separate overtime charges are required for music if the band is requested to stay for the additional hour. This additional fee is generally discussed between the host and the bandleader. Under no circumstances should the band be permitted to play overtime without first consulting and receiving permission from management.

Cancellations

As already mentioned, a caterer may impose certain penalties on a customer who decides to cancel a booking, such as not refunding the deposit or charging the customer for expenses incurred on his behalf up to the point of cancellation. Depending on the circumstances surrounding the cancellation, the caterer may choose not to enforce this policy. Nevertheless, it is a good idea to discuss the repercussions of cancellation with a customer beforehand so that (1) he cannot say he was not informed in the event the penalties are imposed and (2) to discourage cancellations in the first place.

Now what if the shoe is on the other foot? May the caterer cancel the affair for any reason? May the caterer change the facilities or function room? Caterers usually reserve the right to cancel any affair, when it may not be feasible for legitimate reasons for a caterer to hold the function: for example, if the client does not live up to the agreements or conditions of the contract; violates an agreed-upon house rule; or when because of an act of God, labor strike, or any incident beyond the control of management the caterer cannot perform the function. Caterers may change a client's facility or function room to another smaller or larger facility under certain conditions such as when the number of guests varies excessively from the original commitment. The assigned room may also be changed in instances as when a malfunction, e.g., a broken air-conditioning unit, faulty heating system, or flooding, prevents the use of the contracted room. To protect the caterer, cancellation clauses should be placed into the conditions of contract.

It is apparent that, throughout all negotiations with clients, the salesman's role is an important one. Although making the sale is his primary function, he also acts in a public relations capacity, since his contact with customers extends beyond the point of sale. For this reason, the selection of your sales team should be based not only on track record but also on ability to deal with people effectively. Remember that in most cases the salesperson who first interviews a customer will be the only person that customer deals with until the function takes place. He represents you, your business, and your business philosophy. Make sure the people you hire will do just that.

Final Bills

With the salesman out of the picture, the responsibility of checking and presenting the final bill to the client at the conclusion of a function falls on the headwaiter. His first job in this regard is to obtain the final head count. He can make this determination by simply deducting the number of empty place settings from the total number set up for the affair. Since this is often an unreliable method because guests who may be elsewhere can be overlooked, the headwaiter should instruct all waiters to tally and report to him the number of guests at their station as a means of counter checking. (Waiters should make a second tally while dinner is in progress to account for any guests who may have arrived after the initial count was made.) After notifying the chef so that the exact number of meals can be prepared, the headwaiter should check the number of guests attending against the final guarantee. If the numbers differ greatly either way—many more or many less than guaranteed—the headwaiter should speak to the person in charge immediately if the policy regarding deviations from the final guarantee calls for it. This will preclude misunderstandings later when the final bill is presented.

The final bill can be prepared by the banquet or accounting department from the contract and checked by the headwaiter to make sure that any extra items ordered by the host but not listed on the contract can be

Bill

ABC Catering
120 Main Street
New City, N.Y. 10956

☐ Customer copy
☐ File copy
☐ Accounting Department

Name of function Retirement Dinner for Mr. Stephen McConnell

Name of person in charge Mr. Patrick Cahill

Address 230 West 23rd Street

New York, New York 10011

Phone Office: (212) 354-2000   Home: (516) 765-3311

Date of function Friday, January 23, 19XX

Name of room Blue Room and Foyer

Time 8 PM to 1 AM

No.	Item	@	Totals
278	Cocktail Hour	$ 4.50	$ 1,251.00
278	Hors d'oeuvres ☒ Butler ☐ Buffet	3.50	973.00
278	Food Covers	14.00	3,892.00
	Cake		
	Toast		
	Unlimited Liquor		
	Cocktails per quart		
30	Bottles of Rye (Seagrams 7)	28.00	840.00
30	Bottles of Scotch (Dewars)	30.00	900.00
	Bottles of		
	Bottles of		
	Extras (Food or Beverage)		
	TOTAL FOOD & BEVERAGES		7,856.00
	17% Gratuities on above		1,335.52
	8% City and State Tax on above		628.48
278	Coat Room Checking	.50	139.00
2	Lounge Attendants	35.00	70.00
1	Music Charges: 5 Piece Band (4 Hrs.)		600.00
	Music Overtime per Hour (if applicable)		

Fig. 5-11. The final bill.

1	Large Floral Centerpieces	30.00	30.00
29	Regular Floral Centerpieces	20.00	580.00
	Floral Pedestals/Sprays		
	Floral Aisle Baskets		
	Floral Canopy		
	Aisle Runner		
	Rental (Chapel)		
	Rental (Room)		
	Bridal Suite		
	TOTAL		11,239.00
	LESS DEPOSITS		1,000.00
Payment Received by: *M. Jones — Headwaiter*	BALANCE DUE		10,239.00
Date: 1/23/XX			
THANK YOU FOR YOUR VALUED PATRONAGE!			

Fig. 5-11. The final bill (*continued*).

included. All extra items and services not given in the contract should be documented, so that a record of them can be produced should the customer question any extra charges on the bill.

The final bill for the retirement dinner presented earlier in this chapter (Case A) is given in Fig. 5-11 and completes, for the time being, the file for this function. But hopefully not for the account. Although the profits garnered from this function cannot be fully ascertained immediately, the caterer can see from the final bill that substantial revenue was generated by this affair and will take the steps outlined in this chapter to make sure that the client becomes a repeat customer. Read on for more guidelines on this and other aspects of the sales effort of the successful catering operation.

Chapter 6

Developing and Increasing Sales

Every caterer will ask, "How can I increase my sales?" or "Why should my competitor (sometimes with an inferior facility) do more volume?" The answer lies in the fact that high-volume operations aggressively solicit business from both inside and outside the operation and immediately follow up all leads in order to book potential clients ahead of their competition. The entire operation works as a team to keep repeat clients satisfied, and also to actively solicit new clients and other sources of business to increase sales. Successful caterers constantly and persistently merchandise, promote, and sell their facilities, products, and services.

The Educated Sales Staff

Before a salesman can effectively sell anything, he must be thoroughly familiar with his clientele, area, operation, competitors, and his own products and services.

Know Your Clientele

To better understand their needs and desires, find out who they are:

What type of clientele do you get?
Where do they live?
What age groups are most prominent?
What are their most common occupations?
What is the average income level?
How far and by what means do they travel to your operation?
What type of functions do they require?
How often do they come to your operation?
How much are they willing to spend?
Why do they book (or not book) with you?

61

Know Your Area

Do a complete study on your area to better understand its demographics.

What types of businesses are in your area?
Industry?
Utilities?
Governmental agencies (local, state, federal)?
Educational facilities?
Religious groups?
Recreational facilities?
Historical sites?
Residential characteristics (owned or rented homes or apartments)?
Office buildings?
Shopping facilities?
Sporting facilities?
Entertainment?
Hotels and lodging?
Restaurants?
What is the growth rate of the population?
What is the growth rate of business?
How many building permits are issued?
What is the per capita income?
What are the business, home, school, and personal tax rates?
What access is available to catering establishments?
What are the traffic counts and patterns?
Climatic conditions?
Zoning laws?
Other pertinent information?

Know Your Operation

Get to know the physical characteristics of your plant both inside and outside.

What is the number, size, dimensions, and capacity of parking facilities; entrances; lobby; checking facilities; bars; cocktail areas; function rooms; theater-style meeting rooms; classroom-style meeting rooms; stages; dance floors; bridal rooms; dressing rooms; chapels?

Which rooms get used most? Least? For what reason?

What is the full range of the kitchen facilities?

What equipment is available?

List your advantages and mention them to customers. For example, good location; good parking facilities; largest seating capacity in area; newly decorated rooms; no pillars or posts to obstruct view; raised platforms or stages.

List your disadvantages and play these down to customers. For example, small lobby; limited parking; limited access to men's and ladies' lounges; some rooms not completely private; small dance floor.

Know Your Competitors

Get to know their strengths and weaknesses.

How many are there in your area?
Who are they?
Where are they located?
What types of facilities do they offer?
How many function rooms do they have?
What is the seating capacity for each room? Total capacity?
What type of service do they use?
What type of menus and prices do they offer?
Do you have a recent copy of their menus?
What is their price range for breakfast, lunch, and dinner?
Do they offer package plans?
What is included in their package plans?
What is their price range for functions such as weddings, anniversaries, bar mitzvahs, etc.?
Do they charge room rentals? How much?
What promotions do they use?
What are their advantages? For example, free parking; newly decorated rooms; large seating capacity.
What are their disadvantages? For example, high prices; average food and service; constant change of ownership and personnel; limited parking.

Know Your Product and Services

Let a client know what you have to offer and sell it. A salesman should be able to confidently answer any question a client may pose in relation to food, beverages, and service.

Know your banquet menus and prices.

Be able to recommend appropriate foods, beverages, and services to a client.

Know the proper preparation and presentation of these items.

Know what extra or special services are available.

Know what extra charges are to be applied.

Know what items you can promote to improve an affair and increase revenues.

Know the outside services and contacts that you recommend, including their prices.

Promote your advantages! For example, use of fresh products, not frozen; reasonable prices; "seconds" on entreé course; free glass of wine with dinner; free cordial after dinner; professional service staff; clean operation; free services such as valet parking; good reputation (show letters of appreciation from previous clients).

The Effective Sales Program

Regardless of the size of your operation, your objective should be to increase your sales figures over that of a previous period. To accomplish this, first compile sales figures from a previous period (e.g., last year) and then set a goal (dollar figure) for an upcoming period (e.g., this year), breaking the figures down into food sales, beverage sales, and revenue generated by additional service. In setting this goal, make sure that it is realistic, e.g., attainable by your sales personnel. Plan your strategy and carry it out systematically.

Step 1

Make a list of all the different groups that patronize your establishment most often and the types of functions most often held:
Professional groups
Fund-raising groups
Business organizations
Trade organizations
Weddings and engagements
Bar mitzvahs
Anniversaries

Step 2

After the list is completed, pick one group at a time and compose a list of prospective sources or leads such as past files, referrals, yellow pages, Chamber of Commerce, and newspaper clippings. Record the names and addresses of these potential clients. For example, to obtain leads on potential engagements or weddings the following sources should be contacted:
Newspapers (engagement or wedding announcements)
Bridal consultants
Bridal shops
Formal wear shops
Published bridal and engagement lists
Photographers
Musicians
Florists

Department stores (bridal registries)
Limousine services
Jewelers
Travel agencies
Clergymen

Step 3

After your list of sources is complete, contact each one by a direct mail or phone. Tell them in your communication what your services are and that you would appreciate any referrals. If any of these sources requires a commission or a reciprocal business arrangement within reason, do not hesitate to comply.

Step 4

Contact those sources who have responded to your mailings by phone. If they show interest, invite them to see your operation. It may also be advisable to phone those sources who have not responded to your mailing to find out the reason why they have not contacted you. Even though they have not responded to your mailing, they still may be interested in providing leads. Again and again, in salesmanship the important value of the follow-up cannot be overemphasized.

Step 5

Review progress weekly and continue to follow up all leads.

After the wedding and engagement leads have been exhausted, start a sales campaign on another group, e.g., professional groups. Go through the same steps of procuring leads through contacting professional groups such as physicians, lawyers, dentists, accountants, architects, engineers, etc. Refer to trade journals, periodicals, professional organizations, and other sources. Organize a mailing and follow up on any potential function until all leads have been traced. Then start on another group or segment of your business. Do this until all groups and functions have been solicited. Repeat as often as possible throughout the year. Keep in mind that certain functions or groups may require more frequent solicitation than others because of the nature or volume of business it may provide. In many operations, the wedding business may be a major source of revenue and would command more effort in solicitation.

Plan a sales program on a yearly basis and break it down into monthly intervals and discuss progress being made at weekly meetings. Next to each date put down your strategy; for example, for the solicitation of wedding and engagement business, the following sequence might be listed:

January 7—Solicit sales for weddings and engagements.

January 14—Compile list of sources of leads from various contacts for direct mailing.

January 21—Send out mailings to sources received.

January 28—Contact any responses to mailings by phone. Contact responses not received.

February 4—Review results. Solicit next category—professional groups.

It is important that every salesperson be aware of his responsibility for the initiation and success of the sales program. Records should be kept on each month's progress to compare to last year's monthly sales. Each salesman should be rated as to the progress of his sales over last year's. Consistent checking, periodic evaluations at weekly and monthly meetings during the entire length of the sales program, and measurement of the final sales results targeted for the operation must be supervised by a responsible individual or department head. The salesman who shows consistent increases should be rewarded for his efforts with a promotion, bonus, or other incentive to keep interest and motivation high.

Teamwork is essential for the overall success of the program. Each person at every level has a responsibility to do his job thoroughly to make each function a success. Any person who fails to give his all lowers the effectiveness of the entire program.

The operation whose salesmen are most active in going after the sales is generally the most successful. Here are a few suggestions for approaches a salesman might try in soliciting and increasing business.

Review local newspapers daily for any announced parties. Find out and contact the person in charge of each function. For repeat or annual functions, ask your client to book or reserve a tentative date for his next function as soon as the current affair has been completed or the final bill has been paid. See Fig. 6-1 for a sample letter. Systematically send letters and make telephone calls to rebook past clients and solicit new leads.

Solicit functions well in advance of their intended dates. Seek contacts for Christmas parties during the summer months; baseball leagues during the football season, etc. See Fig. 6-2 for a sample letter.

To promote your facilities and services, send letters of congratulations (see Fig. 6-3) to people who have received promotions or awards, been elected to office, retired, become engaged, have upcoming anniversaries, etc.

Run promotions during your slow season. During a period when your wedding business slacks off, run an ad for a special wedding price break. Run this ad well in advance of the month or months you wish to promote.

Have a bridal fashion show during your slow season to expose your operation and services. Invite a bridal shop to put on this show and also invite all outside or house services to put on demonstrations or displays.

ABC Catering
120 Main Street
New City, N.Y. 10956

Date _____

Name of Person in Charge
Organization or Company
Address
City, State, Zip

Dear _____:

I trust that you and your guests were satisfied with the (breakfast,
luncheon, reception, or dinner) you held last (day, date). To insure
that we will have similar accommodations available for you, we are
holding, on a tentative basis, the following reservation:

(Name of Organization or Company) _____

(Type of Function) _____

(Name of Room) _____

(Day, Date, Time) _____

(Approximate Number of Guests) _____

Since we are already receiving requests for this time next year, we
would appreciate your confirming this date at your earliest
convenience.

We wish to express our sincere appreciation for your past and
continued patronage. Should you wish to discuss any novel ideas
to personalize your next party, whether it be menu, service, decor,
or other arrangements, please feel free to discuss them with us.

Sincerely yours,

Name
Title

Fig. 6-1. Letter soliciting repeat function.

ABC Catering
120 Main Street
New City, N.Y. 10956

Date _____

Name of Person in Charge
Organization or Company
Address
City, State, Zip

Dear _____:

You may think we are premature in contacting you at this time
regarding your annual (Christmas/New Year) party, but we are
already beginning to receive inquiries for these dates.

Since we do value your patronage, to assure you of your preferred
date, we would like to ask you to consider making a tentative
reservation, subject to a later final decision, to reserve the
necessary accommodations for your group.

Time seems to pass quickly and your reservation now will assure you
of the best possible date and private banquet facilities necessary
for the kind of party your group will appreciate having during the
holiday season.

I appreciate the opportunity of bringing this matter to your
attention and I do hope that I will be hearing from you shortly.

Sincerely yours,

Name
Title
Banquet Department

Fig. 6-2. Letter soliciting holiday function.

Find out who books functions for various organizations. Most large
organizations have someone in the personnel department or public relations department handling their functions. Remember, it may not always
be a person connected with top management who decides where the
function will be held. Whoever it may be, get to know them and show
these key people your appreciation for their patronage.

ABC Catering
120 Main Street
New City, N.Y. 10956

Date _____

Name of Person in Charge
Organization or Company
Address
City, State, Zip

Dear _____:

Congratulations on your (nomination, election, appointment,
promotion, etc.) We were extremely pleased to hear of your recent
achievement.

We would appreciate your considering us for any upcoming event you
plan. We have a wide range of accommodations to offer and, if you
should need any assistance in planning, I will be pleased to assist
you at your convenience.

Again, my sincere congratulations and best wishes for your continued
success. I remain,

Cordially yours,

Name
Title
Banquet Department

Fig. 6-3. Letter offering congratulations.

Be active in your community. Join various community groups and
clubs such as the Rotary, Kiwanis, Lions, Masons, and Elks to create a
positive image for community relations. Often, social contacts made
through these organizations lead to potential business opportunities.

Invite various local groups and organizations to visit or tour your
facilities. Show them what you have to offer. Promote and display your
talent, e.g., have the chef demonstrate a food display or arrangement.

Contact the county, state, and federal organizations in your area for
any upcoming functions, elections, meetings, etc.

Contact fund-raising groups such as political parties, churches, tem-
ples, hospitals, and charitable organizations for breakfasts, lunches, dinners, fashion shows, etc.

Contact various social groups or organizations for annual affairs, meetings, dances, and other possible functions.

Contact religious groups and organizations for required religious or social functions.

Contact professional, semi-professional, club, university, college, high school, grade school, Little League, and other sponsored sports teams and leagues for possible meetings, award dinners, or other functions.

Contact recreational facilities or businesses such as bowling alleys, tennis courts, skating rinks, sporting shops, and trophy manufacturers, for possible award, league, or social events.

Contact nonprofit organizations and businesses for annual meetings or other regularly held functions.

Contact fraternal or ethnic groups and clubs for social functions and meetings.

Contact department heads, the ladies' auxiliary in hospitals, fire departments, police departments, etc., for social functions, graduations, fund-raising functions, benefits, etc.

Contact local schools for graduations, lunches, meetings, class reunions, and social events. Send letters and invite all principals and senior and junior class advisors to visit your operation and reserve their prom dates one year in advance.

Check the list of your competitors' clients and functions. Contact the person in charge of the function immediately after the function is completed. If for some reason they were not satisfied with their arrangements or are looking for a new location for their next function, invite them in to see your facilities. If they had a problem with another caterer, take a special interest in seeing that the problem is not repeated.

In summation, contact any and all possible sources of business.

The Successful Advertising Program

Each operation will have a varying amount of money to spend for advertising. Most caterers generally have some funds set aside for advertising. To get the best results for the lowest cost, analyze which form of advertising will be most effective. For the small caterer who has limited funds, it may be advisable for him to put his limited resources directly into improving his operation or providing unique features. This will hopefully produce word-of-mouth advertising. The large or more established caterer, on the other hand, may be able to allocate a segment of its sales, perhaps between 2 and 4%, to an advertising program.

Your advertising message should tell your potential clients what you have to sell and what you want them to buy. It is wise to allocate a large portion of your advertising budget to the sale of affairs that return high profits. For example, in certain areas, weddings may be lucrative, so a large segment of the budget should go for promoting the wedding business.

Consider using media that will be in contact with the public year round to get best results, for example, the yellow pages and newspapers. When planning ads, there are often deadlines to meet, so it is important that they be submitted on time. To keep your name in front of the public, the following channels of advertising should be considered.

Telephone directories are a relatively inexpensive advertising medium and help direct clients to your operation. Since potential clients often search for services in telephone directories, a caterer should be listed in both the white and yellow pages, and an attractive display ad should be placed in the yellow pages. The yellow page listing should be placed under "Caterers." Use your telephone company representative to help you with suggestions as to the layout and organization of a creative ad.

Newspaper and magazine advertisements are beneficial because the client visualizes and retains the message given. Contact your local newspaper and magazine ad representative to get their rates and help set up your ad. Rates will be based on the size of the ad, position, number of lines, and the frequency of appearance. Magazines have the added advantage of being kept in the home or office for longer periods of time and are bought for a specific reason or by a specific group of readers. Find out which type of magazine readership will best serve your purposes.

Ads should be placed in the entertainment, restaurant, or catering section of the paper or magazine. Do not hesitate to seek a certain amount of free advertising, that is, articles, reviews, and editorials about your establishment especially in those publications in which you have placed ads. Since many of your events may be newsworthy (political debates, election returns, award dinners, celebrities attending or speaking at functions, etc.), it would be advisable to contact the local media well in advance to get complete coverage for these events.

Radio and television advertising can be expensive, so carefully evaluate the potential results of these modes of advertisement before making a commitment. Commercials or spot announcements vary in rates as to station, channel, time, frequency, and length of ad. Check into discount rates offered by stations for air time that has not been sold. Let your radio and television stations' representatives help you write your script for best results.

Direct mail, although costly, is an effective way to advertise and promote your business to a particular individual. Letters, brochures, postcards, handouts, and flyers may be used to thank clients, send congratulations, and promote your operation, ideas, or services to potential clients. To cut mailing expenses, inquire about bulk mail rates from your post office.

Outdoor signs and billboards may be used to advertise your operation and functions. They should be made of quality materials, visible from all directions. They may be painted, illuminated, electronic, portable, or stationary and should reflect the style of your operation. A professional sign manufacturer and painter should be consulted for best results.

Posters should be displayed in your lobby, rest rooms, restaurant, or other high-visibility areas to promote banquet functions.

Promotional giveaways, such as balloons, key chains, matches, menus, stirrers, etc., which are freely distributed to the public, are also a useful means of advertising.

Besides paid advertising, there are two other areas that are important in promoting sales: personal contacts and your employees.

Personal contacts are the most inexpensive and most effective means of advertising. A special effort should be made to satisfy your current clients. Get to know them personally and their likes and dislikes. Don't disappoint them. You want to turn them into repeat business, and you want them to recommend your operation to others. Be present for their functions and stay until they are completely satisfied. After the function is completed, book upcoming future affairs. Show your appreciation by thanking them personally and following up with a personal call and a thank you letter. Some caterers make it a policy to give their key accounts a token of appreciation such as a free dinner for two or the family; a bottle of liquor; a box of quality cigars. An annual function may be held with food, beverage, and music to which all key clients are invited. The expense for these promotions is generally charged to the advertising and promotion budget.

Your employees will advertise your operation because they directly reflect your attitude to the customer. They should be polite and well trained, have a neat, clean appearance, and wear good-fitting uniforms. Employees can be your best salespeople: often potential clients will ask employees about the operation to find out if it is reputable. Employees who are happy in their working environment and whose employer gives good value will always give a good recommendation to their friends or other potential clients.

Remember that an operation cannot turn around or change overnight. It takes time and effort to get results, but by having a determined sales crew willing to pursue a sales program and advertising campaign, your operation definitely should begin to show positive results within a reasonable period of time.

The Inevitable Loss of Business

Despite all of your efforts, as outlined in this chapter, you will lose business at some time or another. Whether it it is a past client who elects to go to your competition with his next function or a new customer who after visiting your premises decides not to book with you makes no difference. Either way you have lost an account.

It is essential that you analyze closely the reasons for losing an account, since more often than not lost business indicates that a problem exists. You will want to rectify the problem, especially if it is one that is cited repeatedly by customers. In order to be able to effectively analyze reasons for losing business, you will need to document them. One way is to prepare a report of lost business (Fig. 6-4).

□ General manager
□ Director of catering
□ File copy

Report of Lost Business

Name of organization: _____

Type of function: _____

Size of function: _____

Estimated revenue: _____

Contact's name: _____

Title: _____

Address: _____

_____

Phone: Office _____ Home _____

Name of competition selected: _____

Reason given for loss of business: _____

_____

Salesman's recommendation for future solicitation: _____

_____

_____

Follow-up date: _____

Date: _____ Salesperson: _____

Fig. 6-4. Report of lost business.

The problems that will be indicated most frequently on these reports and their solutions are as follows.

1. *Problem.* Lack of available dates and openings forcing a customer to go elsewhere.

Solution. Maintain a lost business book that records the type of function, the name of the person in charge, the organization, the number of persons attending, and the requested day, date, and year of each lost account so that, in the event the date becomes available due to a cancellation or change of date, it can be made available to this inquiring customer.

2. *Problem.* Prices are too high and you have overpriced your banquet menus in comparison to competition.

Solution. Analyze your price structure and put it in line with that of your competition. Your prices may be too high because control over spending is too liberal or too much ordering is being done for each party. The remedy to these problems is to set up a tight control system to avoid leakage and pilferage. Also, do comparison buying by checking with several vendors as to best price and quality.

Perhaps staffing is heavy or overloaded in relation to the amount of business performed. In catering, only a certain number of employees should be required for each job. Perhaps your employees are not producing at their required capacities. More productive output with less personnel will reduce labor costs. Combining several operations into a teamwork concept helps cut labor costs and eliminates the hiring of additional high-cost help, for example, the pantry man and dishwashers should help the chef prepare and serve dinner.

3. *Problem.* The caterer continues to offer the same menus for each affair, which causes a decline in business, especially for the "repeat" customer.

Solution. Change banquet menus periodically with new and varied offerings to satisfy the demands of the repeat customer. Ask your chef for recommendations or innovative ideas to increase customer acceptance. Use cookbooks and subscribe to trade publications, recipe card files, or other food publications for new ideas.

4. *Problem.* There are complaints about the poor quality of the food served.

Solution. First, buy the best-quality merchandise available. Then hire a competent and professional chef and kitchen staff to check, prepare, and produce the best possible product. Because of the proportionally small amount of money spent in relation to the number of guests served, it is poor business to hire cheap, inexperienced, and incompetent help who will ultimately cause disastrous results. Establish incentive plans for the chef and other key employees as a reward if business increases or if waste is reduced, yielding better food cost percentages.

5. *Problem.* Service was poor or inadequate.

Solution. Whether the service was careless, slow, indifferent, discourteous, or unprofessional, the problem can be solved by establishing a training program to correct these deficiencies. Service personnel must be shown how to properly approach, correctly serve, and please customers to the point where they may overlook other problems like average food.

6. *Problem.* The customer complained about bad arrangements or poor and shoddy facilities.

Solution. Avoid overcrowding, poor table and seating arrangements, poor heating, air-conditioning, and ventilation problems, using a small dance floor, or any other physical defect that will create customer complaints. Avoid problems by proper planning and by repairing or redecorating rooms periodically (every five years). Do not procrastinate in repairs or improvements because you will lose revenue due to these oversights. Lost business will shortly be greater than the cost of improvements.

7. *Problem.* Unsanitary conditions existed, such as dirty or spotted glassware, silverware, dishware, ashtrays, linens, men's and ladies' lounges, function rooms, etc.

Solution. Initiate a training program and cleaning schedule. Stress that a customer's first impression is of the operation's cleanliness or lack of it. Make sure that the necessary cleaning equipment and supplies are provided to do the job properly. Charge your service personnel with setting up a function completely and being responsible for clean rooms, serviceware, and linens. Demonstrate simple cleaning techniques, such as holding glasses over steamed water (a chafing dish is good) and drying before setting on tables. Basically, demonstrate to all personnel the importance you place on running a clean operation.

Whatever customer complaints are registered on the report of lost business, make sure that they are given top priority and that the problems are corrected quickly. If this is done, there is less chance that your business will continue to lose business.

Chapter 7

Agenda for Weekly Sales Meetings

It is important for meetings to be held on a weekly basis with the appropriate personnel in attendance in order to review and evaluate past, current, and future functions. The personnel who will be required to attend these meetings will depend on the individual operation and its organizational structure. For example, in a relatively small operation (see Fig. 7-1), there might be one person in charge of overseeing the entire operation (banquet manager), and he may meet with the owner or general manager alone, with the assistant banquet managers attending as necessary. In a larger organization (Fig. 7-2), that one person in charge of the entire banquet operation who is responsible to the general manager is usually the director of catering. He holds weekly meetings with his subordinates (e.g., banquet manager, assistant banquet managers, and banquet sales representatives). Whatever the structure of your operation, weekly meetings conducted in an orderly and logical manner will assure a smooth-running business.

Evaluating Past Functions

It is essential to review the various aspects of functions that have already been held, since what you do in the future depends on what you learn from the past. The following topics should be explored.

1. *Profit or loss.* Determine the final cost of a function and compare it to income produced. If a loss occurred, the function should undergo closer scrutiny to determine the reason, especially if a number of functions have been showing losses of late. Compare the final guest count to the number originally expected, since very often not meeting the minimum attendance requirements of a particular function room can be a source of financial loss.

2. *Labor and food costs.* It is necessary to single these out of the total cost of a function, since these costs are being used as the basis for prices being currently quoted to inquiring customers.

ORGANIZATION   RESPONSIBILITIES AND DUTIES

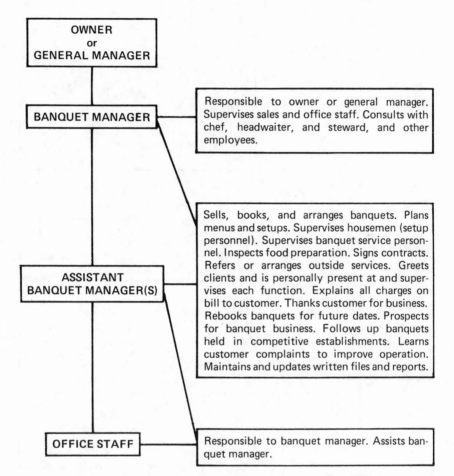

Fig. 7-1. Organizational structure for a small catering operation.

3. *Quality of food and service.* Discuss possible solutions to problems encountered and ways of implementing them. Invite staff members to offer suggestions and ideas.

4. *Customer comments.* Compile questionnaires returned by customers of recent functions and discuss any negative reactions. If there is more than one customer complaint about a certain food item or some aspect of your service, determine the cause and rectify it.

5. *Condition of rooms and equipment.* Report any needed repairs or equipment replacement that became apparent during a recent function. Determine customer liability if any.

ORGANIZATION   RESPONSIBILITIES AND DUTIES

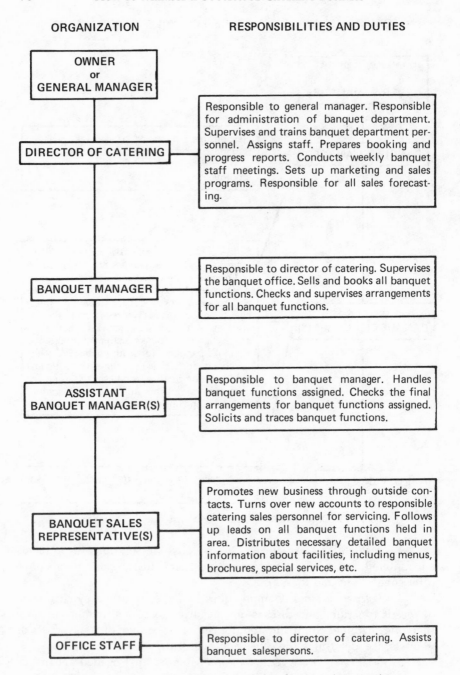

OWNER or GENERAL MANAGER

DIRECTOR OF CATERING

Responsible to general manager. Responsible for administration of banquet department. Supervises and trains banquet department personnel. Assigns staff. Prepares booking and progress reports. Conducts weekly banquet staff meetings. Sets up marketing and sales programs. Responsible for all sales forecasting.

BANQUET MANAGER

Responsible to director of catering. Supervises the banquet office. Sells and books all banquet functions. Checks and supervises arrangements for all banquet functions.

ASSISTANT BANQUET MANAGER(S)

Responsible to banquet manager. Handles banquet functions assigned. Checks the final arrangements for banquet functions assigned. Solicits and traces banquet functions.

BANQUET SALES REPRESENTATIVE(S)

Promotes new business through outside contacts. Turns over new accounts to responsible catering sales personnel for servicing. Follows up leads on all banquet functions held in area. Distributes necessary detailed banquet information about facilities, including menus, brochures, special services, etc.

OFFICE STAFF

Responsible to director of catering. Assists banquet salespersons.

Fig. 7-2. Organizational structure for a high-volume catering operation.

ABC Catering

Week of Sunday ___September 15th___ Through Saturday ___September 21, 19XX___

DAY	DATE	NAME OF ORGANIZATION	TYPE OF FUNCTION	NO. OF PERSONS	TIME	ROOM	SALESMAN
SUN	Sept. 15	XYZ CORPORATION	Coffee and Danish	75	8:30 AM- 9 AM	Rose Foyer	P.M.
			Meeting	75	9 AM-5 PM	Rose	
			Lunch	75	12 Noon- 1 PM	Rose Foyer	
WED	Sept. 18	CBD SALES CORP.	Cocktail Hour	150	12 Noon- 1 PM	Orchid	C.B.
			Lunch	150	1 PM	Orchid	
SAT	Sept. 21	Morris-Anderson Wedding	Cocktail Hour	100	7 PM-8 PM	Rose Foyer	P.M.
			Lunch	100	8 PM- 12 Midnight	Rose	

Fig. 7-3. Weekly function sheet.

Reviewing Current Functions

The functions that will be held in the coming week should also be the subject of this meeting. It is essential to touch base at this time with everyone involved in the execution of upcoming affairs to insure that all will go smoothly. The following points should be covered.

1. *Weekly function sheet.* All the functions to be held in a particular week should be assembled on this form (Fig. 7-3) and distributed to the appropriate personnel. With so many functions at various planning stages, it is important to officially notify all key personnel of approaching functions. Review the requirements of each function and make sure they are being met. Daily function sheets may be issued to keep track of events on a daily basis and to list functions on your bulletin board prior to guest arrival.

2. *Missing menus or menu changes.* Indicate the functions for which menus are outstanding and remind the salesman who booked the function to call the customer. Make sure all appropriate personnel know about changes that have been made in a menu.

3. *Final guarantees.* Determine for which functions you still need the final guest count. Since the customer is asked for this number no later than 5 days prior to the function, this information should be available for most functions to be held in the upcoming week. If any are missing, the salesman who booked the function should call the client.

4. *Work order forms.* Be sure that these have been drawn up for all functions. Distribute to personnel in charge of ordering or purchasing. Each will need to refer to this form to perform his particular tasks, e.g., the chef will extract information on all food items, the housekeeper all linens, etc.

5. *Work schedules.* Determine whether any additional help will be needed for any upcoming function. Also discuss the need for any overtime.

6. *Floor plans.* Make sure that a floor plan has been drawn up for each function. Also ascertain whether the customer has submitted his guest list and table assignments so that place cards may be prepared.

7. *Rehearsals.* Schedule any rehearsals needed, e.g., for wedding ceremonies.

Surveying Future Functions

With the evaluation of past functions and the review of current functions out of the way, it is time to turn the meeting's attention to future business. You will probably want all personnel involved in sales to be present for this portion of the meeting to discuss the following issues.

1. *Banquet guidelines.* As costs to the caterer increase, so must his

prices. Also, the minimum attendance required for each function room may change as prices fluctuate. When changes need to be made in either menu pricing or minimum attendance requirements, new guidelines need to be drawn up and distributed to each salesman (see Fig. 7-4). Once established, these guidelines will help utilize space to the maximum and will assure that each function produces the income needed to make a profit.

2. *Bookings.* Review all definite and tentative bookings acquired in the past week. Compare to bookings of a similar period, e.g., last year, to gauge progress. Review all open dates, especially those prime dates you would like to see booked. Check banquet inquiry reports and discuss game plan for follow-up by sales personnel. Also set goals for amount of business expected to be brought in based on same period last year.

Minimums for Attendance and Menu Price

NAME OF ROOM <u>STARLIGHT ROOM (Maximum Seating Cap-500)</u>

Period of Time	Minimum Number of Persons	Minimum Menu Price
A. During Months of *January, February, March, July, August*		
(1) *Weekdays* (Monday through Friday)		
LUNCH	200	$4.50
DINNER	300	6.50
(2) *Weekends* (Saturday, Sunday)		
LUNCH	250	$5.00
DINNER	350	7.50
B. During Months of *April, May, June, September, October, November, December*		
(1) *Weekdays* (Monday through Thursday)		
LUNCH	250	$5.00
DINNER	350	7.50
(2) *Fridays*		
LUNCH	250	$5.00
DINNER	350	8.00
(3) *Weekends* (Saturday, Sunday)		
LUNCH	300	$5.50
DINNER	400	8.50

Fig. 7-4. Banquet guidelines.

3. *Estimates.* Review estimates drawn up in the past week. Discuss items or services that a number of customers seem to be interested in at the present time, as well as those that are not selling. Determine whether these are usual trends for the time of year or type of function or whether definite changes in menus or services offered should be considered.

4. *Referrals.* Discuss current and potential sources. Review any new leads received in the past week.

5. *Advertising and marketing program.* Discuss current target group and progress being made in program to solicit their business. Also set up timetable for initiating program to solicit another group.

6. *Lost business.* Determine cause of business lost in the past week and come up with suggestions to prevent future losses. Do the same for any cancellations of functions that were already booked.

Some Tips on Conducting the Meeting

It may not be feasible to cover all of the above-mentioned points at each weekly meeting, but a systematic approach should be employed to periodically cover them all. Determine which topics are the most important for weekly review in your operation and then make every effort to insure that they are covered. Remind all attendees to come to these meetings prepared with all the information necessary to report, analyze, compare, discuss, etc. It might be a good idea to distribute the agenda prior to each meeting to insure that all personnel do come prepared.

SECTION III

Functions and Menus

What type of functions will you hold at your catering establishment and what will be on the menus? Although a great deal depends on what your customers want, the degree of versatility and innovativeness you will want for your operation is ultimately up to you. In this section, the many kinds of functions and parties your customers will request are reviewed, with special attention given to the wedding and bar mitzvah, two of the most profitable. In many cases, suggested menus are offered. Also, the many ways you can add flair and individuality to food and beverage presentation and service are discussed. First, though, let's explore the many facets of planning and pricing menus and package plans.

Chapter 8

Planning and Pricing Banquet Menus

Banquet menus inform the customer what food and beverages are available at what price and in so doing serve as an important link between the caterer and the client. Printed menus should look and sound interesting, imaginative, and elegant. Menu copy should be descriptive, clear, and easy to read.

Planning the Menu

Menu planning should be a team effort. Before the menu is printed, the chef should be consulted for suggestions and to confirm that kitchen equipment and staff are adequate and skilled enough to handle the demands of the menu; the maitre d' or headwaiter should be consulted to assure the proper training of the service staff and to guarantee the availability of adequate dining facilities and serviceware; the input of supervisory personnel should be encouraged to insure a soundly managed and smooth-running function.

Since ease of preparation and speed of service are essential in serving many guests in a short period of time, banquet menus should be kept simple. This will also help limit food, labor, equipment, and operating costs while insuring a superior end-product with efficient controls and less complications throughout the entire affair.

Each item on the menu should have eye appeal and offer an overall balance in taste, color, texture, and shape. Banquet foods should be attractively arranged and presented to arouse the interest of the guests and spur favorable comments and reactions.

The following are some points to remember when composing banquet menus:

1. Food must have popular appeal. Avoid spicy, sharp, or unusual tasting and looking foods, e.g., lamb, pork, fish, and curried sauces. If a client requests an item that does not have universal appeal, tactfully make the customer aware that many of his guests may not care for it. An unwise menu selection will prevent a segment of the guests from being

displeased. An exception would be a customer or group requesting ethnic foods or a theme menu.

2. Do not clutter the banquet menu. It should read like a business card. A limited selection of entrées will make the choice seem more personalized.

3. Foods should not be duplicated on a menu. For example, carrots as a vegetable and carrot cake for dessert or similar sauces such as charon or bearnaise. Also, if a wedding cake is to be served, do not serve another cake or pastry for dessert.

4. Incorporate liquor, wine, and beer into the menu selection whenever possible to increase beverage sales.

5. Offer menu substitutions for every function in the event a guest cannot eat the chosen entrée.

6. Keep records of what menu items are popular in your area. Make substitutions where needed. Record the number of favorable and unfavorable comments. Compare the sale of items, keeping in mind that higher-priced items tend to sell less frequently than lower-priced ones.

7. Use boneless meats whenever possible.

8. Use locally grown items for both interest and price.

9. Butler style (hand-carried) hors d'oeuvres should not be messy and drippy or contain shells, bones, or other inconveniences.

10. If soups are on a menu, offer a selection of clear, thick, and creamed types.

11. Include only one starch or fried item per entrée.

12. List menu items in the order they will be served. Each entrée should be priced to include all courses, e.g., appetizer, soup, salad, etc.

13. If menu items are unusually expensive or require special services and skills, additional charges should be listed next to them. For example: Shrimp cocktail, $3.00 extra.

14. A varying price range should be offered for each menu so that each customer's budget can be accommodated.

15. Menu items should not be listed in price from lowest to highest but should be mixed so that customers do not notice the increasing prices. The most profitable items should be placed on or near the top of the list of entreés.

16. Gratuities and sales tax should be listed separately on the bottom of the menu and not included in the menu price, to avoid creating customer resistance to price.

17. List extra charges on the menu for smaller numbers of guests to compensate for low income or extra labor charges.

18. Include on the menu the number or percent of additional portions that will be available for guests who arrive in excess of the client's guarantee.

19. State deadlines for final arrangements and confirmed guarantees on the menu.

20. Eliminate any items that may cause unnecessary production or service problems for large groups, such as soufflé potatoes.

21. Consider using convenience foods to control labor costs, and to avoid waste.

22. Calculate how much skilled and unskilled labor and time goes into each item.

23. Utilize leftovers or trimmings.

24. If possible, limit your customer's selection to one entreé for each function. This will speed preparation and service.

25. Advertise and use only top-quality foods and merchandise.

26. Do not oversell or overpromise on your menus.

27. When an operation has several types of food operations on the same premises, distinguish banquet menus from other menus by including the word "banquet" in the heading, such as "banquet breakfast" or "banquet dinner."

28. Use your menus as advertising. Put your name, address, telephone number, logo, and days and hours open on the menu to help promote business.

Pricing Banquet Menus

In pricing menus, be mindful of all the costs involved in the purchasing, receiving, storing, issuing, preparing, finishing, and serving of each proposed item, and, to guarantee a proper return on investment, price menus to insure that an adequate profit is garnered. Pricing banquet menus is simpler than most other menus, since most costs can be forecasted and controlled because of known quantities and expenses in catering. There are many methods that can be used to determine menu selling prices. Two of the most common approaches are: (1) basing your prices on those of a competitor; and (2) using food cost percentage factors and markups.

Using a competitor's prices: There are many pitfalls to this approach. Who says your competitor's prices are accurate? How do you know he is making a profit? How do you know his business expenses? His labor, overhead, or a multitude of other variables may make his profit margin quite different from yours. However, since customers will compare the prices of several competitors, these prices must not be totally ignored but should be considered when planning and pricing a banquet menu.

Food cost percentage factors and markups. Depending on the desired food cost percentage, raw food costs are calculated and multiplied by a factor, namely 2 (50% food cost percentage), $2\frac{1}{2}$ (40%), 3 (33%), 4 (25%), etc. The desired food cost percentage should take into account direct and indirect costs and profit. The word "should" is used because this method can be too general a system, since a profit will not be realized if the factor did not cover all costs.

Obviously, neither of these two methods of menu pricing is satis-factory. It is best to actually price each menu item yourself and then compare it to similar operations to see if the determined price is competi-tive. In pricing a menu, remember that any costs that have been forgotten will reduce your profit. As laborious and time-consuming as this method may be, it is necessary in order to arrive at true menu prices. When this approach is properly followed and periodically (quarterly) reviewed in relation to market conditions, prices, labor costs, and other related ex-penses, a constant and accurate profit level will be maintained. Menu prices need not be completely revamped each and every time food, labor, or operating expenses increase. Rather, establish a percentage figure of increase as the point at which to raise menu prices. For example, when total costs have increased 5%, increase menu prices accordingly. To calculate what a customer should be charged, as mentioned earlier, all the components that make up the total cost of a menu item must be deter-mined. To do this, first project the total food and labor cost and deter-mine the total operating expenses. Then determine the desired profit. Finally, add the desired profit to the total actual costs.

Projecting the Total Food Cost

Establish standard recipes and accurately cost out each menu item to get an exact portion cost. Since costing and portioning are done on the finished product, it becomes important to find out what, if any, losses occur in preparing a menu item. For this reason, prior to costing, yield tests should be conducted on any items for which a loss of weight will occur. Loss of weight, namely shrinkage and waste, usually occurs during such processes as trimming, boning, cooking, roasting, slicing, toasting, evaporating, or freezing. These losses must be accurately and periodically calculated and deducted from the total weight or volume to determine an accurate net yield. If trimmings, bones, fat, or other salvageable portions are used to make other products, then credits should be extended to the original item for its byproducts. Yield tests need not be performed on items on which no loss occurs, that is, on products that are bought and served in the same state or weight, such as convenience foods.

For example: After roasting a 10-pound (160 ounces), oven-ready, boned and tied roast top sirloin of beef, which is purchased at $2.80 per pound, a yield test indicates that the loss amounts to 28 ounces. This amount is deducted from the original 160 ounces. In addition, losses through slicing, tasting, and waste are determined to be 24 ounces. The net amount or yield is now reduced to 108 ounces. Note that the usable price per pound is not the original $2.80, but $4.12 because of a 32% loss (28 ounces + 24 ounces). An example of a yield test and costing sheet on the roast top sirloin of beef appears in Fig. 8-1.

ITEM: <u>Roast Top Sirloin of Beef, Choice, Oven Ready, Boned and Tied</u>

ID # _____ DATE: _____

Yield Test

	Quantity/ Unit	Unit Loss	Usable %	% of Loss
GROSS WEIGHT/VOLUME	160 oz.		100	
MINUS PREPARATION LOSS		− 0 oz.		− 0%
MINUS COOKING LOSS		−28 oz.		−17%
MINUS SERVING LOSS		−24 oz.		−15%
TOTAL LOSS	−52 oz.		−32%	
NET YIELD	108 oz.		68%	

COSTING SHEET

INGREDIENTS	Quantity	Unit Price	Total Cost
Roast Top Sirloin O.R.	10 lbs.	2.80	$28.00
8 oz. onions Mirepoix 4 oz. celery 4 oz. carrots	1 lb.	.25	.25
Brown Stock	1/2 Gal.	1.50 per Gal.	.75
Salt & Pepper	to taste		.05
Garnish	27 ea.	.05	1.35

Recipe: Preheat oven to 350°F. Place mirepoix in roast pan. Place oven-ready roast on top of mirepoix. Season lightly with salt & pepper. Turn after 1 hour. Continue roasting until meat thermometer reaches 130°F (rare) or 140° (medium) — about 1 hour. Remove roast, deglaze roast pan with brown beef stock. Strain through fine cheesecloth and china cap. Add salt and pepper to taste. Slice each serving 4 oz. per person

TOTAL COST:	$36.40
NET YIELD	108 Oz.
PORTION SIZE:	4 Oz.
NO. of PORTIONS	27
COST PER PORTION	$1.12
COST PER UNIT	.28

Fig. 8-1. Yield test results and costing sheet.

One method that can be used to calculate cost per portion is as follows:

(A) $\dfrac{\text{Purchase price per unit}}{\text{Net yield percent}} = \text{Cost per usable unit}$

$\dfrac{\$2.80}{.68} = \$4.12 \text{ per usable lb}$

(B) $\dfrac{\text{Total unit weight/volume}}{\text{Portion size}} = \text{Number of portions per unit}$

$\dfrac{16 \text{ oz}}{4 \text{ oz}} = 4 \text{ portions per lb}$

(C) $\dfrac{\text{Cost per usable unit (A)}}{\text{Number of portions per unit (B)}} + \dfrac{\text{Cost of additional ingredients}}{\text{Number of portions}} = \text{Cost per portion}$

$\dfrac{4.12}{4} = 1.03 + \dfrac{1.08}{27} = .09$

$1.03 + .09 = 1.12 \text{ Cost per portion (4 oz)}$

(D) Cost per portion ÷ Portion sizes = Cost per unit

$1.12 \div 4 \text{ oz} = .28 \text{ Cost per unit (1 oz)}$

For the sake of accuracy, condiments, sauces, spices, and garnishes should always be calculated in the costing. It becomes especially important that kitchen personnel responsible for serving an item are made aware of and follow through with the correct portion sizes to yield the correct number of portions for each item. For example, in the preceding example, it is essential that each serving of roast beef be exactly 4 ounces to maintain the proper number of portions. If, for example, a vegetable requires a 3-ounce portion, then a 3-ounce scoop or ladle should be used. This will be effectively done only through constant checking and supervision at each function. When calculating the total menu cost, do not overlook any item that is part of the complete menu: rolls, butter, relish trays, coffee, beverages, cream, sugar, etc. If an additional amount of food is calculated for each function or meal to compensate for emergencies such as last-minute arrivals, spillage, accidents, or other unforeseen situations, this overage or percentage must be figured into the total food cost. To assure that the proper prices and charges are being used, it is advisable to take the corrected purveyors' invoices to compare each item and tally the total food costs relating to each function.

Projecting the Total Labor Cost

Analyze the labor cost by keeping payroll records for each function. Include any and all costs that relate to each function—administrative, service, preparation, sanitation, and maintenance personnel. These amounts should include such extras as overtime. Employee meals may be considered as a benefit and placed under payroll costs or may be placed under food cost as a net cost, depending on the meal policy of the operation.

Projecting Your Total Operating Expenses (Overhead)

Analyze all costs needed to run the business for each affair. The following is a list of some costs that should be considered:

Rent	Fuel
Taxes	Electricity
Insurance	Advertising
Heat	Repairs
Water	Maintenance
Depreciation	Telephone
Breakage and	Laundry and
replacement of equipment	linens
Paper goods	License fees
Permits	Bad debts
Printing	Equipment rentals
Donations	Miscellaneous
Garbage removal	costs
Professional fees	
(accountant, lawyer, etc.)	

Operating costs can be assigned a percentage or can be converted to a dollar amount on a per-portion or meal basis. Operating costs are best taken from existing figures on your profit and loss statement. Another method may be to take a three- or four-month trial period to determine an accurate average overhead cost.

Determining the Desired Profit

A fair return on the dollar is the prime objective, always keeping in mind that prices must be competitive to attract business. This percentage or dollar value should be added into the total cost for the final step.

To illustrate the steps required for menu pricing, assume it is necessary to cost out a dinner for 100 guests. The costs are as follows:

Step 1: Total food cost

Item	Cost per portion	×	Number of portions (100)
Appetizer	.20		$20.00
Soup	.15		15.00
Dinner	.90		90.00

Vegetable	.12	12.00
Starch	.10	10.00
Salad with dressing	.15	15.00
Dessert	.20	20.00
Coffee	.08	8.00
Misc. (rolls, butter, etc.)	.10	10.00
Total food cost	2.00	200.00

Step 2: Determine the total labor cost

4 Waiters at $30.00	=	$120.00
2 Dishwashers at $20.00 each	=	40.00
1 Cook at $45.00	=	45.00
1 Office person at $20.00	=	20.00
1 Manager at $50.00	=	+ 50.00
Total payroll expense	=	$275.00

Step 3: Total overhead or operating expense

This can best be done by analyzing and determining all operating expenses from the profit and loss statement and relating them to a percentage of total selling prices. First, arrive at a constant percent for overhead, which, of course, varies from operation to operation. This fixed percent is derived by adding each individual percent of the following items: payroll taxes, direct operating expense, advertisements, utilities, entertainment, repairs and maintenance, general and administrative expenses, rent and depreciation. After this percent is determined, the second step is to convert this percent to a dollar figure for the overhead cost.

For example, if the overhead percent is determined to be 15% and the desired dollar value of profit is $100 (see Step 4), the menu price and overhead cost in dollars would be determined as follows:

(A) Total price = Food cost + Labor cost + Overhead cost + Desired profit
    100%   = $200   + $275   + 15%   + $100
    1.00   = $575 + .15
    1.00 − .15 = $575
         .85 = $575
    Total price = $675

To convert the percentage of overhead cost to a dollar value, use the following equation:

(B) Overhead cost = Total price − Food cost − Labor cost − Desired profit
              = $675   − $200   − $275   − $100
              = $100

Step 4: Desired profit. This can be a dollar amount or percentage of all costs that the caterer determines to be a reasonable return for the meal served.

Step 5: Menu price.

Total food cost	$200.00
Total labor cost	275.00
Total overhead cost	100.00
Total profit	100.00
Total price	675.00

Menu price = Total price ÷ No. of guests
= $675 ÷ 100
= $6.75

Forecasting can be an accurate way of anticipating the cost of food, labor, and overhead prior to an affair. Later, after the affair is over, the caterer can then compare to anticipated costs. By doing so, he can keep effective controls on preparation, production, waste, pilferage, and labor. If this is done conscientiously, it will produce money-saving results and make the operation cost-efficient.

Analyzing Each Account

After the final bill is paid by the client, an analysis of the function should be performed to determine its profitability. This will help management make the proper adjustments in menu pricing. As mentioned previously, if the profit margin is lower than anticipated or if a loss occurred, costs should first be scrutinized before raising prices. Analysis of each function is also important to evaluate an account as to the desirability of future bookings. That is, the more profitable a function, the greater preference it should receive as to choice of prime dates and times. In so doing, management is assured the highest possible dollar return from future functions.

Banquet Beverage List

Sales from liquor, wine, and beer are the most profitable source of income for a catering establishment. Liquor sales produce more profit than food sales because liquor costs, waste, and spoilage are lower; labor costs, such as bartenders, in relation to sales are lower; and beverage markups and profit margins are higher. Without liquor sales, many operations would find it difficult to operate profitably. The more profitable operations generally have a higher ratio of liquor sales to food sales. For this reason, many caterers find it necessary to be licensed to dispense alcoholic beverages. Salesmen should be encouraged to sell alcoholic beverages for any function whenever feasible to increase sales and profits.

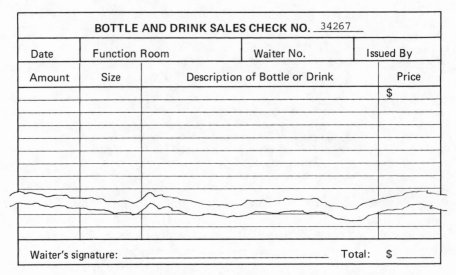

BOTTLE AND DRINK SALES CHECK NO. _34267_			
Date	Function Room	Waiter No.	Issued By
Amount	Size	Description of Bottle or Drink	Price
			$
Waiter's signature: _____		Total: $ _____	

Fig. 8-2. Bottle-and-drink salescheck.

In catering, even though full-bottle sales bring less revenue per bottle than individual drinks, it is preferred, since it saves time, is easier to sell, serve, and control, can be priced attractively, and has less waste and spillage problems. Since customers who purchase full-bottled goods tend to pour more generously for their own drinks, bottled goods are consumed more quickly. As noted earlier, fifths are usually preferred to quarts because customers find the lower price more attractive.[1] If a customer requests quarts, then an additional charge is added to compensate for the adjustment.

All setups including mixers, sodas, garnishes, and ice are included in the selling price of the bottled goods requested. Bottled goods can be served prior to and/or during the function and charged on the final bill or can be sold on a cash basis. If bottle sales are on a cash basis, it becomes one of the few times in catering when cash is transacted. Individual drinks may also be requested, served, priced, and paid for on a cash basis. To prevent pilferage or inaccurate recording of cash liquor sales, a numbered bottle-and-drink salescheck should be made out in triplicate by the person in charge of issuing liquor (bartender, wine steward) and signed by the waiter for the amount, size, description, and price of the item requested (see Fig. 8-2). One copy should be retained for the accounting department for auditing purposes.

[1]With the conversion to the metric system, the terms "fifth" and "quart" are no longer accurate but will probably still be referred to for some time by customers. However, since the price structure for the new bottling system differs from that for fifths and quarts, customers should be made aware that they are purchasing 750 ml bottles (25.4 ounces) instead of fifths (25.6 ounces) and 1 liter bottles (33.8 ounces) instead of quarts (32 ounces). And, of course, in this book, the terms fifth and quart are used loosely to mean the 750 ml and 1 liter sized bottles.

Liquor is no different than food in that each individual bottle or drink must be costed accurately with all expenses and profit added before a price can be determined. Banquet liquor sales fall into three categories: bottled goods, mixed drinks, and individual or straight drinks. Costing sheets should be classified and made out for each one of these three categories to determine the proper selling price. In order to control costs, it is important that management check the bartenders to see that they pour the exact amount of liquor in ounces for each recipe. It is advisable that a chart be made available for all drinks to familiarize the bartenders with the prescribed amounts.

Examples of the various beverage costing sheets are given in Figs. 8-3, 8-4, and 8-5.

Another method that can be used for beverage costing is as follows:

1. Determine the number of drinks obtained from each bottle:

$$\frac{\text{Bottle capacity in ounces}}{\text{Drink size in ounces}} = \frac{33.8 \text{ (liters)}}{1.5 \text{ oz}} = 22.5 \text{ drinks per bottle}$$

A loss of from $\frac{1}{2}$ to $1\frac{1}{2}$ ounces of liquor per bottle due to spillage, returns, overpouring, or alcohol left in discarded bottles should be included.

Date: _____			No.: __A____
Brand name	**Size**	**Unit Cost**	
Seagram Seven 86	4/5	$5.10	
Canada Dry Club Soda	1 Qt.	.40	
Canada Dry Ginger Ale	1 Qt.	.40	
Ice	3 Lbs.	.05	
Garnishes		.05	
Total beverage cost ÷ Beverage cost percent* =		$6.00 ÷ 20% (.20)	
Selling price per bottle =		$30.00 (fifth)	

*Beverage cost percentage is determined by management after calculating and tallying the desired profit and all costs, and analyzing competitors' pricing.

Fig. 8-3. Beverage costing sheet (bottles).

Date: _____   No.: _B_____

Name of drink: _Manhattan Cocktail_____

Type of glassware: __Cocktail Glass_____   Size: ____3 oz.__

INGREDIENTS				
ITEM	BRAND NAME	SIZE	UNIT COST	
RYE	4/5 Seagram Seven 86	1½ oz.	* .30	
SWEET VERMOUTH	MARTINI-ROSSI	3/4 oz.	.03	
CHERRY		1 ea.	.02	

Total beverage cost ÷ Beverage cost percentage   .35 ÷ 20% (.20)

Selling price per drink $1.75

Method of preparation: Stir all ingredients well in shaker glass
with cracked ice and strain into a chilled 3 oz. cocktail glass.
Serve with maraschino cherry.

*To find the unit cost per drink first find the number of drinks per bottle and then the unit cost per bottle.

(1) $\dfrac{\text{Bottle capacity in ounces}}{\text{Drink size in ounces}} = \dfrac{25.6\ (4/5)}{1.5} = 17$ drinks per bottle (4/5's)

(2) $\dfrac{\text{Cost per bottle}}{\text{No. of drinks per bottle}} = \dfrac{5.10}{17} = .30$ Unit Cost per Drink

Fig. 8-4. Beverage costing sheet (mixed drinks).

2. Determine the selling price per bottle:

$\dfrac{\text{Cost per bottle}}{\text{Beverage cost percentage}} = \dfrac{9.00}{25\%\,(.25)} = \$36.00$ (selling price per bottle)

3. Determine the selling price per drink:

$\dfrac{\text{Selling price per bottle}}{\text{No. of drinks per bottle}} = \dfrac{36}{22.5} = \$1.60$ (selling price per drink)

4. Add cost of mixers, sodas, and garnishes by using average sales
mix analyzed from a specific period of time.

Selling price per drink   = $1.60
Average cost of mixers, sodas, garnishes   =   .15
Final selling price per drink   = $1.75 each

Some catering operations will average out the cost of various groups of drinks. For example, if the average price of mixed drinks (manhattans, martinis, whiskey sours, etc.) is $2.00 and the average price of straight drinks is $1.50, then all drinks would be priced at $1.75. A one-unit pricing system is less confusing and helps speed cash transactions. Fancy drinks (flamingos, frozen daiquiris, etc.) requiring extra liquor or labor costs would be grouped in a higher price structure, for example $2.50 per drink.

All liquor, wine, and beer must be controlled from the moment you purchase it to the moment the client pays for it. Only responsible persons should order, purchase, and issue alcoholic beverages and possess liquor room keys. Printed forms rather than verbal communication should be used for keeping track of the liquor supply. Liquor rooms should be set up with a perpetual inventory. Use *bin cards* to show amounts, brand

---

Date: _____   No.: _C_____

Name of drink: Rye and Ginger Ale _____

Type of glassware: Highball Glass _____ Size: 6 ounces ____

Ingredients				
Item	Brand name	Size	Unit Cost	
RYE	4/5 SEAGRAM SEVEN 86	1 oz.	.20	
GINGER ALE	CANADA DRY	3 oz.	.04	
ICE			.01	

Total beverage cost ÷ Beverage cost percentage =   .25 ÷ 20% (.20)

Selling price per drink   1.25

Method of preparation: Fill 6 ounce highball glass with 2 cubes of ice, pour 1 oz. Rye, add 3 ounces ginger ale and stir.

Fig. 8-5. Beverage costing sheet (straight drinks).

		Issued to Banq. Rooms						Total Amt. Issued	Balance on Hand	Signature

Bin Card

Brand name: <u>Dewars White Label</u>   Size: <u>Fifths</u>

Dealer's name: <u>Star Distributors</u>   Price: <u>$7.10</u>

Date of Delivery & Issue	Amount Received	A	B	C	D	E		Total Amt. Issued	Balance on Hand	Signature
5/1	12								12	
5/2		5	1	1				7	5	a.c.
5/3			1	2	1			4	1	e.b.
5/4	24	3	1	1				5	20	e.b.
5/5		2			1	1		4	16	a.c.

Recommended Inventory: <u>24</u> Bottles

Fig. 8-6. Bin card.

names, and sizes that were received and issued, as well as what balance remains. These cards will show instantly what needs to be ordered, what items move fastest, and what, if any, shortages exist. An example of a bin card appears in Fig. 8-6.

Whenever liquor is issued to an individual banquet room, a requisition should be filled out in triplicate. Utilize numbered liquor requisition and consumption sheets (Fig. 8-7) for this purpose. One copy should be signed and kept by the person issuing the merchandise, one by the receiver of the goods (head bartender, headwaiter), and the third copy should go to the accounting department. All requisitions should be issued and checked by the director of catering or the banquet manager for each function. The auditor will calculate the beverage consumption for each function by adding the amount of liquor, wine, and beer issued and subtracting any returns.

A potential sales value for each bottle of liquor should be established. When liquor will be sold on a per-drink basis, this figure, also known as the standard sales value, is calculated by multiplying the estimated number of drinks per bottle by the selling price of each drink.

No. _____

Name of Function: _____

Person in Charge of Function: _____

Name of Room: _____   No. of Guests: _____

Day, Date of Function: _____   Time: _____

Bin No.	Brand Name	Size	No. Issued	No. Returned	No. Sold (A)	Unit × Cost	= Total Cost (B)	Unit Value @ Selling Price (C)	Potential Sales (A x C)	Actual Sales (D)	*Dollar Overage	*Dollar Shortage
						$	$	$	$	$	$	$
TOTAL							$	$	$	$	$	$

*Overage—When Actual Sales are Higher than Potential Sales

*Shortage—When Actual Sales are Lower than Potential Sales

Total Beverage Cost (B) $ _____

Total Beverage Sales (D) $ _____   = _____

Beverage Cost % for function _____ %

Requisitioned By: _____

Issued By: _____

Received By: _____

Fig. 8-7. Liquor requisition and consumption sheet.

When liquor is sold by the bottle, the potential sales value of the bottle is simply the established selling price.

The potential sales value indicates the dollar amount that should actually be received when the bottle is sold. To assure that the proper charges have been made and collected, the revenue received on the sale of the bottle (actual sales value) is reconciled with the calculated potential sales value. This will highlight any shortage or overage. Minor differences can be expected especially when liquor is sold on a per-drink basis. All major differences should be completely investigated. Dollar shortages that show up on the banquet requisition and consumption sheet are usually attributed to improper charges made, improper collection made, cash theft, pilferage of liquor, carelessness, inconsistent pouring, deviation from standard recipes (overpouring), or breakage.

Overages usually indicate improper charges or collections were made or that standard recipes were not followed (underpouring). This added revenue has the potential to hurt business, since it is a sign that somewhere along the line the customer was shortchanged.

Never permit an employee to take any leftover liquor that a patron has been charged for. Any remaining liquor should be returned to the point of issue, the liquor room or bar, and any partial or full bottle should be placed on a memo for credit. One copy of the credit memo goes to the auditor and the other to the point of issue (liquor room or bar). Storage of partially filled bottles may be against state legislation. Therefore, separate storage lockers for opened bottles may be necessary.

To help increase beverage sales, place a banquet beverage list on every table for all functions especially when no liquor has been presold or contracted. An example of a banquet beverage list is given in Fig. 8-8.

Since wines are becoming increasingly popular and consumed more frequently at cocktail hours and banquet functions, it is advisable to have a banquet wine list available for potential inquiries. Encourage salesmen to sell wine for all functions, since wine commands high markups and profits and adds to the enjoyment and improves banquet food functions. Wine markups usually range from two to four times the bottle cost. The current trend is to lower the markup to make the selling price more attractive and create higher volume. Wine sales can be exceptionally profitable, especially at functions for which customers have contracted for unlimited liquor (no wine or beer included) and wine is sold separately. This will increase liquor revenue while decreasing the overall liquor consumption of the function.

Keep the banquet wine list simple and brief, listing about a dozen wines to complement the range of banquet food items offered. Limited selections will help keep expensive inventories low and be easier to control. Special or more expensive wines may be made available on customer request. Since most wines are sold at the contract stage (well

SCOTCH
Dewars White Label	25.00
Teachers	25.00
J & B	25.00
Grants 8 Years	25.00
Cutty Sark	25.00
Black and White	25.00
Johnnie Walker Red	25.00
Johnnie Walker Black	30.00
Chivas Regal	30.00

RYE
Seagram's Seven Crown	22.00
Four Roses	22.00
Schenley Reserve	22.00

CANADIAN
Canadian Club	25.00
Seagram's V.O.	25.00
Schenley O.F.C.	25.00
Seagram's Crown Royal	35.00

IRISH
Old Bushmill	25.00

BOURBON
Old Grand Dad	25.00
I.W. Harper	25.00
Jim Beam	25.00
Old Forester	25.00
Old Fitzgerald	25.00
Early Times	25.00
Wild Turkey	28.00

SOUR MASH
Jack Daniels	30.00

GIN
Gordon's	22.00
Seagram's Gin	22.00
Tanquaray	25.00
Beefeater	25.00

VODKA
Wolfschmidt	22.00
Smirnoff	25.00

RUM
Bacardi	22.00
Ronrico	22.00
Meyers	25.00

BRANDY/COGNAC
Hennessey Brasarme	35.00
Martell 3 Star	35.00
Remy Martin VSOP	40.00

CHAMPAGNE AND SPARKLING WINE
Domestic	10.00
Gold Seal Brut	12.00
Great Western	14.00
Cinzano Asti Spumanti	14.00
Chauvener Red Cap	16.00
Moet and Chandon	25.00
Piper Heidsieck, Extra Dry	30.00
Mumm's Cordon Rouge	30.00

A Complete Wine List is
Available Upon Request.

VERMOUTH
Dry or Sweet	12.00

COCKTAILS
Manhattan	1.50
Martini	1.50
Whiskey Sour	1.50
Scotch Sour	1.50
Daiquiri	1.50
Champagne (domestic) glass	1.50

BEER
Domestic	1.00
Imported	1.50

SOFT DRINKS
Splits	.75
Quarts	1.50

ABOVE BOTTLED GOODS ARE PRICED AS FIFTHS. AN ADDITIONAL CHARGE WILL BE MADE FOR QUARTS. CLUB SODA, GINGER ALE, AND ICE ARE INCLUDED IN PRICING. BOTTLE AND INDIVIDUAL DRINK PRICES DO NOT INCLUDE GRATUITIES OR TAX.

Fig. 8-8. Beverage list.

before the function), there is sufficient time to order most wines in advance. Train sales personnel to make the proper suggestions for the best wine at the best price for the dinner selected. To maximize wine sales, it is good merchandising to let the customer sample the wine prior to selection, so that the customer will be assured beforehand of the acceptability of the wine.

It is important that wines be served in proper glassware and at proper temperatures. Service personnel should be instructed by the headwaiter on the proper presentation and pouring of wine prior to each function.

Assign a bin number to each selection on the banquet wine list. This will facilitate controlling wine issues and help customers who may find ordering by name difficult.

Any wine may be served as long as it is palatable and complements a dish. There is no reason why red wines should be served only with red meats or white wines only with white meat and fish. In most cases, common sense will dictate that light, dry, younger wines be consumed before heavier, full-bodied, aged, or sweet wines.

Chapter 9

Package Plans

To facilitate sales, most caterers offer their clients package plans by which most components of a function are grouped together and offered for one all-inclusive price per person. Simple yet comprehensive in nature, package plans are popular with customers and operators alike. For the customer, the total cost for the entire function is easily calculated by multiplying the cost per person by the number of guests. By combining all the separate aspects of the function into a single unit, package plans prove useful to management by increasing sales, saving time, and aiding in the organization of the affair.

The following paragraphs offer some helpful guidelines that should be considered when constructing and pricing a package plan. A typical package plan is offered in Chapter 11 on weddings.

Analyze your area and clientele closely. Check which type of functions are held most frequently and consequently are most conducive to being structured into the package plan format. Incorporate the basic items, arrangements, and services that are being requested and sold elsewhere into your package plan. Thus, the consistent inquiries and repetitive demands made by customers will determine how simple or elaborate your package plan should be for your particular area. However, to compete effectively, your package plan must be made more attractive than the competition's by offering a better or more varied plan. Incorporate different, unique, and more elaborate foods, services, and arrangements while keeping within the same or preferably lower price range than the competition.

Examine what price range is most acceptable for your area. Keep in mind that the more items placed into the package plan, the higher the final cost per person. Be careful not to overprice your plans. It may be to your advantage to sell a lower-priced plan initially and thus attract a larger market, and then at a later date attempt to sell additional items to build your total sales. This can be done effectively by training your sales personnel to sell these extra items to a customer when discussing the final arrangements since they are generally easier to sell as the affair draws near. However, under no circumstances should a customer feel that he is being pressured or that he was initially deceived as to the final charge, which may become substantially higher than anticipated. All extra items should be sold on the basis that they will enhance or insure the success of an affair.

If no customer resistance is encountered initially to your package plan price structure, then it may be feasible to add additional items until it becomes evident by the customer's reaction that you have incorporated too many items, Any extra or additional item like music, photography, limousines, or other outside service should be closely scrutinized as to being sold separately, outside the plan and at a later date, in order to keep the initial package plan price within an attractive and acceptable range.

While customers generally shop around when planning an affair, they often do not closely examine the content, value, or differences among the package plans offered by various caterers. Incorrectly assuming that all package plans are basically identical in what they offer, many customers are primarily affected by the quoted prices. It is advisable for the caterer or salesman who offers better value to be familiar with the differences between plans and to use this knowledge as an advantage in selling a package plan to a customer.

Construct several complete package plans with different price structures especially in areas where diversified income levels exist. In the event a customer is not receptive to a higher-priced package plan, then another less expensive plan should be offered until the price range is acceptable and falls within the customer's budget. This reduction in price can be accomplished by eliminating or reducing certain parts of the initial package plan; for example, the "unlimited liquor" that might be part of a package plan can be changed to a "choice of one bottle of rye or scotch for each table of ten persons." This substitution can reduce the cost per person by as much as $4.00. The reduction of certain items or services may actually provide management with more profit if the reduction eliminates an expensive high-cost item or service. However, do not lower or reduce the cost of a package plan to the point where, because of the lack of working capital, the overall catered affair becomes ineffectual and leaves a poor reflection on your ability as a caterer to produce a successful affair. There comes a point for every caterer when he should refuse a function because of the lack of potential profit, unless he is willing to subsidize an affair for promotional, charitable, or other personal reasons. Nevertheless, never execute a poor or inadequate affair just for the sake of doing a function.

The price of a package plan should be structured so that, regardless of what main course or dinner a customer selects, the same amount of profit is made by management, e.g., the coq au vin package should produce the same amount of profit as the filet mignon package, the only difference for management being that the purchase and selling price for the filet mignon will be higher. Of course, since gratuities for service personnel are generally based on a percentage of the total selling price of the affair, a higher-priced entreé will render greater gratuities.

Price ranges for package plans should vary depending on the demand for services according to season, day, or time. For example, when booking requests for Saturday nights greatly outnumber requests for Friday or Sunday evenings, which in turn outnumber Saturday afternoon and weekday requests, then it is advisable to establish three separate price structures to compensate for the demand factor. This pricing system gives the customer an incentive, in the form of a price reduction, to select less attractive or desirable time periods. This helps management utilize the facilities to the maximum and opens the more desirable and valuable prime dates for other higher-income-producing functions.

If package plan prices are predetermined and permanently printed on the menu, and only Saturday evening affairs command premium prices, then mention this on the bottom of the package plan as follows: "Prices are 15% higher for Saturday evening functions."

To stimulate or promote sales in slack or off-season periods, package plans should be advertised as being lowered or reduced in price. By keeping the business operating at an acceptable capacity during these slack times, even though at a lower profit margin, expensive key employee turnover and re-training programs can be avoided.

Allowances or price reductions should be considered in situations in which a customer may justifiably eliminate or reduce an item or service that would normally be included in the package plan. Customers may often request a price reduction or change for a legitimate reason, such as, a party where liquor is included in the package plan and a certain number of children or minors have been invited. In this case, it should be the policy of management to make a price allowance for those minors who are not permitted by law to consume alcoholic beverages.

Allowances or price reductions can also be offered in conjunction with the number of guests to be invited to the affair. For example, in a package plan priced at $22.00 per person for 100 guests, charges may be prorated on a sliding scale such as: $21.75 per person for 125 guests; $21.50 per person for 150 guests; $21.25 per person for 175 guests; $21.00 per person for 200 guests, etc. This price structure reduces the price per person by one dollar for every 100 additional guests. Even though per-person prices decrease, management makes more profit due to the additional number of guests.

When writing or constructing a package plan be certain that all items, arrangements, services, and other information are clearly described. Avoid any question or doubt that may arise in the customer's mind due to lack of description, misquote, or the use of vague terminology, especially when dealing with prices, amounts, additional services, and other items and conditions mentioned on the menu. Additional charges for overtime, French or Russian service, deluxe premium brands of liquor, flambe' desserts, after-dinner cordials, gratuities for service staff, additional gratuities for supervisory personnel, taxes, or any other charges for any item or service rendered should be explained clearly or presented in written form to a customer in order that no misunderstanding will occur, especially when the final bill is presented.

Choices within the various food courses can be directly printed on the menu, or a notation can be simply made on the menu that a "choice" exists and will be further explained by the salesman.

There are advantages and disadvantages to both methods. The advantage of having the items printed on the menu is that time is saved in making final arrangements, since the customer will likely have made a selection before meeting the salesman. The disadvantage is that if adverse price or market conditions affect the availability or cost of a product chosen from the printed menu, then the loss will more than likely have to be assumed by the caterer to avoid creating customer dissatisfaction. The advantage to stating that a choice is available and will be explained is that a salesman can persuade a customer to make choices he knows are best for purchasing reasons and easiest for the kitchen and service staff to produce and serve efficiently with best results. The disadvantage is that it takes more time for both the salesman to present the choices and the customer to make a selection.

For ease of preparation and to cut costs by limiting the selection and amounts needed, the salesman should try to standardize the menu selections for similar functions; for example, try to elicit the selection of the same vegetable for all functions. This is especially true in volume operations.

Be sure that all facets of the package plan are completely explained and described to the customer. For example, when discussing unlimited liquor, be sure to mention whether champagne, wine, or beer is included (usually available on a request basis) or, if it is not, explain what the charges will be for the amounts of these items consumed. Describe what types of liquor, mixers, sodas, and juices are available. Describe what type of service is given—whether rolling bars or waiters taking individual drink orders at the tables. This latter system is more efficient in that more personnel can be utilized to give maximum service in taking orders and delivering individual drinks to patrons at their tables. This service should also provide for stationary bars in the function room for those who want to leave the table area for a drink. This service can never be criticized because liquor is always available either at the tables by waiter service or at the bar(s) by bartender service. Portable bars can also be effective when rolled from table to table as long as adequate space is allowed for the carts between tables, but the success of this service will rely solely upon the effectiveness and speed of the bartenders.

A package plan should contain a list of complimentary items offered at "no cost to a customer" as an inducement or selling point. Such items would include colored linens, lace overlay cloths, free parking, bridal dressing rooms, bridal suites, seating and direction cards, engraved cake knives, or other items, no matter how insignificant they may appear. These complimentary items will help sell the affair by making the customer feel that these are extra benefits that he will receive if he selects your package plan.

Whatever the package plan, it should include a notation that other customized package plans and prices are available. A customer should never be made to feel that there is no flexibility in any of the plans or arrangements offered. Never allow a customer to leave your premises without a package plan that has been structured for his budget and personal requirements, unless the customer has too little money to spend to guarantee the operation a certain profit.

Chapter 10

The Various Types of Parties and Functions

Inquiring customers will make varying demands of the caterer. Requests will range from a limited or low-budget affair to a completely elaborate and expensive one. It is the task of the catering salesman to arrange a high-quality affair while staying within the customer's budget and achieving a reasonable profit for the operation.

Customers should never be permitted to force the price level below the point where a reasonable profit can be made, nor should quality be negotiated for price, since the guests, as potential customers, will evaluate the caterer's performance by the total affair and will not be aware of the price arrangements. Nevertheless, management should not always analyze parties solely on the basis of immediately generated income but may compromise at times and book functions that will return smaller immediate profits but may lead to other potentially more profitable parties.

Separate menus should be composed for each type of affair, especially those that are in high demand and are requested often. This will save time for both the salesman and client, and at the same time help establish and standardize menu precosting. Many food and beverage items should be duplicated on several menus, as shown in the examples in this chapter, to facilitate food purchasing and preparation for all affairs. A customer may, on occasion, request a special menu or particular item other than that which has been offered. Management should be able to adapt to the customer's wishes by either providing the special items or offering alternate backup menus.

The following is a list of the types of functions:

Anniversary party
Bachelor party
Bar or bas mitzvah
Breakfast
Communion breakfast
Bridal dinner or luncheon
Brunch

Champagne wedding brunch
Birthday party
Sweet sixteen party
Buffet
Business meetings and seminars
Boxed meals
Christening
Cocktail parties
Coffee break
Confirmation
Convention
Dance
Debutante ball
Dinner party
Engagement party
Farewell or "bon voyage" party
Fashion show
Fund-raising party
Funerals
Gourmet dinner
Graduation party
Holiday party
Luncheon
Outdoor party
Prom
Rehearsal dinner
Retirement dinner or luncheon
Reunion
Shower (bridal or baby)
Sport function
Supper
Theme dinner and costume party
Tea
Trade or promotional party
Wedding

Most of these functions are detailed in this chapter; weddings and bar mitzvahs are discussed in greater depth in Chapters 11 and 12.

Anniversary Parties

These parties produce high income, since food, liquor, and many extras are usually requested at these happy gatherings. The silver (25th) and golden (50th) are the most often celebrated anniversaries. Although less in demand, the following anniversaries are occasionally celebrated with a catered affair: 1st (paper), 5th (wood), 10th (tin), 15th (crystal), 20th (china), and 35th (coral). The symbolic material should be incorporated into the decorations and theme of the party.

Champagne and other liquor arrangements can easily be sold separately or incorporated into the package plan for an anniversary. The festivities usually take the form of a luncheon, dinner, or buffet with either formal or informal seating arrangements and with liquor being served at the cocktail hour, during the meal, and/or after dinner. An anniversary cake can be sold separately or substituted as a dessert course. These cakes can either be tiered and topped with an ornament or else arranged as a single tier or sheet cake with the appropriate inscription.

A fully decorated dais table is usually set for the guests of honor. Music is often requested for an anniversary party. As at a wedding, the master of ceremonies often conducts a formal introduction of the anniversary couple, a first dance, and a cake-cutting ceremony.

An example of a complete anniversary party follows:

ANNIVERSARY PARTY

Cocktail Hour
To be served one hour prior to dinner

Unlimited Cocktails to Include
Manhattans, Martinis, Bacardis, Whiskey Sours, Scotch Sours, Rye, Scotch, Vodka, Gin, Bourbon, and Rum with all the necessary Soda and Mixes

Unlimited Hot and Cold Hors D'Oeuvres
A beautiful selection of assorted hors d'oeuvres served on silver trays with butler service

Your Anniversary Dinner Includes
Champagne Toast
Pineapple Fruit Basket
Soup du Jour

Choice of Anniversary Dinner:
  A. Coq au Vin   _____per person
  B. Roast Stuffed Vermont Turkey,
     Giblet Gravy, and
     Cranberry Sauce   _____per person
  C. Roast Prime Rib of Beef   _____per person
  D. Filet Mignon, Sauce
     Bearnaise   _____per person

Bouquetière of Vegetables
Choice of Potato
Mixed Green Salad with a Choice of Dressing

Decorated Anniversary Cake

Coffee, Tea, Decaffeinated Coffee

Unlimited Rye, Scotch, Vodka, Gin, Bourbon, and Rum Will Be Served from Rolling Bars throughout the Entire Dinner

All Gratuities for Waiters Are Included in Above Prices

Also Provided at No Additional Cost Are the Following:

Choice of Colored Linens and Napkins
Choice of Colored Candles and Table Fern
Beautifully Decorated Anniversary Head Table
Silver Candelabras for Anniversary Head Table
Place Cards and Direction Cards
A Bridal Dressing Room
A Captain to Conduct and Supervise Your Anniversary Party
A Beautifully Decorated Gift Table

8% Sales tax not included in above prices

Breakfasts

These are good income-producing functions that add exposure to the operation during a normally slack period—early morning. The key to a successful breakfast is to serve plenty of coffee immediately as the guests are seated at their tables and to continue serving it throughout the entire affair. Additional amounts of coffee should be figured in the preparation and service of breakfasts, usually two or three cups extra per person. Items such as juice, Danish pastries, rolls, bread, bagels, butter, cream cheese, and jam should be placed on the tables immediately so that guests are not kept waiting for service.

Breakfast must be served hot and quickly. Hard-to-prepare items should be eliminated from the menu. To increase speed of service, all food items should be pre-plated in the kitchen or served on platters. It may also be advisable to offer additional amounts of food in chafing dishes for guests who desire seconds. This system avoids customer complaints of insufficient food. Buffet-style breakfasts are suggested when a selection of foods is to be served.

An example of a banquet breakfast menu follows.

BANQUET BREAKFAST

Your Choice of Table Service or Buffet

No. 1. _____ per person

Fresh Orange or Grapefruit Juice	Assorted Danish Pastries
Creamy Scrambled Eggs	Hot Rolls with Farm Butter and
Crisp Bacon, Ham, or Sausage	Assorted Jams
Home-Fried Potatoes	Coffee, Tea, Sanka, or Milk

No. 2. _____ per person

Fresh Orange or Grapefruit Juice
Breakfast Steak
Scrambled Eggs
Hash Brown Potatoes

Assorted Danish Pastries
Hot Rolls with Farm Butter and
    Assorted Jams
Coffee, Tea, Sanka, or Milk

No. 3. _____ per person

Continental Breakfast
Fresh Orange or Grapefruit Juice
Assorted Danish Pastry

Hot Rolls with Farm Butter and
    Assorted Jams
Coffee, Tea, Sanka, or Milk

No. 4. _____ per person

Fresh Orange or Grapefruit Juice
Fresh Nova Scotia Salmon
Pickled Herring

Bagels, Rolls, and Cream Cheese
Assorted Danish Pastries
Coffee, Tea, Sanka, or Milk

No. 5. _____ per person

Fresh Orange or Grapefruit Juice
Mushroom, Western, Spanish, or
    Cheese Omelette
Home-Fried Potatoes

Assorted Danish Pastries
Hot Rolls with Farm Butter and
    Assorted Jams
Coffee, Tea, Sanka, or Milk

A $20.00 labor charge must be added for groups under 30 persons. 17% Gratuity and 8% Sales Tax are additional.

Bridal Dinners or Luncheons

These are usually small functions prior to the wedding arranged by a bride for the purpose of presenting her gifts to her attendants. Cocktails or champagne should be suggested prior to the dinner or luncheon. The color scheme of the bridal party can be incorporated into the linen and other decorations used. If no color scheme is requested, pink or white is always acceptable. If a cake is ordered, it is usually decorated with miniature dolls resembling the bridal party, or a large doll cake can be made and decorated in the colors the bridal party has selected.

Brunch

This meal falls between 10 A.M. and noon and includes a combination of breakfast and luncheon foods. Since many people understand and interpret brunch to be different things, the salesman must be sure the client totally understands what is being offered for brunch. The most popular brunch items include the following: various types and styles of eggs, quiches, pancakes, waffles, crêpes, french toast, steak, bacon, ham, sausage, fresh fruit, fruit juices, fried potatoes, fish such as herring, rolls, bread, bagels, Danish, muffins, butter, jam, cream cheese, honey, coffee, tea, and milk. Brunches can be served as a sit-down affair in which the menu is predetermined and then served at the table. However, brunch is very popular and appealing when done up as a buffet especially when customers want a more relaxed and less formal affair. To increase sales, liquor should be incorporated into the menu and sold as an "eye opener."

Champagne Wedding Brunches

These are popular because they offer a less expensive alternative to the typical wedding reception and also make it less formal. The major ingredients of a wedding brunch are abundant champagne and a complete brunch menu, including dessert and/or a wedding cake. Flowers and music are usually included to make the affair more festive.

To add showmanship and flair, items like omelettes and crêpes can be prepared by a chef dressed in a white uniform and standing on a platform with portable burners. Hot fillings for these omelettes and crêpes can be placed in chafing dishes and served by the service personnel.

An example of a banquet brunch menu follows.

BANQUET BRUNCH
Your Choice of Table Service or Buffet

BEVERAGE SUGGESTIONS

Screwdriver	Champagne Cocktail
Bloody Mary	Bull Shot
Vodka and	Irish Coffee
Grapefruit Juice	Jamaican Coffee
Orange Blossom	Fresh Strawberry
Asti Spumanti with	Daiquiri
Fresh Strawberry	Fresh Banana
Gimlet	Daiquiri

ENTRÉES

Rib Steak with Two Eggs
Eggs Benedict
Omelettes: Mushroom, Cheese, Jelly, Ham,
      Fine Herbes, Spanish
Smoked Nova Salmon Platter
Scrambled Eggs and Chicken Livers
Potato Pancakes, Sour Cream, Lumpfish Caviar
French Toast and Canadian Bacon

All entrées include fresh-squeezed Orange Juice, Fried Potatoes, Bagels, Rolls, Cream Cheese, Butter, Jelly, Coffee, Tea, Sanka, and an array of Babka (coffee cake).

DESSERT *(choice of one)*

Fresh Strawberries with Port and Whipped Cream
Fresh Melon with Lime Wedge
Chocolate Mousse
Apple Fritters with Vanilla Sauce

SPARKLING WINES

Korbel Brut
Asti Spumanti
Mumm's Extra Dry
Great Western Extra Dry

A $20.00 labor charge must be added for groups under 30 persons. 17% Gratuity and 8% Sales Tax are additional.

Sweet Sixteen Party

These birthday celebrations, usually for a young lady, should incorporate foods that teenagers prefer such as pizza, hamburgers, fried chicken, frankfurters, and french fries as well as popular beverages such as soda and punch, which can effectively be served from fountains. A pink, heart-shaped, sweet-sixteen cake decorated with pink birthday candles is customarily served for dessert. An additional ice cream dessert is always acceptable and can be provided with the cake at an additional cost. Pink is the predominating color choice for linens, flowers, and cake decorations. Dancing to contemporary live music is often provided when young men are invited. Novel ideas are particularly popular, e.g., a jukebox stocked with current music and activated by coins that have been distributed to the teenage guests. A gift table is always furnished for the birthday presents. When parents or adults are in attendance, they should be seated in a separate area removed from the teenagers. Adults can be sold a different menu with liquor arrangements.

Buffets

A very popular type of informal and relaxed affair, a buffet offers a wide selection of interesting foods. Eye appeal is the key attraction at the buffet line, and this is achieved by the effective use of contrasting and complementing shapes, colors, forms, and volumes of foods presented. To enhance the food presentation, it is suggested that such serving and display pieces as the following be used:

Silver and copper chafing dishes
Silver and copper cooking equipment
Silver serving trays
Antiques
Punch bowls
Samovars
China and crystal display pieces
Candelabras
Floral arrangements
Tallow sculptures
Ice carvings
Specially decorated or lighted tables

A typical buffet will offer a wide variety of hot and cold foods such as appetizers, entrées, assorted cold meats, salads, cheese platters, fresh fruit arrangements, assorted breads and rolls, and baked goods and desserts served with coffee, tea, or milk. A hot carving station can be added to the buffet for an additional fee. Appetizers can be placed on the buffet or at the table if it is necessary to seat the guests prior to opening the buffet. Desserts can be served from the same table as the buffet, from a separate table, or tableside from a rolling cart. A sample buffet menu follows.

BANQUET BUFFET

(for 100 or more guests)

HOT CHAFING DISHES *(choice of 5)*

Seafood Newburg	Veal Scallopini a la Marsala
Chicken Chasseur	Pepper Steak
Beef Stroganoff	Stuffed Cabbage
Manicotti Marinara	Clams Casino
Sweet and Sour Pork	Cheese Ravioli with Meat Sauce
Shish Kabob	Rice Pilaf
Boneless Cornish Game Hen with	Buttered Noodles
Fruit	Macedoine of Vegetables
Sliced Tongue Polonaise	

COLD PLATTERS *(choice of 4)*

Italian Antipasto	Smoked Beef Tongue
Roast Breast of Turkey	Sliced Virginia Ham
Chicken Galantine	Sliced Roast Beef
Assorted Fish Platter	Corned Brisket of Beef
Liver Pâté Maison	Veal Medallions

SALADS (choice of 5)

Waldorf Salad	Red Wine Gelatin Salad Mold
Salad Nicôise	Marinated Mushrooms
Spinach, Bacon, Water Chestnut Salad	Three Bean Salad
Tossed Green Salad with Assorted	Caesar Salad
Dressings	

INTERNATIONAL CHEESE PLATTER

Emmenthaler, Danish Blue, Camembert, and Italian Fontina
Cheeses served with Assorted Party Breads

CHEF'S HOT CARVING TABLE (choice of 2 items)

additional charge of $2.00 per person:
Roast Top Sirloin of Beef, Corned Brisket of Beef, Roast Turkey, Hot Pastrami

Macedoine of Fresh Fruits

Assorted French Pastries
Rolls and Butter
Coffee-Tea-Sanka

Luncheon _____ per person   Dinner _____ per person

17% Gratuity and 8% Sales Tax applicable to all food and beverage consumed.

Business Meetings and Seminars

Business clients like to periodically gather selected groups together outside of their own environment. These meetings often heavily feature food. Therefore, separate rooms or attached areas are best suited for these occasions so that the meeting may be conducted and the dining area set up simultaneously. A typical business meeting or seminar may include some or all of the following, depending on the demands or budget of the client:

Room	Activity	Time
A	Coffee and Danish Breakfast	8:30 to 9:00 A.M.
B	Meeting	9:00 to 10:30 A.M.
A	Coffee Break	10:30 to 10:45 A.M.
B	Meeting	10:45 to 12:00 noon
A	Lunch	12 noon to 1:00 P.M.
B	Meeting	1:00 to 2:30 P.M.
A	Coffee Break	2:30 to 3:00 P.M.
B	Meeting	3:00 to 5:00 P.M.
A	Cocktail Party	5:00 to 6:00 P.M.
B	Dinner	6:00 to 7:00 P.M.

When no food is required for a business meeting, then a room rental is charged for the space used. Room rental policies vary and are determined by each operation as to the relation between the space used and the food income generated, i.e., a higher room rental may be charged if little or no food is ordered. Room rentals may be reduced or eliminated completely depending on the competition of the area and the labor and overhead expenses incurred.

Two items that are repeatedly needed at meetings are podiums and lecterns. Podiums are free-standing, chest-high speaker's rostrums. A lectern is a speaker's rostrum that is placed on the head or dais table. It is advisable to display the logo of your establishment conspicuously on the front of each of these rostrums to capitalize on the "free" advertising that may be obtained when photographs that are taken appear in the newspapers. Customers will often request a raised speaker's area for better vision and exposure. This can easily be provided by placing platforms under the podium or speaker's table.

Hunter green felt conference cloths are commonly used to both provide a "cushion" effect for writing comfort and to hide the exposed legs of the conference tables. Other basic items that should be furnished at these meetings are: water pitchers and glasses, ashtrays, pencils, and writing pads. Standard audio equipment should be provided by the caterer for these meetings— microphone, podium, or lectern. However, when additional or excessive amounts of audiovisual equipment is needed, such as projectors, overheads, screens, and tape recorders, then it becomes the responsibility of the person in charge of the meeting to rent this equipment from either an audiovisual equipment rental agency or from the caterer who may be stocking these additional items as an investment for rental purposes.

The two types of seating arrangements requested for business meetings are theater or auditorium style and classroom or schoolroom style.

For *theater or auditorium style,* chairs are arranged facing a speaker's podium or head table. Approximately four inches should be allowed between chairs for comfort. To estimate the seating capacity of a theater-style arrangement, divide the square footage of the total seating area by eight. An example of a theater-style configuration appears in Fig. 10-1.

Classroom or schoolroom style is required when writing or notetaking is part of the meeting. For comfort and writing room, one person needs two feet of table space, e.g., a six-foot table seats three and an eight-foot seats four. The most popular sized conference table is 72 inches long and 18 inches wide. Thirty inches between conference tables gives adequate chair space. To estimate the seating capacity of a classroom style arrangement, divide the square footage of the total seating area by ten. An example of a classroom-style configuration is given in Fig. 10-2.

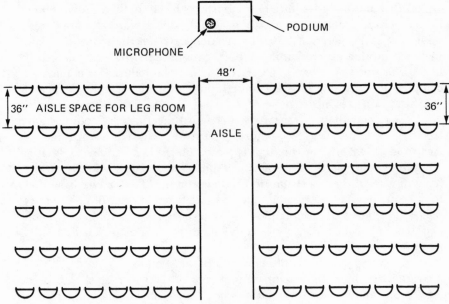

Fig. 10-1. Theater or auditorium style seating arrangement.

Boxed Meals

These are take-out lunches or dinners for picnics, sporting events, social affairs, or business gatherings. Boxed lunches or dinners can be made very simple or elaborate depending on the requirements or budget of a customer. An example of a lunch box menu follows:

A. *Lunch Box 1*
Choice of 2 sandwiches: roast beef, turkey, pastrami, or ham
French pastry
Swiss cheese with crackers
Banana
Apple
Packed in a box with a paper napkin, salt, and pepper
_____ *each*

B. *Lunch Box 2*
Celery, radishes, and carrot sticks
One-half roasted chicken
Choice of 2 sandwiches: roast beef, turkey, pastrami, or ham
Potato salad and cole slaw
French pastry
Swiss cheese with crackers
Banana

Apple
Packed in an attractive carton with napkin, salt, pepper, spoon,
fork, knife
_____ *each*

C. Other Boxed Lunches can be made up by special order.
Beverages can also be provided.

Cocktail Parties

This type of party is very popular for various reasons. It is relatively
easy to arrange, generally inexpensive, and usually informal in nature
with no set seating arrangement. Cocktail parties can be arranged as
separate affairs on an hourly basis or can be held prior to a luncheon or
dinner function. Late afternoon and early evening are the most popular

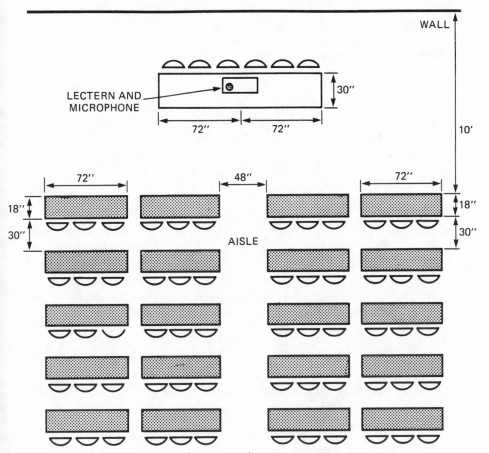

Fig. 10-2. Classroom style seating arrangement.

times for most cocktail parties. A combination of food and beverage (liquor) is usually sold. Due to limitations, customers may request only liquor for their cocktail hour. At such times, limited inexpensive tidbits may be provided by management at nominal cost or offered gratis as a complimentary gesture.

The two types of service used for the food segment of a cocktail party are butler and buffet.

Butler style is the most popular mode of food presentation for a cocktail hour. It is used at the less expensive type of cocktail hour. A limited but adequate selection of assorted hot hors d'oeuvres and cold canapes is generally offered. The average consumption rate for hors d'oeuvres at cocktail parties is six to eight per customer per hour. Service personnel (butlers) pass these hors d'oeuvres or finger foods on silver trays, which include paper doilies, toothpick frills, sauce containers or holders if needed, and paper cocktail napkins. Only hors d'oeuvres that are easy and convenient for the customer to handle should be served, since one of their hands will usually be occupied with a drink. This type of cocktail offering should never require plating. Hors d'oeuvres that are messy, greasy, have bones, hot shells, or other inconveniences should be eliminated from the selection to better facilitate handling. Trays of attractive and colorful cold canapes should always be available as fill-ins, when there are waiting periods for the hot hors d'oeuvres to be heated or other service delays in the kitchen. Most salesmen try to sell a selection of half hot hors d'oeuvres and half cold canapes, but this may vary according to customer preference or perhaps because of handicaps in preparation or kitchen equipment that will favor a higher percentage of one type over the other.

Buffet style is a more expensive and substantial cocktail party in that it offers a full selection of assorted hot chafing-dish items, cold platters, salads, cheeses, and fruit arrangements. A large buffet table is arranged with small-sized plates, silverware, and napkins. An adequate amount of small cocktail tables are set for the guests, and service personnel are available to serve and clean up the cocktail area. Customers who request a buffet-style cocktail party usually have more money to spend on their affair or may simply want to give a more elaborate presentation to their guests than that offered by the simpler butler-style cocktail selection. Some customers may want additional items or decorations incorporated into their buffet such as hot carving tables, ice carvings, desserts, etc. These are extras and are added to the buffet at an additional cost.

An example of a cocktail party menu follows.

COCKTAIL PARTY

A. A delightful selection of assorted Hot Hors d'oeuvres and Cold Canapes passed butler style on silver trays for one hour.

HOT HORS D'OEUVRES

Angels on Horseback	Honey-Dipped Fried Chicken
Stuffed Mushrooms Escargot	Shrimp Puffs
Pineapple Fritters	Glazed Ham Cubes
Miniature Quiche Lorraine	Skewered Sausage and Peppers

COLD CANAPES

Salami Pinwheels	Assorted Canapes with Foie Gras,
Deviled Eggs	Caviar, Smoked Salmon, and
Stuffed Cherry Tomatoes	Herring
Roquefort Cheese on Toast	

_____ per person (average of 8 hors
d'oeuvres per person)

B. For those who wish to have a more substantial and elaborate cocktail hour, may we recommend our buffet-style cocktail party for one hour.

CHAFING DISHES *(choice of 5)*

Seafood Newburg	Veal Scallopina à la Marsala
Chicken Chasseur	Pepper Steak
Beef Stroganoff	Stuffed Cabbage
Manicotti Marinara	Clams Casino
Sweet and Sour Pork	Cheese Ravioli with Meat Sauce
Shish Kabob	Rice Pilaf
Boneless Cornish Game Hen with	Buttered Noodles
Fruit Sauce	Macedoine of Vegetables
Sliced Tongue Polonaise	

COLD PLATTERS *(choice of 4)*

Italian Antipasto	Smoked Beef Tongue
Roast Breast of Turkey	Sliced Virginia Ham
Chicken Galantine	Sliced Roast Beef
Assorted Fish Platter	Corned Brisket of Beef
Liver Pâté Maison	Veal Medallions

SALADS *(choice of 3)*

Waldorf Salad	Red Wine Gelatin Salad Mold
Salad Nicôise	Marinated Mushrooms
Spinach, Bacon, Water Chestnut Salad	Three Bean Salad
Tossed Green Salad with Assorted	Caesar Salad
Dressings	

INTERNATIONAL CHEESE PLATTER

Emmenthaler	Camembert
Danish Blue	Italian Fontina

Served with Assorted Party Breads

_____ per person

17% Gratuity and 8% Sales Tax applicable to all food and beverage consumed.

Some caterers sell hors d'oeuvres or canapes by the piece or by the tray—for example, 50 hors d'oeuvres per tray. Whatever way the customer chooses to purchase hors d'oeuvres, he should be made aware prior to the function that, on an average, guests consume approximately two hors d'oeuvres or canapes per 15 minutes (8 per hour).

Since today's clientele is becoming more and more aware of the selection of liquor by brand names, it is no longer advisable to offer inferior brands for economy's sake. Like food and service, the brand of liquor offered is a reflection on the reputation and quality of goods used by the caterer. Offer a wide selection of name brands to the host for good value. If premium brands are requested, then an additional charge should be made. Since portable bars are used in most function rooms, a limited but adequate selection of liquor should be extended to the host to insure quick and prompt service by the bartenders to the attending guests. Exotic or fancy drinks should be avoided when discussing the liquor arrangements with the host. This will insure that the bartenders are not handicapped by complicated mixtures, and the host can be assured that, by their elimination, the guests will be served faster and not be kept waiting for drinks. Where a permanent or built-in bar exists, the selection can be made larger and more varied because of the nature and completeness of the stocked bar.

Liquor may be sold on an unlimited, consumption, or cash basis.

Unlimited liquor is an arrangement whereby the caterer extends an "unlimited" amount of liquor to the customer for a flat or fixed charge per guest based on an hourly rate. Customers like this concept of "free-flowing" liquor without limitation, and caterers find this type of service easy to sell and quite simple to calculate. All mixers, sodas, juices, and garnishes needed for the liquor setup should be included in the price of this arrangement. Beer and wine may be built into the price structure or may be sold separately. Many caterers will freely include these items into their unlimited plan at no charge, since it reduces the amount of hard liquor consumed, and only a limited number of guests will prefer these drinks over hard liquor.

For every function at which liquor is dispensed, a liquor consumption sheet should be made out after each affair by the bartender in charge. This report will indicate the total amount of liquor, wine, and beer consumed. The cost figures for the alcohol consumed should be compared to the actual amount of revenue received. Be careful not to offer this unlimited liquor plan to certain groups or organizations that are reputed to consume exceptionally large amounts of liquor. Rather, these groups should be sold liquor on a consumption basis.

Table 10-1. Cocktail Party Unlimited Liquor Price Structure (Hourly Basis)						
	½ Hour	*1 Hour*	*2 Hours*	*3 Hours*	*4 Hours*	*5 Hours*
1. Butler style						
Hors d'oeuvres	$1.75	$3.00	$5.00	$6.00	$6.50	$6.75
Unlimited Liquor	2.25	3.75	6.00	7.50	8.25	8.50
Total Food & Beverage	4.00	6.75	11.00	13.50	14.75	15.25
17% Gratuity	.68	1.15	1.87	2.30	2.51	2.59
8% Sales Tax	.32	.54	.88	1.08	1.18	1.22
Total Per Person	5.00	8.44	13.75	16.88	18.44	19.06
Bartender Charge*	X	X	X			
2. Buffet style						
Buffet	4.50	6.50	11.00	12.00	12.50	12.75
Unlimited Liquor	2.25	3.75	6.00	7.50	8.25	8.50
Total Food & Beverage	6.75	10.25	17.00	19.50	20.75	21.25
17% Gratuity	1.15	1.74	2.89	3.31	3.53	3.61
8% Sales Tax	.54	.82	1.36	1.56	1.66	1.70
Total Per Person	8.44	12.81	21.25	24.37	25.94	26.56
Bartender Charge*	X	X				

*Bartender Charges (X) apply to those cocktail parties where total revenues, because of price or the limited amount of guests attending, do not sufficiently cover the labor costs of the needed number of bartenders. Thus, additional bartender fees are charged to the customer for each bartender (based on one bartender per 50 guests). Example: $25.00 charge per bartender per 4 hour job which includes setup of bar, service, and cleanup period for cocktail party.

Prices may be rounded to the nearest five-cent figure to ease calculations and negotiations.

Price incentives or reduced rates can be given to customers who require cocktail parties beyond the initial hour, on the premise that customers will consume less liquor and food per hour as the party is extended in time.

For quick reference to price quotes, especially when customers inquire frequently for cocktail party information, a chart like the one given in Table 10-1 can be composed to show the total price including both gratuities and tax.

Liquor is sold on a *consumption basis* when a customer has a small budget and wants to serve only a limited amount or a specific number of bottles or drinks in order to control the amount or cost of liquor consumed by his guests. The customer is charged for exactly the amount of liquor consumed. During the cocktail party when the predetermined amount has been consumed, the person in charge of service (headwaiter) informs the host that the supply of liquor has been depleted. It then becomes the decision of the host as to whether to stop at this point or to continue with the party and add additional liquor. Additional liquor should only be provided after authorization has been given by the host and should never be done arbitrarily or without the host's consent. This is best handled by having the headwaiter obtain the signature of the host for any additional liquor served and placed on an additional request

Table 10-2.

Consumption Chart

(Converted From Dollar to Liquor Amounts)

Cocktail Hour Selection Item	Price per Bottle	Total Dollar Amounts to Spend											
		$194	$358	$504	$610	$702	$804	$896	$1002	$1148	$1230	$1322	$1448
Btls. Scotch	$24.00	3	7	8	11	13	14	16	19	20	22	24	26
Btls. Canadian Rye	24.00	1	3	4	5	6	7	8	9	10	11	12	13
Btls. Vodka	22.00	1	1	2	2	2	3	3	3	4	4	4	5
Btls. Gin	22.00	1	1	2	2	2	3	3	3	4	4	4	5
Btls. Bourbon	24.00	1	1	2	2	2	2	2	2	3	3	3	3
1/2 Btls. Sweet vermouth	5.00	1	1	2	2	2	2	2	2	3	3	3	3
1/2 Btls. Dry vermouth	5.00	1	1	2	2	2	2	2	2	3	3	3	3
Qts. Whiskey sours	10.00	1	3	4	5	6	7	8	9	10	11	12	13
Qts. Scotch sours	10.00	1	1	2	2	3	3	4	4	5	5	6	6

Above Btld. Liquor is priced according to fifths.
Prices include setups (sodas, mixers, juices, and ice)

Note: Wine and beer can also be included in cocktail hour selection when applicable.

sheet. This will avoid any misunderstanding or controversy when the final bill is presented. The host should also be shown the number of full bottles displayed prior to the cocktail hour and also the empty or partially full bottles after the cocktail party so as to avoid any disagreement as to the amount of liquor consumed by the guests. Beer and wine can be added to this type of cocktail party and charged according to consumption. All the necessary soda, mixers, juices, and garnishes can be added into the price of the bottled goods of liquor or can be charged for separately on a consumption basis.

Vermouths can be incorporated into the cocktail party for those guests who may want drinks such as manhattans or martinis and can be charged for on a half- or full-bottle consumption rate. Mixed drinks like whiskey sours or scotch sours can also be incorporated into the cocktail party and charged according to the amount of liquor, juices, and other ingredients needed to mix these drinks, or they can be sold on a premixed basis such as by the quart or gallon consumed. However, it is management's decision whether to make these drinks to order or on a premixed basis. Appearance, speed, and acceptability are factors to consider in making this decision.

Customers requesting liquor on a consumption basis may approach a salesman in different ways. One may request a certain number of drinks to be given per person. Perhaps another has a certain budget or fixed amount of money to spend on the entire cocktail party and wishes to know how much liquor is available for this amount. The former case is easily calculated as follows: A customer has 100 guests and he wishes to purchase two drinks per person, at the average cost per drink of $1.50, which comes to a total of $300.00 (100 × 2 × 1.50 = $300.00). Sometimes customers may request that tickets be issued to the guests and the bartender collect one as he serves each guest a drink. At the end of the cocktail hour, the host is charged according to the number of tickets collected. In the latter case, a customer may want to spend exactly $360.00 for liquor and would like to know the actual amount of bottled liquor this will entitle him to receive. Assuming that our average bottle (fifth) price of liquor is $24.00, then he would be entitled to 15 bottles of liquor ($360 ÷ 24 = 15 bottles).

The consumption chart in Table 10-2 can be designed to give the salesman a quick reference as to how much liquor is exchanged for dollar amounts the client may wish to spend. This chart should be constructed with the tested preference of the various types of liquor demanded by the clientele in your particular area. The following chart was based on an area where the sequence of highest demand was scotch, rye, vodka, gin, and bourbon, respectively.

Once the party has begun and the trend for one brand of liquor unexpectedly appears greater than another, then simply replace or exchange tbe more requested types of liquor for the least keeping the same number of total bottles on hand. Any adjustments or trends during a function should be brought to the attention of the host. Bartender fees should be charged whenever the liquor revenue does not substantiate the absorption of the labor cost or when the number of attending guests does not produce a high enough income to pay for the services of the bartender(s).

Liquor is sold on a *cash basis* when a host, for reasons of his own, does not provide for liquor arrangements on an unlimited or a consumption basis and where the guests will not object to paying for their own drinks on an individual basis. Since no liquor revenues should be overlooked because of the high profit level, bars should always be available on a cash basis especially when enough volume exists to make it feasible to hire bartenders. Normally, additional bartender fees are charged if a cash bar is requested by the host. In order to control the money flow and to unburden bartenders and allow them to handle more drink orders, it may be advisable to hire a cashier to handle the cash transactions or exchange tickets for the customer's cash. Of course, if the host requests the services of a cashier for control purposes, then this cost is added to the final bill.

Coffee Breaks

These are sold primarily to business meetings, seminars, conventions, or other group functions where light foods and beverages are requested to refresh the participants during a pause in their activities. An example of the type of items incorporated in a coffee break is shown in the following menu.

COFFEE BREAK

Coffee, Tea, or Milk	_____	each
Assorted Danish Pastries	_____	each
Bottle of Iced Coca-Cola or 7-Up	_____	each
Assorted Cookies	_____	per lb.

Prices Per Gallon

Fresh Brewed Coffee (Approximately 25 cups)	_____
Special Blended Tea (Approximately 25 cups)	_____
Fresh Fruit Juice (Approximately 25 glasses)	_____
Freshly Squeezed Orange Juice (Approximately 25 glasses)	_____

A $15.00 labor charge must be added for groups under 30 persons.

All prices are subject to a 17% Gratuity and 8% Sales Tax.

Conventions

Conventions are the highest income-producing functions a catering operation can hold provided there are hotel or motel accommodations available with meeting room facilities attached. Conventions should take preference over all other functions because they generate such high incomes from function room rentals, guest room rental charges, room service, and food and beverage from the restaurant, bar, and banquet facilities. A daily convention report such as shown in Fig. 10-3 should be made out in detail for each convention.

Name of convention: _____

Day and date: _____

Person in charge: _____

Type of function	No. of Persons	Name of room	Time
Breakfast	50	Rose	7—8 A.M.
Registration		Orchid	9 A.M.—5 P.M.
Exhibits setup		Main	9 A.M.—5 P.M.
Coffee break	200	Rose	9:45—10 A.M.
Luncheon	200	Rose	12—1 P.M.
Seminar	200	Diamond	1—3 P.M.
Coffee break	200	Rose	3—3:30 P.M.
Lecture/discussion	200	Diamond	3:30—5 P.M.
Dinner	200	Rose	6—7:30 P.M.
Exhibits dismantled		Main	7—11 P.M.

SUMMARY

Total Food Income $ _____

Total Beverage Income $ _____

Total Function Room Rental $ _____

Total Guest Room Income $ _____

Total Daily Convention Income $ _____

All Charges Billed To

Name _____

Address _____

_____ ZIP_____

Telephone   Home _____

Office _____

Fig. 10-3. Daily convention report.

Detailed information and instructions for exhibit setups, floor plans, and room diagrams should be correlated with the daily convention report. Also, compose a complete list of equipment to be used in each function room. This equipment will accompany the daily convention report and would include such items as blackboards, easels, podiums, lecterns, microphones, projectors, blackout switches, extension cords, tables, and head tables on platforms. It is also wise to include instructions for requested security arrangements including the opening and locking of doors. In summation, the daily convention report should be as accurate, detailed, and complete as possible so no point is overlooked.

Prior to the convention, arrangements should be made through the receiving department for the delivery and storage of incoming convention goods. All these items must be tagged with proper identification and dates for future use.

Dances

Usually held by social, religious, or organizational groups either for profit or purely for enjoyment, dances often only require liquor arrangements, which are furnished on a cash or on an unlimited basis. Room rental fees are usually charged additionally for such functions. When dances require both liquor and food, it will be the policy of the operation as to whether or not room rentals are charged in addition to the food and beverage ordered. In cases in which dinners, buffets, or other substantial food revenues are received, then the room rental is generally waived. Sometimes, dances will require only limited or light foods such as cold platters, light buffets, or suppers. Specialty dances such as barn dances, holiday dances, or ethnic dances should take on the theme and decorations of that particular party to make it festive. Good music and entertainment, if not arranged by the organizers, should be recommended by the caterer to assure a successful dance.

Dinners

The most often requested type of meal for evening affairs, sit-down dinners are generally preferred as the format for formal affairs, since the guests are served directly at the table by waiters so that no waiting or standing on lines occurs as with buffets. When music arrangements are provided, then these functions are classified as dinner/dances. A dinner usually includes the following: a cold appetizer, soup, salad, entrée, starch, vegetable(s), dessert, and beverage. Courses may be added, eliminated, or substituted depending on the requirements and budget of each customer. For example, an intermezzo may be added in the form of a sherbet or cordial, such as crème de menthe, served prior to the entrée to cleanse and refresh the palate.

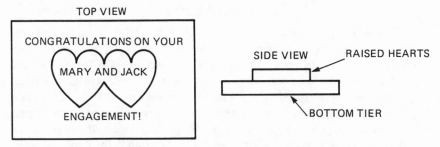

Fig. 10-4. Sample cake for engagement party.

Wine is popular at dinners. Other liquor arrangements can also be provided either prior to the dinner in the form of a cocktail reception, during the dinner, on an unlimited basis, or on a per-bottle or per-drink consumption basis, and after dinner as cordials. Of course, liquor can be made available at all times on a cash basis.

Dinner menu prices should vary in order to be within the budget range of most customers. An example of a banquet dinner menu is given in Chapter 11 for a wedding.

Engagement Parties

These celebrations most often take the form of a cocktail party, luncheon, dinner, or buffet. Champagne, liquor, and punch bowls or fountains are easily sold for these festive occasions. Music for dancing and floral arrangements are often requested for these functions. An engagement cake is always part of the affair, with a popular design to coincide with the theme of the party, such as a heart or interlocking hearts (see Fig. 10-4).

Since guests may bring gifts to the party, a gift table should be provided near the couple's table. An engagement party should receive special attention, since it is not only a high-income-producing affair but may also lead to booking the even more lucrative wedding reception.

Farewell or "Bon Voyage" Parties

These are given for someone about to depart on a trip or who is moving out of the area and are usually organized by the friends or relatives of the guest of honor. They are often surprise parties. These celebrations can be arranged as cocktail parties, luncheons, dinners, or buffets. Because of the festive nature of these affairs, liquor arrangements are always incorporated into the affair, especially champagne as a toast. In addition to the food and liquor arrangements, a cake is suggested, appropriately inscribed. The cake can be shaped to form a ship, house, plane, or other appropriate configuration.

Fashion Shows

These are popular fund-raising or purely social events organized usually by a women's religious, professional, or social group. Fashion shows can be held in conjunction with a brunch, cocktail party, lunch, dinner, or buffet. They can also be arranged as less expensive affairs where pastries or assorted finger sandwiches are served with coffee and tea. To make the affair more festive, and to generate additional liquor revenue, champagne and various cocktails such as manhattans, martinis, whiskey sours, and scotch sours can be incorporated into the package. These cocktails are usually served prior to the fashion show, as the guests arrive and are being seated at their respective tables. Light foods and pastries are best served during the intermission or at the completion of the fashion show. One pastry per person is generally sufficient. Extra coffee is usually called for.

If no liquor arrangements have been made, a cash bar should be made available prior to the function so guests can order drinks. Since women tend to order mixed or fancy drinks, bartenders should be prepared to handle these often-complicated and time-consuming drinks.

Where the income is not sufficient to insure a profit from the limited food and beverage requirements of a fashion show, it may be advisable to charge a room rental fee including charges for the linen, labor involved in setting up and cleaning the room, and other overhead expenses.

To run fashion shows effectively, the following equipment and facilities should be made available for each function:

1. Dressing rooms or partitioned or screened-off areas convenient to the stage or display area with sufficient coat racks, hangers, mirrors, dressing tables, and chairs
2. A ramp or runway that should lead directly from the stage area where a permanent stage exists
3. A podium and microphone for the commentator who coordinates and describes the fashions
4. A piano or piped-in or taped music
5. A theater spotlight to follow and accent the models

Certain precautions must be taken when booking a fashion show. Most fashion shows are arranged through a professional fashion house. Make certain that the client has a *definite* commitment from such a fashion house, since the better ones, similar to caterers, require bookings well in advance to hold a show. To cut costs, some fashion houses are no longer providing models free of charge to display their clothing, but are solely furnishing the garments. In such cases, the organizers of the show are responsible for the garments exhibited. Make certain that the client is aware of his/her responsibility not only for the garments but also for

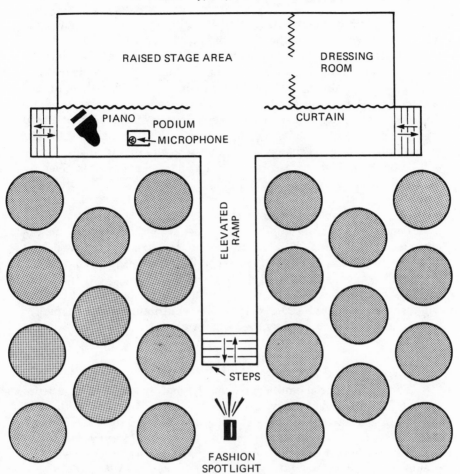

Fig. 10-5. Sample setup for a fashion show.

providing models and commentators. Good lighting is a necessity and the room must be bright to effectively display the fashions. To avoid complaints, especially in large rooms where the fashion ramp or display area is far from certain sections of the room, it is wise to install additional platforms or raised areas with steps where the visibility is poor, so that the models and fashions can be brought closer to the guests. See Fig. 10-5 for a typical fashion show setup.

Fund-Raising Functions

Held by religious, business, and political groups, hospitals, unions, charities, and other organizations whose main purpose is to raise money for a specific cause, these events are sold as testimonial dinners, luncheons, or breakfasts. Fund-raising affairs usually honor a well-known and influential person to aid in the selling of tickets. These tickets are sold at a higher price than given to the caterer for his goods and services so that a profit is realized by the organization. The ticket price is determined usually by a committee, which is formed to organize and sell these tickets. A caterer must get prior guarantees or commitments as to head count on this type of party, since many times people buy tickets and do not attend the functions. Hence, the head count can be lower than tickets sold. The person or committee in charge must be made aware that food and service will be provided and charged for the final guarantee or counts given by the deadline date. Any percentage under or over the final number of guaranteed guests must be made as clear as possible prior to the affair to avoid any disagreement as to final charges.

Fund-raising organizations may publish a journal to generate extra revenue. These journals sell ads to various business, professional, and labor organizations and charge rates according to the size and color of the page or advertisement taken. Often, the caterer will be asked to buy an ad in the journal. This is not only good public relations and advertising, but will also be considered as a tax-deductible contribution. The charge for such an ad can be deducted by the caterer from the final bill.

Gourmet Dinners

These are special multicourse meals that customers or societies request for an unusual dining experience. Gourmet dinners are usually high-costing affairs with elaborate menus accompanied by fine wines and after-dinner cordials. Special serviceware, such as gold service and linens, should be made part of this elegant service. Additional service personnel should be hired to make it an outstanding event. An example of a gourmet dinner menu follows.

GOURMET DINNER

Caviar Beluga Malossol sur Glace
Consommé Double Royal
Homard du Maine Parisienne
Coeur de Filet de Boeuf Flambé à la Fine Champagne
Pommes Château
Bouquetière de Légumes
Salade Marseillaise
Fromage de Brie de la Normandie
Soufflé au Grand Marnier
Café

_____ per person

Gratuity and Sales Tax are additional to above prices.

Holiday Parties

These festivities are held for the usual holidays as well as for holidays celebrated by certain groups or nationalities, including Columbus Day, Easter, Valentine's Day, and St. Patrick's Day. Special decorations should always be used to enhance the spirit of these holiday events and periods. Menus should be constructed to comply with the foods of the specific holiday. An example of a holiday banquet dinner menu follows.

THANKSGIVING DINNER

Celery   Olives   Radishes

Supreme of Fresh Fruit in Hawaiian Pineapple Baskets

Consommé Double Amontillado

Roast Vermont Turkey with American Dressing,
    Giblet Gravy and Cranberry Sauce

Brussel Sprouts with Chestnuts   Creamed Onions
Puree of Turnips   Candied Yams Imperial
Whipped Potatoes   Baked Idaho Potato

Pilgrim Salad (choice of dressings)

Pumpkin Pie Chantilly
Mince Pie
Cheddar Cheese with Fresh Fruit Bowl
Assorted Mints and Nuts
Coffee, Tea, Milk
Hot Rolls, Breads, and Creamy Butter
Jugs of Apple Cider

_____ per person

17% Gratuity and 8% Sales Tax are applicable to all food and beverage consumed.

Luncheons

Fast becoming a popular type of banquet function because prices are more reasonable, luncheons usually include a choice of cold appetizer or soup, entrée, starch, vegetable(s), dessert, and coffee and tea. If requested, a salad course can be included at additional cost. The type of luncheon served will depend on who is attending, e.g., ladies' luncheons will often require lighter or more dietetic types of foods, while a men's luncheon will require heavier or more substantial foods. Cocktail and liquor arrangements should be sold and offered prior to the luncheon in the form of a paid cocktail hour or cash bar. Since wine is becoming more popular and acceptable, it should be suggested for all luncheon selections.

An example of a banquet luncheon menu follows.

BANQUET LUNCHEON

APPETIZER (choice of one)

Supreme of Fresh Florida Fruits
Melon in Season, Wedge of Lime
Half Grapefruit
Consommé
Chilled Double Tomato or V-8 Juice
Eggs à la Russe
Soup du Jour
Antipasto
Jumbo Shrimp Cocktail Supreme
Alaskan King Crab Seafood Cocktail

SALAD .50 Additional (choice of one)

Tossed Green Salad with Tomato Wedges
Spinach Salad with Sliced Mushrooms
(choice of dressing included with above salad)
Roquefort Dressing (.50 extra)

ENTRÉE (choice of one)

Sliced London Broil, Sauce Chasseur
Seafood Crêpe à la Maison
Roast Prime Rib of Beef, au Jus
Chef's Mixed Salad Bowl, Choice of Dressing
Broiled Sirloin Steak, Maitre d'Hotel
Filet of Sole, Sauce Vin Blanc
Roast Top Sirloin of Beef, au Jus
Broiled Chopped Tenderloin Steak, Sauce Bordelaise
Yankee Pot Roast, Marchand de Vin
Boneless Breast of Chicken, Bourguignonne
Fruit Salad with Cottage Cheese or Sherbet

POTATO (choice of one)

Rissole	Duchesse
Stuffed Baked	Home Fried

VEGETABLE (choice of one)

Broccoli Mimosa	String Beans Provencale
Glazed Baby Belgian Carrots	Fresh Garden Peas and Pearl Onions

DESSERT (choice of one)

Assorted French Pastries	Chocolate Mousse
Rainbow Ice Cream or Sherbet Parfait	Peach Melba
Apple Pie with Cheddar Cheese	Black Forest Cake

BEVERAGES   Coffee, Tea, Milk

If less than 20 persons, a $30.00 service charge will be applied.
Add 17% Gratuity and 8% Sales Tax.

Outdoor Parties

Promoting outside functions should be considered where there is sufficient property or acreage surrounding the catering operation. The availability of outdoor parties will increase revenues especially during the slower periods or summer months of your indoor catering operation. By installing temporary tents or permanent pavillions with bandstands or platforms and portable dance floors, an attractive and desirable setting is created for all types of groups and organizations to hold outdoor parties. Outdoor sporting and game facilities such as ball fields, volleyball and badminton courts, horseshoe pits, etc., can be easily and inexpensively installed for customer participation. Special barbecue charcoal grills and pits, clambake pits where cooking can be done New England style with seaweed on hot stones, or iced clam bars can be permanently constructed to lend flair to these functions. Chafing dishes should be utilized to easily serve most hot food items. Liquor bars can be permanently constructed under protective covering, and liquor can be sold on a cash basis. Beer for outdoor parties can be sold separately on a half-barrel basis. Music may be contracted for separately if requested.

Barbecues, clambakes, or picnics can be arranged and sold to large groups on a daily basis. These affairs might include breakfast, lunch, a clam bar, and dinner for a fixed price per person. A corresponding reduction in price can be made if any segment of the function is eliminated or reduced. Unlimited coffee, tea, milk, and soda should be served throughout the entire affair. Additional items such as lobsters, crabs, and various fish can be incorporated into the all-day affair at an additional cost or substituted for items in the same price range.

Special children's prices or allowances can be offered for those in attendance under a certain age especially when families are attending these functions.

The following format can be used for this type of affair.

ALL-DAY OUTDOOR BUFFET

BREAKFAST
(served from 10 A.M. to 12 Noon)

Chilled Orange and Grapefruit Juice
Soft Country Scrambled Eggs with
   choice of Link Sausage, Ham, or
   Bacon
Danish Pastry
Breakfast Rolls
Marmalade
Freshly Brewed Coffee (all day)

LUNCH
(served from 12 Noon to 3 P.M.)

Barbecued Chicken
Barbecued Spare Ribs
Italian Sausage and Peppers
Hamburgers on Buns

Frankfurters on Buns
Corn on the Cob
French Fries
Iced Watermelon
Rolls and Butter
Soda (all day)

CLAM BAR
(served from 3 to 5 P.M.)

Clam Broth and Chowder
Iced Cherrystone and Little Neck
   Clams with Cocktail Sauce
   and Lemon wedges
*Jumbo Shrimp Cocktail

DINNER
(served from 5 to 6 P.M.)

*Charcoal Broiled Steak
Potatoes Charcoal
Choice of Fresh Vegetable
Mixed Green Salad (choice of
   dressing)
Apple Pie with Cheddar Cheese
Rolls and Butter

$30.00 per person   Add 17% Gratuity and 8% Sales Tax.
*Tickets will be issued for these items for control purposes. All other items are served in unlimited quantities. These parties not available for less than 100 persons.

Proms

These senior high school functions usually require a dinner or buffet and also have music for dancing. Soft-punch bowls and soda fountains are popular beverage displays for these affairs prior to and during the meal, since no liquor arrangements are provided because of the age group of the guests. Although no liquor revenue is obtained from this function, it is important that special attention be given to the food, service, and other arrangements because many of these graduating students will remember this affair and, if satisfied, will be potential customers for weddings and other affairs within a few short years. These functions should be booked on weekdays so that other higher-income-producing parties can have the more desirable weekend dates.

Rehearsal Dinners

Given for the entire bridal party after rehearsing the wedding ceremony, the expense for this dinner, conditions permitting, is generally absorbed by the groom's parents, since most other expenses of the wedding are paid for by the bride's parents. To lower the cost of this affair, it could be arranged as a luncheon or perhaps a light supper or buffet. Liquor and wine arrangements are usually requested or easily sold for this type of function. If the wedding ceremony is to take place on the premise, then it is management's function to direct and conduct the rehearsal for the bridal party.

Retirement Dinners or Luncheons

Usually sponsored by an employer, whether a company, union, or other organization, this dinner or luncheon honors the retiring employee with a customary award of service or gift. The budget for this type of function will be delegated to the person in charge of the function who will determine the food and beverage requirements and arrangements. Since it is a happy farewell party, a cocktail hour or other liquor arrangements are generally made, budget permitting. If not, then a cash bar should be opened to capitalize on this additional revenue. Often a good luck or farewell cake is ordered with an appropriate inscription. Usually, a dais or head table with floral arrangements is requested for the guest of honor, and a lectern with a microphone is required for the speeches and presentations.

Reunion Parties

These are functions where friends and families come together from various locations to hold a celebration or group gathering. The two most popular gatherings are class and family reunion parties. For most class reunions, tickets are usually sold for a dinner function so as to keep the price of the tickets low and insure a large turnout. Liquor arrangements are most often sold separately on an individual or cash basis. Liquor should always be made readily available for these parties, since the consumption is usually high for these happy reunions.

Family reunions are usually budgeted affairs and their food and beverage requirements will be determined by the amount of finances available.

Showers

As surprise parties given by the female friends of a bride-to-be or expectant mother, showers require a gift table because of the many presents that are brought. Over the gift table a shower umbrella, usually made of papier-mâché, is hung. This umbrella may be supplied by the caterer, but most often it is furnished by the women arranging the party. A microphone is often needed for larger showers so that when the gifts are opened, usually after the food and beverages have been served, everyone will hear the comments made by the bride or mother-to-be.

Showers can be organized as cocktail parties, luncheons, dinners, buffets, or suppers. Champagne, cocktails, punch bowls or fountains, or other liquor arrangements can be sold on an unlimited or consumption basis for these surprise occasions. Bar facilities should be made available on a cash basis especially when no liquor arrangements have been made for the men who will be arriving later to escort the women home.

Specially decorated cakes are appropriate for both types of parties. "Happiness on Your Shower" or "For Baby" can be inscribed atop the cake, which might be in the shape of an umbrella, a pair of baby shoes, or a crib according to the type of shower held.

Showers are important functions and should be executed with care, since many of the attending guests may be potential clients for future parties, especially weddings.

Sports Functions

These are luncheons or dinners that are held by baseball, football, bowling, basketball, or some other team or league. A prominent sports figure is often invited to give a speech. Trophies are often given to the participants, and so a table may be needed to display these awards. When youngsters are involved in these functions, then the dinner or luncheon is usually low budgeted. Limited menus are popular with soft beverages and ice cream included. Liquor arrangements should be made available on a cash basis for the attending adults.

Suppers

Usually late-evening affairs, these functions feature light snacks, sandwiches, or heavy meals and are held for groups arriving after an outing or show held elsewhere. Cocktails or liquor arrangements are successfully sold for these functions.

Teas

Usually held in the afternoon, teas commonly require tea, coffee, Danish, finger sandwiches, sweet rolls, croissants, brioche, cookies, and mints.

When music and dancing are incorporated, these affairs are called tea dances. These dances are usually held on Sunday afternoons and liquor arrangements are popular. An example of a tea menu follows.

TEAS

For tea or coffee service, a samovar is provided on a draped table with cups and saucers, lemon, cream, and sugar	_____ per gallon
	or_____ per person
Finger Sandwiches	_____ per person
Danish Pastry and Sweet Rolls	_____ each
Assorted Cookies and Mints	_____ per person
Trays of Danish Pastry, Sweet Rolls, Croissants and Brioche (24 pieces)	_____ per tray

Theme Dinners and Costume Parties

These are popular festive and fun social affairs. The caterer must be imaginative and flexible enough to decorate and provide the necessary menus and service that might be requested for these unusual functions. Often the caterer will be consulted by the organizer for menu and costume suggestions. An example of one such menu follows.

GALA LUAU DINNER

Pineapple Aloha

Seafood Curry Served in Coconut Shells

Native Tossed Abaco Greens (choice of island dressings)

Roast Stuffed Suckling Pig Carved by Our Chef Before Your Eyes

Assorted Paradise Island Vegetables

Sweet Potatoes

Fried Plantains

Treasure Island Parfait

Coffee, Tea, Milk

Whole Round Loaves of Dark Breads Served with Fresh Butter Balls

An Assortment of Island Fruits Displayed at Each Table

_____ per person

17% Gratuity and 8% Sales Tax are additional.

Trade or Promotional Shows

Since these functions include exhibits or displays, they provide an excellent source of income for a catering operation especially when scheduled during normally slow periods. There are hundreds of different shows that can be booked, each producing revenues and providing excellent exposure due to the large number of persons attending. Such shows as the following may be organized: antique, appliance, automobile, art, boat, bridal, camping, ceramic, coin, flower, gem, photography, and stamp shows.

In order for any of these shows to be successful, full cooperation must be established between management and the show's organizers as far as the use and setup of the facilities are concerned.

The promoter or organizer of the show usually seeks large indoor facilities so that sufficient income can be made by both renting booth space and by charging an admission fee. The promoter's expense comes in organizing and setting up contracts to the individual displayers, as well as in advertising the show. The caterer makes his income by charging the organizers a rental fee for the use of the facility, plus whatever additional revenue can be made by providing cash bars and food arrangements for both customers and exhibitors. Checking and parking arrangements can be provided and charged for on an individual basis by the caterer. Clean-up arrangements after the show are the responsibility of the caterer and should be calculated in the room rental charge. Additional individual room rentals can be realized when the caterer has hotel or motel facilities available. To successfully book and promote this type of business, the catering facility must be fairly large and must be easily accessible for goods and displays to be delivered. Sufficiently wide doors, high ceilings, exceptionally good lighting, and adequate outlets and electrical wiring are essential. A diagram should be made of every room that can be utilized for shows. Include in this diagram the dimensions of the room, the door widths and heights, ceiling heights, chandelier heights, the positions of all electrical outlets, dimmers or light switches, mike jacks, and any other information that may be useful to a promoter who wishes to set up the room for a show.

Chapter 11

Weddings

Millions of dollars are spent each year on catered wedding receptions. In many cases, clients save for years in anticipation of hosting an elaborate wedding. To successfully book and execute a wedding, the caterer must be familiar with the entire scope and organization of this type of affair. It is equally as important to know how to properly conduct a wedding ceremony and bridal introduction as it is to know how to properly prepare and serve food and beverage.

Some couples may want an informal or fun-filled reception, while others may request a more reserved, dignified affair. Each couple's tastes and requests will be different, so each wedding must be handled individually. In any case, always react to each customer in a positive manner. Sell them "their" type of affair whether it be formal or informal; with alcoholic beverages or without; buffet or Russian service; package plan or individually priced. To be competitive, the caterer must be able to accommodate a customer's every request and whim from the rehearsal and actual conducting of the ceremony to the cutting of the wedding cake and throwing of the bouquet and garter.

By servicing all aspects of a wedding, the caterer will be assured of a fair share of this lucrative market. For example, a couple may wish to be married on your premise. The caterer who frequently receives such requests should either reserve a room that can be easily converted into a chapel or, if the business warrants, construct a permanent chapel. On-premise weddings offer the opportunity for the caterer to make additional money from the chapel room rental, flowers, aisle runners, and whatever other incidentals may be needed. On-premise ceremonies are popular because everything is held under one roof. Guests do not have to travel from the ceremony to the reception. This, of course, saves time and eliminates travel arrangements and limousine expenses. As an added touch to an on-premise ceremony, the caterer can set aside a "hospitality room" for guests who arrive early. Juice, coffee, tea, Danish, and cake may be offered as part of the package plan, on an individually priced basis, or gratis to help book the affair.

Saturdays and Sundays are the most popular days for weddings. Afternoon affairs, usually from 12 to 5 P.M., are usually sold at a lower rate than evening affairs, which generally range from 7 p.m. to as late as possible. Overtime rates are generally applied after five hours. In most locations, May and June traditionally have been the most desirable months for weddings, but September and October have been gaining in popularity. It is a common practice to offer special rates for functions held during off-season months. Brunches and informal weddings, usually lower-income-producing affairs as compared to formal functions, are generally booked for mornings or afternoons of slack periods. A minimum of one hour is needed between functions to clean and reset the room. Proper timing is important to prevent affairs from running over.

The Rehearsal

All the participants in the wedding can be called together for a wedding rehearsal conducted by the banquet coordinator or headwaiter. Usually held just a few days prior to the actual ceremony, so that all procedures remain fresh in the minds of the participants, the rehearsal may be accompanied by a luncheon or dinner. Only when no previous arrangements have been made should a rehearsal be scheduled for the day of the function.

During the rehearsal, all the major participants in the wedding will be acquainted with positions and procedures for the lineup, entry, ceremony, and exit. Spacing, timing, and cues to watch for are also discussed. If a participant is unable to attend the rehearsal, it is the responsibility of the client to inform the absent party of what they missed.

The bridal party processional should be conducted at a slow, but not a creeping, pace. The recessional should be faster, but not at a running pace. For appearance sake, the shortest ushers and bridesmaids are positioned first in line, the tallest last.

Any special request or deviations from traditional wedding procedures should be discussed with the banquet representative and clergyman prior to the affair, no later than the rehearsal. Since ceremonial or religious rituals differ from faith to faith, it is advisable for the banquet representative to consult with the clergyman as to what procedure will be followed. Certain clergymen may want to conduct the entire service without the caterer's assistance, while others may request that the caterer organize the entire proceedings up to the point of the actual ritual. In all cases, the clergyman always has the final say as to how the ceremony will be conducted.

While the ceremony itself is customarily executed by a member of the clergy, the caterer assumes the responsibility for organizing the processional, recessional, receiving line, entrance into the reception hall, cutting of the cake, and throwing of the bouquet and garter. There are numerous variations to these ceremonies, but the standard formats usually followed will be discussed here.

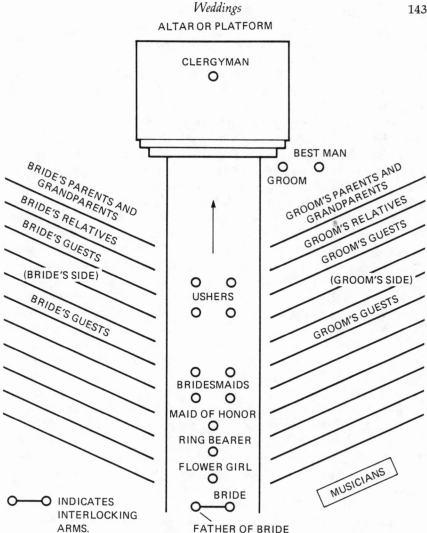

Fig. 11-1. Processional for a Christian wedding.

The Christian Wedding

Processional

The processional immediately precedes the wedding ceremony and is conducted as follows (see also Fig. 11-1).

The ushers seat the arriving guests. A general rule of thumb is to have one usher for every 40 to 50 guests. The first pews are for the parents and grandparents of the bride and groom. The bride's parents, relatives, and friends are seated on the left side; the groom's are seated on the right. Seats closest to the aisle should be left vacant for the bride's parents. The second and succeeding pews should be reserved for the next closest relatives of the bride and groom. The next unreserved pews are for the invited guests of the bride and groom.

After all the guests are seated, an usher escorts the bride's mother down the aisle to her seat in the first pew. The usher returns to the rear of the room. The caterer's representative then rolls out the aisle runner. The guests rise as the clergyman enters from the rear or side, taking his position at the head of the room, altar, or platform. He then faces the congregation. The groom and the best man enter in the same manner as the clergyman, and the groom stands to the clergyman's left and the best man to the groom's left. They both face the clergyman.

Music is played and the processional begins. The ushers walk slowly down the aisle in pairs (with several yards between pairs) and proceed to the right side in front of the first pew or row. The bridesmaids follow slowly in pairs (or single file) and proceed to the left side in front of the first pew or row. Bridesmaids and ushers may also pair off and stand together, with half of them to the right side, the other half to the left.

The maid or matron of honor walks slowly down the aisle and stops at the first or second pew, where the best man meets her and escorts her to the left side of the altar or platform (clergyman's right) facing the clergyman. The best man returns to the right side facing the clergyman. The honor attendant may also go directly to her position left of center without being escorted by the best man. If a ring bearer and flower girl are included in the bridal party, they proceed down the aisle next. The ring bearer, usually carrying the ring on a pillow, enters first and walks slowly down the aisle, positioning himself to the right of the best man. The flower girl proceeds down the aisle just before the bride, slowly dropping floral petals in her path. She then goes to the left of the maid of honor.

The bride enters on the right side of her father, holding his right arm with her left. This is the more traditional procedure; the bride may also walk down the aisle on her father's left. Together they walk slowly down the aisle as the music plays the appropriate wedding march. They stop at the first or second pew. The father removes the bridal veil, if worn, and kisses his daughter. The groom walks from the front to meet her. The father steps aside to permit the bride to take the groom's left arm. The couple proceeds slowly to the center of the altar or platform directly in front of the clergyman (Fig. 11-2). The bride's father goes to the first pew and is seated next to his wife.

The clergyman begins the ceremony. The maid of honor takes the bridal bouquet and the best man gives the ring(s) to the groom at the proper time. The ceremony concludes with a kiss and both bride and groom turn and exit the room with the maid of honor assisting the bride with ber gown and train.

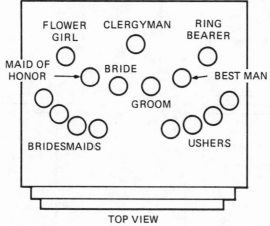

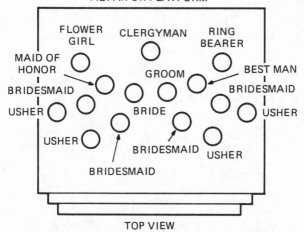

Fig. 11-2. Positioning of bridal party for a Christian wedding.

Recessional

The recessional (Fig. 11-3) is conducted in reverse order to the processional. People leave the ceremony in the following sequence:

1. Bride and groom
2. Flower girl and ring bearer
3. Maid of honor and best man
4. Bridesmaids and ushers in pairs
5. The parents of the bride and groom
6. The relatives of the bride and groom
7. The friends of the bride and groom

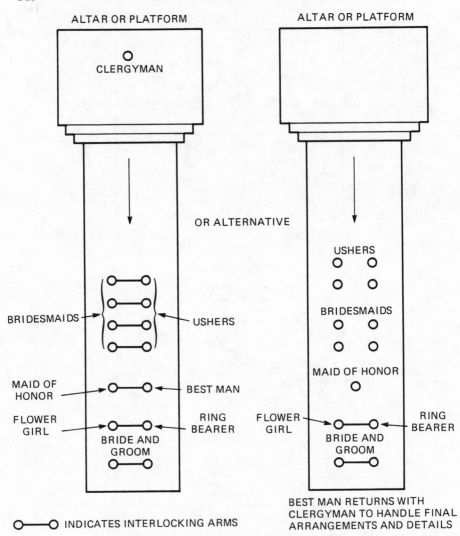

Fig. 11-3. Recessional for a Christian wedding.

In certain instances, the maid of honor and bridesmaids will leave after the ring bearer, followed by the best man and ushers. The clergyman may request that the best man return with him to handle any final details or arrangements.

As the bridal party is filing out of the chapel, the banquet coordinator should begin to arrange the receiving line.

The Jewish Wedding

Processional

There are three branches of Judaism: Orthodox, Conservative, and Reform. Each has its own rules and regulations pertaining to wedding ceremonies. For example, the Orthodox segment requires that men and women be separated by a partition during the service, while the Conservative and Reform branches allow men and women to be seated together. It is important for the caterer to know these and other distinctions among the three branches so as not to offend any client. To insure strict observance of established procedures, some congregations do not permit members to hold ceremonies outside the synagogue.

For a rabbi to properly conduct a wedding ceremony on a caterer's premises, certain items are needed. The *huppah* is a four-posted floral or fabric canopy underneath which the wedding ceremony is performed. It symbolizes the sanctity of the bridal chamber of the wedded couple. Under the huppah, a small table is draped on which three items are placed for the rabbi: a bottle of kosher wine; two wine cups or glasses (should be provided by the caterer in the event the rabbi or the parents do not bring their own); and a fragile glass wrapped first in paper, then in a cloth or napkin. This last item is placed on the floor at the conclusion of the ceremony, at which point the groom breaks it with the heel of his shoe. This symbolizes the sorrow of the Jewish people being evicted from Jerusalem and the destruction of their temple with their pledge to always remember it. Caterers should provide yamulkas (skull caps) for the male guests as a symbol of their respect for God. A draped table outside the entrance to the chapel should be set up with the yamulkas laid out neatly so that each man may take one and place it on his head before entering the chapel. Most caterers will charge on extra fee for souvenir yamulkas that have the names of the couple and date of the wedding imprinted on the inside.

Upon arriving, the guests are seated by the ushers on the proper side. Unlike the seating arrangements for the Christian wedding, the groom's family and friends sit on the left while the bride's sit on the right. The catering coordinator lines up all participants in order of their entry into the room (see Fig. 11-4).

The rabbi enters first, usually with the introduction of the wedding music. He is positioned either at the beginning of the processional or he may enter through a side door. In either case, he goes directly underneath the huppah behind the table and faces the congregation. If a cantor (a liturgy specialist and singer of religious chants) is used, he will lead the congregation in song and accompany the rabbi. Both men can enter

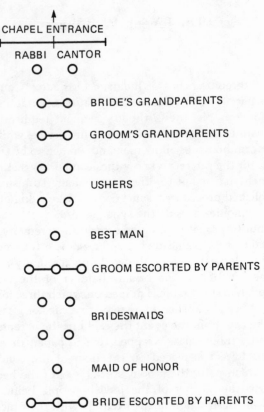

Fig. 11-4. Processional for a Jewish wedding.

together and stand side by side under the huppah. A musician to accompany the cantor is usually furnished by the cantor or by the caterer if requested. Usually a short rehearsal is required for this prior to the ceremony.

After the rabbi positions himself under the huppah, the ushers escort the grandparents to the first row, which has been reserved for them. The ushers regroup at the rear of the chapel and enter together in pairs. They walk at a slow pace to the front and stand side by side to the left in front of the huppah facing the rabbi. The best man walks a few feet behind the ushers and goes to the left side of the huppah, facing the rabbi. The groom now enters with his parents on each side holding his arms. Unlike the Christian wedding, the parents partake in the actual ceremony. They proceed down the aisle and stand underneath the huppah. The groom approaches the table and stands slightly to the left of it in front of the best man and faces the rabbi. The parents pass to the left of the groom and stand perpendicular to the side of the table equidistant from the rabbi and the groom.

Now that the groom's party has entered the chapel under the direction of the catering coordinator, the bride's is next. The bridesmaids enter slowly either in pairs or single file and position themselves opposite the ushers on the outside fringe of the huppah facing the rabbi. The maid of honor now comes down the aisle and stands under the huppah to the right side opposite the best man facing the rabbi. She may also stop at the first or second row, where the best man meets her and then escorts her to her position under the huppah. The bride, on the cue of the musician(s) and catering coordinator, proceeds slowly down the aisle, escorted by her parents. They stop at the first or second row, where they wait for the groom to join them. The bride takes the arm of the groom, who she sees this day for the first time, and is slowly escorted under the huppah. Both stand directly in front of the table facing the rabbi. The parents now move to the right side of the bride and stand facing the side of the table or opposite the parents of the groom (see Fig. 11-5).

The rabbi begins the ceremony, blesses the wine, and gives it to the groom and then the bride to sip. This symbolizes the act of sharing their lives together. The ring ceremony is performed with the best man giving the ring to the groom, who places it on the bride's right index finger. It is transferred to the left ring finger after the ceremony is completed. The rabbi usually addresses the couple and congregation with a short talk. He may also read the ketubah (marriage contract), which has been previously signed by the witnesses and given to the bride. Several blessings are read by the rabbi and, if a cantor is used, religious chants periodically will be sung throughout the ceremony. The signal for the conclusion of the ceremony is the groom crushing a glass with his heel with the congregation responding with "mazel tov," which means "good luck."

Recessional

The recessional now takes place with the parties leaving in pairs in the following sequence:

1. Bride and groom
2. Bride's parents
3. Groom's parents
4. Maid of honor with the best man
5. Bridesmaids with the ushers

The grandparents along with the rabbi and cantor should be permitted to leave shortly after the recessional to be allowed to give their congratulations to the bride and groom. The banquet coordinator should begin to arrange the receiving line for the oncoming congregation.

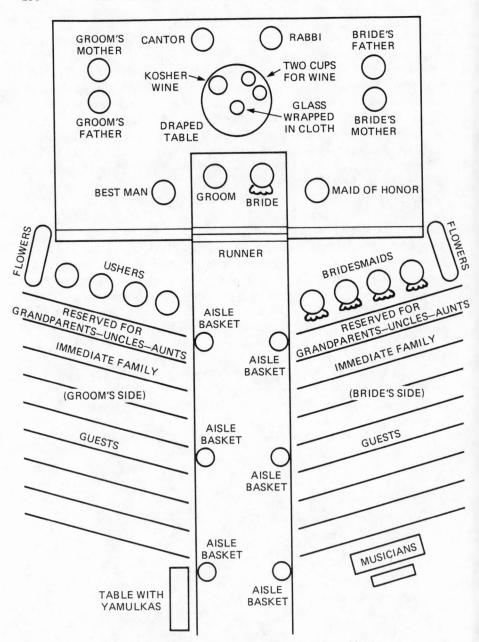

Fig. 11-5. Positioning of bridal party for a Jewish wedding.

The Receiving Line

Because there is so little time between the conclusion of the ceremony and the arrival of the guests at the receiving line, the banquet coordinator must act quickly. To avoid crowding, the receiving line is never set too close to the doors through which the guests must walk. It is advisable to set the line in the open and as close to the cocktail or refreshment area as possible. This will allow the guests to offer their congratulations and proceed directly into the reception area. If too heavy a backup of guests occurs, some of the guests may be led to the refreshment area and asked to return after the line has thinned. This will also aid in the serving of cocktails and other refreshments.

The sequence for the receiving line is: bride's mother, groom's father, groom's mother, bride's father, bride, groom, maid of honor, bridesmaids. An alternative to this line-up would be the bride's mother and father, groom's mother and father, bride, groom, maid of honor, bridesmaids. The best man and the ushers are generally not included in the receiving line unless the bride requests their presence.

As the guests pass through the line, they are introduced individually, and their names are passed down the line. If the name of a guest is lost or a person on the receiving line does not know the identity of a guest, it is permissible to ask the name and then continue to pass it along the line.

Although not often requested, an announcer, a person who introduces the guests to the mother of the bride, may be hired for the occasion.

By the time the last guest has passed through the receiving line, the cocktail hour or reception should be in full progress. The bridal party may take this time to refresh itself in a private room. Champagne, cocktails, and hors d'oeuvres may be served to the bridal party by service personnel. However, some brides may want the bridal party to join the cocktail party rather than wait in a private room. Photographs may be taken at this time. If a rehearsal had not been held, this time may be used for a brief run-through of the procedure for entering the function room, which is usually empty during the cocktail hour.

Introduction of the Bridal Party

When the cocktail hour is over, the guests are directed to the banquet room, and the catering coordinator organizes the bridal party to be introduced to the reception. The caterer usually consults a wedding list (Fig. 11-6), submitted by the bride along with her final arrangements one week prior to the function, to check the sequence of entry into the room. There should be two copies of the wedding list, one going to the master of ceremonies, bandleader, or whoever will announce the bridal party, and the other to the headwaiter who arranges the bridal party outside the banquet room in the proper sequence.

When the guests are seated, the headwaiter gives the signal to the master of ceremonies that the bridal party is set and the band starts to play. The master of ceremonies introduces each couple, starting with the tallest usher and bridesmaid, who enter the room arm in arm and proceed directly to the cake table situated in front of the bridal table. When they reach it, they separate and stand approximately six feet apart facing each

FOR THE INTRODUCTION OF THE BRIDAL PARTY

NAME: _____

DAY, DATE OF WEDDING: _____

ROOM(S) ASSIGNED: _____

PLEASE FILL IN THE FOLLOWING INFORMATION AS COMPLETELY AS POSSIBLE. WRITE THE NAMES AS YOU WISH THEM TO BE ANNOUNCED INTO THE FUNCTION ROOM. IF THERE ARE ANY CHANGES PLEASE INDICATE THEM ON THE FORM OR ON THE SPECIAL REMARKS (last section).

TALLEST USHER: _____

BRIDESMAID: _____

NEXT TALLEST USHER: _____

BRIDESMAID: _____

NEXT TALLEST USHER: _____

BRIDESMAID: _____

BEST MAN: _____

MAID/MATRON OF HONOR: _____

RING BEARER: _____

FLOWER GIRL: _____

BRIDE AND GROOM'S MARRIED NAME: _____

BRIDE'S FIRST NAME: _____

NAME OF FIRST DANCE (Favorite Song): _____

ARE PARENTS DANCING? _____ yes _____ no

IF SO, GIVE NAMES OF BRIDE'S PARENTS: _____

GROOM'S PARENTS: _____

IS GRACE TO BE SAID? _____

IF SO, GIVE NAME OF PERSON TO SAY IT: _____

TOAST TO BE SAID BY: _____ (Best Man)

Fig. 11-6. Wedding list for introduction of bridal party.

DO YOU WISH A CAKE CUTTING CEREMONY?   _____ yes   _____ no

DO YOU WISH TO THROW THE BRIDAL BOUQUET?   _____ yes _____ no

DO YOU WISH TO PLACE THE GARTER? _____ **yes** _____ **no**

DOES THE BRIDE WISH TO DANCE WITH HER FATHER? _____ yes _____ no

PLEASE LIST SPECIAL SONGS REQUESTED DURING YOUR FUNCTION:

_____

_____

_____

_____

PLEASE LIST ANY OTHER SPECIAL REQUESTS OR REMARKS:

_____

_____

_____

Fig. 11-6 (Cont'd)

other. Then the rest of the ushers and bridesmaids are introduced and do the same, forming an aisle. Next the maid of honor and best man are introduced and stand next to the last bridesmaid and usher. If a ring bearer and flower girl are introduced, they can either be introduced individually or as a couple. In the latter case, they enter arm in arm, separate, and stand next to the maid of honor and best man, completing the formation of the aisle.

The bride and groom are then introduced for the first time publicly as Mr. and Mrs. As the band plays "Here Comes the Bride," the couple enters the room together, arm in arm, and walks through the aisle formed by the bridal party directly to the cake table. The bridal party may raise hands and bouquets to form an arch over the bride and groom. For military weddings, swords and bouquets may be raised to form the arch. After the bride and groom turn around, the headwaiter takes the bride's bouquet along with the bridesmaid's bouquets to free them for the first dance. He places these bouquets evenly along the edge of the bridal table facing outward to be seen by the guests. The master of ceremonies then announces the couple's first dance as husband and wife. After they dance for a short time, the master of ceremonies then asks the best man and maid of honor, bridesmaids, ushers, and flower girl and ring bearer to join in. After a few moments, the parents of the bride and groom, if they requested to be mentioned, are asked to join in to complete the dancing. If one of the parents is not present for any reason, a close relative may be asked to join in as a partner.

All the guests are then invited to join the bride and groom. The headwaiter summons the bridal party with the bride and groom in the lead behind him to be positioned and seated at the head table. The bride and groom are seated at the center of the bridal table, with the best man seated next to the bride and the maid of honor next to the groom. (At times, the bride may request that the maid of honor be seated next to her and the best man next to the groom.) A bridesmaid is seated next to the best man and an usher next to the maid of honor, alternating bridesmaids and ushers from that point. The waiter for the bridal table now serves the champagne, starting with the bride and groom. When the champagne has been poured for all the guests, the master of ceremonies stops the music and asks the guests to return to their seats. After they are seated, the clergyman, who usually sits to the left of the mother of the bride (unless he is seated at the bridal table, where he is placed to the right of the bride), says grace. In the event that the clergyman is not present, a layperson may be invited to say grace. As grace is being said, everybody in the room stands and remains standing after grace. This may have to be mentioned by the master of ceremonies, since the tendency of the guests is to be seated after grace. The best man is then called upon to give the toast. Shortly before the toast is given, the headwaiter should direct the bride and groom to be seated. After the best man is introduced by the master of ceremonies, he gives his short, prepared speech with raised champagne glass, after which everybody toasts the bride and groom. Everyone is then seated, and there are no further formalities until the cake-cutting ceremony. In certain instances, the bride may request a solo dance with her father, which is usually danced to the tune of "Daddy's Little Girl" and is followed by the groom dancing with his mother to "Mr. Wonderful." This may be done at any time at the discretion of the master of ceremonies.

For a Jewish wedding, the introduction is usually simpler in that only the bride and groom are introduced into the room where everyone has already been seated, including the bridal party. The bride may request to have the parents seated at the bridal table, which is a Jewish tradition as well as a European custom. The bride and groom are introduced into the room and go to the cake table where a short prayer (moitze) is recited over the braided bread (challah) to praise and thank God for his blessings and for giving them the bread made from the soil of the earth. This prayer is usually said by the eldest person present, usually a grandparent, after which the bread is broken and distributed to the bride and groom, who partake in eating a piece of the challah. The remainder of the challah is sliced in the kitchen to be distributed equally to all the tables. The bride and groom now go to the bridal table to be seated by the headwaiter. The wedding toast can be given by the best man at this point or later on.

The Dinner

Since a wedding is a formal affair, a sit-down dinner is usually executed. A complete dinner, including appetizer, soup, salad, entrée, starch, vegetable, and coffee and tea, is usually called for. Dessert is usually omitted, since the wedding cake will be served with coffee, although some customers may request that ice cream be served before the wedding cake is cut. Also, a Viennese table (see details in next chapter) may be requested for more elaborate affairs. Of course, champagne is a must for the toast at almost every wedding reception. Since wedding receptions are usually sold as package plans, a sample menu for a wedding reception is offered in this form.

WEDDING RECEPTION PACKAGE PLAN

Your Wedding Package includes the following:

CHOICE OF WEDDING TOAST

White Champagne, Pink Champagne, Sparkling Burgundy, or Asti Spumante.

CHOICE OF WEDDING DINNER

A. Coq au Vin (Boneless Breast of Chicken simmered in a
   Red Wine Sauce with Sautéed Mushrooms and Pearl
   Onions) $_____ per person

B. Roast Vermont Turkey, House Stuffing, Giblet Gravy,
   and Cranberry Sauce $_____ per person

C. Roast Duckling, Sauce Bigarade $_____ per person

D. Roast Prime Top Sirloin of Beef, au Jus $_____ per person

E. Roast Prime Ribs of Blue Ribbon Beef, au Jus, with
   Yorkshire Pudding $_____ per person

F. Roast Prime Sirloin Steak, Maitre'd Butter
                        or
   Broiled Filet Mignon, Sauce Bearnaise $_____ per person

Above dinners include the following:

CHOICE OF APPETIZER

Supreme of Fresh Florida Fruits	Jumbo Shrimp Cocktail (_____extra)
Melon in Season, Wedge of Lime	Melon with Proscuitto (_____extra)
Chilled Double Tomato or Vegetable Juice	Alaskan King Crab (_____extra) Cocktail

CHOICE OF SOUP

Fresh Garden Vegetable Soup	Consommé
Petite Marmite	Soup du Jour
Minestrone	French Onion

CHOICE OF SALAD

Tossed Green Salad with Tomato   Hearts of Lettuce with Tomato Slices
    Wedges   Caesar Salad   (_____extra)
Spinach Salad with Sliced Mushrooms

The above salads served with a variety
of dressings (Roquefort, _____extra)

CHOICE OF POTATO

Rissole   Duchesse
Baked Idaho, Sour Cream and Chives Au Gratin

Also included are the following: Iced Hearts of Celery, Red Radish Roses, Green
and Ripe Queen Olives, Carrot Spears, Bouquetiere of Vegetables, Assorted hot
Dinner Rolls with Fresh Farm Butter, Choice of Special Ice Cream Desserts, and
Coffee, Tea, and Milk.

Cake: A specially tiered, fully decorated wedding cake with bridal ornament
and choice of fruit filling.

Flowers: A fresh cut floral bouquet centerpiece with choice of colors for
each table of 10 persons.

UNLIMITED LIQUOR

Unlimited premium brand liquors and cocktails are provided within this package
plan to be served continuously throughout the cocktail hour, both during and
after the dinner for a period of five (5) hours.

During the cocktail hour, guests may approach the stationary bar(s) for their
individual selection of cocktails and liquor. During and after the dinner, individual drink orders will be taken at the tables and served directly to the tables by
waiters.

Your personal selection of the following choices is invited:

Manhattan Cocktails   Canadian Rye
Martini Cocktails   Scotch
Whiskey Sours   Bourbon
Scotch Sours   Vodka
Daiquiris   Gin
                    Rum

All the necessary mixers, such as soda, ginger ale, coca-cola, 7-Up, tonic water,
and fresh orange and tomato juices are also provided on an unlimited basis.

GRATUITIES: All gratuities for waiters are provided within this plan.

TAX: 8% Sales Tax is not included in above prices.

WE ALSO PROVIDE AT NO ADDITIONAL COST TO YOU

- Choice of colored linens and fine lace cloths for each table.
- Beautifully decorated bridal table including lace skirting, silver candelabras,
  and special lighting effects.
- A Captain to be at your service and to handle all the arrangements for the
  entire reception.

- Beautifully decorated bridal dressing rooms.
- Free unlimited parking facilities.
- Use of microphone and piano for each room.
- Choice of colored candles and table fern for each table.
- Place cards for seating arrangements.
- Direction cards for guests.
- Complimentary bridal suite for overnight accommodations.

Cutting the Wedding Cake

The wedding cake is the focal point of the entire affair. It must be beautifully decorated and positioned on a draped table where all the guests can readily see it. Wedding cakes come in numerous forms: round, square, oval, rectangular, diamond, and heart-shaped. Fountain cakes (a water fountain of colored water positioned either at the base of or between several tiers) may be sold at an additional cost or included in the package plan. The top tier is decorated with various types of ornamentation given to the bride's mother after the affair is over. This keepsake is often preserved by freezing and enjoyed by the bridal couple on their first anniversary. To help sell functions, caterers who have their own pastry chef may let the bride design or bring in pictures of a wedding cake she wishes to duplicate.

For the best view, the cake table should be positioned in front of the bridal table and rolled out to the center of the dance floor by the headwaiter at the time of the cake-cutting ceremony. The cake table should be set with a bridal cake knife, cake plate, two napkins, and two cake forks.

After the entrée or dessert has been served, the headwaiter summons the bride and groom and shows the bride where to cut her first slice of cake from one of the lower tiers. The groom is instructed to place his right hand over hers to assist in the cake cutting. The photographer will want several pictures of this, so he may assist in positioning the bride and groom for the best photographic results. The band, on cue from the master of ceremonies, announces the cake cutting and the guests join in singing "The Bride Cuts the Cake." After the bride cuts the cake, the headwaiter takes the sliced cake and places it on the plate with a fork. The bride then feeds the cake to the groom, with the groom returning the favor while the guests sing choruses of "The Bride Feeds the Groom" and "The Groom Feeds the Bride." The headwaiter gives the first napkin to the bride and then the second napkin to the groom. The top tier with the ornament is removed and placed with an underliner on the center of the bridal table. The remaining cake is then taken into the kitchen or aside in the function room to be sliced, plated, and served by the waiters.

Most wedding cakes have individual or dual tiers that can be easily disassembled. The supporting pillars for the various tiers are removed as

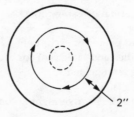

Fig. 11-7. Top view of wedding cake, showing cutting direction.

each tier is laid out individually. Inverted champagne glasses may also be used in place of pillars.

The headwaiter slices the cake. It is helpful to dip the cake knife in a container of hot water for easy cutting. He takes each tier and slices a two-inch width around the entire rim of the cake as shown in Fig. 11-7.

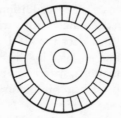

Fig. 11-8. Top view of wedding cake, showing vertical cutting pattern for individual servings.

He then starts cutting pieces vertically, approximately one inch apart, until the entire outer circle is completely cut (Fig. 11-8). He then removes each slice with a spatula onto a plate, and the waiters begin to pick up their required number of servings. The bridal table is served first, followed by the parents' tables. A slice usually measuring 4 by 2 by 1 inch is served.

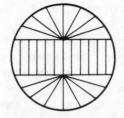
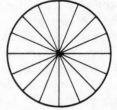

PARALLEL AND WEDGE CUT   WEDGE CUT

Fig. 11-9. Top view of core of cake.

After the outer circle has been sliced, the headwaiter then moves inward to the next two inch rim and cuts a circle around the cake and again cuts vertically for each portion. He continues to do this until the center core of the cake is reached. Here he may cut it in several ways depending on the remaining width. Two such methods are shown in Fig. 11-9.

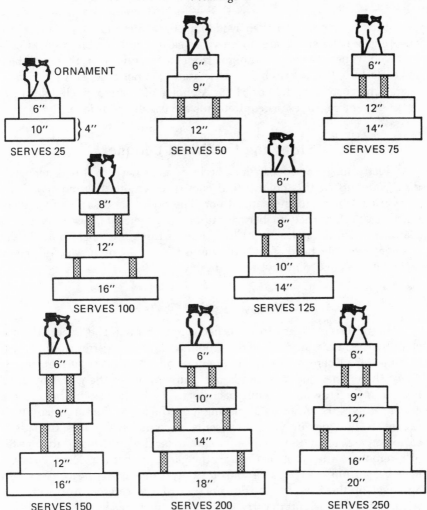

Fig. 11-10. The various wedding cake sizes.

All bakers use different-sized baking pans and forms for their cakes, but an indication of how some cakes are constructed for various-sized functions is given in Fig. 11-10.

Larger cakes may be ordered when the bride wishes to gift wrap additional portions of cake for each guest to take home after the affair has ended. These are usually placed on a draped table near the exit of the function room or near the hatcheck room and distributed by the service personnel to the guests as they leave.

Some customers may want to furnish their own wedding cake. This may or may not be permitted by the management. If permitted, some operations charge a cake-cutting charge of, for example, .25 per person, which includes the service charge for the waiters and cleanup fee.

Most caterers order their wedding cakes from outside bakers, since on-premise bake shops are not always feasible unless volume baking is involved. Where the cake is ordered from an outside baker, there will be a price markup. If a baker charges the caterer .50 per slice, he in turn may charge the customer $1.00 or $1.25. A choice of filling is included in the price, but special cakes or requirements are usually additional.

Throwing the Bridal Bouquet

Just prior to her departure, the bride may wish to throw her wedding bouquet. At this point, the master of ceremonies summons all the unmarried women to the dance floor. The bride stands a few feet away with her back turned to her guests or on an elevated area such as a platform, chair, or stairway. At the count of three, she releases her bridal bouquet over her head. The lady who catches the bouquet according to legend is the next to marry.

Throwing the Garter

If the bride wishes to have her garter thrown, she is seated on a chair by the headwaiter while the groom removes the garter from her leg. The master of ceremonies then summons all the unmarried men to the dance floor. The groom, with his back turned, tosses the garter over his head into the crowd of eligible bachelors. The bachelor who catches the garter receives the privilege of placing it on the leg of the single lady who caught the bouquet, only if she consents, of course. If she does, the lady is seated on a chair by the headwaiter and under the direction of the master of ceremonies, the gentleman places the garter on her leg. These customs may vary from area to area and are only done with the consent and approval of the bride. It is the function of the caterer to execute the wishes of the bride and to carry them out in the tone she sets. After all, it is her day!

After the festivities come to a close, the bride and groom may wish to leave and change into more comfortable attire. The headwaiter should direct them to the bridal or dressing rooms set aside for them (for description, see Chapter 3). After both have changed and last-minute farewells have been exchanged, they leave the affair together in transportation that has been provided or arranged by them. In certain instances, caterers will provide overnight accommodations for the bride and groom at their establishment if hotel accommodations are available, or they may reserve a room in a nearby hotel, which may be included in the package plan.

Paying the Bill

Generally speaking, most of the costs of the wedding and reception are assumed by the bride and her family. For financial or other reasons, the groom and his parents may share the costs of the wedding. This can be done in a variety of ways depending on how much the groom's side wishes to contribute. If, for example, they request to pay half of the expenses of the wedding reception, then this is simply done by dividing the total bill in half. They may request to pay certain parts of the function, for example, the band, flowers, liquor, or all of these. Whatever the decision, this should be discussed and decided upon before the function, with the assistance of the caterer, if requested, so that separate calculations and proper billing can be made for each responsible party.

Chapter 12

The Bar Mitzvah

Generally speaking, the highest single income-producing affair is the bar mitzvah. Held when a boy has reached the age of 13, the bar mitzvah is usually performed in a synagogue or temple on the Sabbath prior to the young man's birthday. It is one of the most important holy days in the life of a Jewish male as well as his parents. To celebrate this memorable day, family and friends are generally invited to a social function held immediately after the religious ceremony has been performed.

In recent years, the celebration of the bat or bas mitzvah has emerged in certain congregations. This ceremony is the female counterpart of a bar mitzvah. The bas mitzvah originally was a simple affair but now receives the same attention a bar mitzvah has always commanded.

The caterer is seldom asked to conduct either of these services on his premises, since the religious ceremonies are usually performed at a synagogue or temple. The caterer, however, may be asked to serve a light snack or refreshment at the synagogue or temple upon the completion of the ceremony. This is known as the kiddush and is comprised of such fare as assorted cold platters, pastries, cakes, wine, and soft beverages. Some traditional cakes served at the kiddush include honey cake, sponge cake, pound cake, strudel, and rugalah. Care must be taken that only kosher foods and equipment are sent to synagogues where glatt kosher rules are observed. (See Chapter 21 for a complete description of kosher catering.)

To ensure a successful bar mitzvah, a plentiful supply of food must be served. Abundance is the key to a successful bar mitzvah, especially as the guests arrive, since they have been at services for a long time. Hors d'oeuvres must be ready to be passed by the service staff as soon as the guests begin to arrive. Extra-hot chafing-dish items must be ready to be served and refills immediately supplied.

The cocktail reception for a bar mitzvah should be set up to include the buffet table(s), the cocktail bars, and a separate children's area.

The buffet will consist of various hot chafing-dish items, cold platters, showpieces, fruit displays, perhaps an ice carving, a carving table, etc. The food can be assembled either on one large table with various pickup points or stations, or else scattered on several smaller tables around the room to disperse the guests. Cocktail tables and chairs should be set up, and the tables may be decorated with linens, flat table ferns, and bud vases to enhance their appearance. Also, be sure to supply ashtrays.

To accommodate any hard or soft drink requests, several cocktail bars should be conveniently located around the room. It is wise to place these bars at opposite ends of the room to avoid crowding. Drinks are usually made available on an unlimited basis throughout the entire affair.

A special separate children's area is set up away from the adults so that both groups can enjoy themselves. The number of children attending a bar mitzvah usually averages out to be about one-fifth the total number of guests. For example, a party of 125 guests will include approximately 25 children under the age of 16. Satisfying these children is most important for the caterer, since many of them may represent potential bar or bas mitzvahs. These children will be asked by their parents how they enjoyed the party. If they were shown a good time, then they will react positively to having their affair at the same establishment. This will become noticeable when the child brings his parents in for an estimate as a result of a past bar or bas mitzvah. If bar mitzvahs are done properly, this business will grow rapidly.

Several things can be done to make the children's area particularly exciting. For example, the area can be decorated in a theme. If the child likes a particular sport like football, or a rock group or star, then large blowups of photographs or posters can be hung around the area. Hanging footballs, helmets, uniforms, goalposts, banners, balloons, and streamers can be arranged to decorate the assigned area. A separate bar to simulate an adult cocktail bar can be arranged with a bartender to mix fancy nonalcoholic drinks. A sign can be hung over the bar with the child's name, for example, "David's Pub" or "David's Place." A separate game, amusement, or arcade room would be ideal and well appreciated. Clowns, Walt Disney characters, magicians, local artists to paint caricatures of each child to take home, and other novelty or entertainment ideas are always recommended. Children's favorite food items such as miniature franks, hamburgers, french fries, soda and punch, cotton candy, popcorn, etc., are very popular. Ice cream carts where children can make their own sundaes with all the trimmings and candy carts decorated with a variety of sweets are features that not only will help make the affair a success but will also command additional revenue. To sum it up, any idea that creates fun or entertainment should be used to promote these affairs. It is the caterer's imagination and execution that make these affairs work, and in most cases they need not be expensive ideas or decorations.

Periodically, a client may wish to have live music throughout the affair and wish to have dancing during the cocktail hour. This may require the placement of a portable dance floor if no dance area exists. After the cocktail hour, a band may be hired on a regular basis, which is usually 20 minutes of music and a 10-minute break per half hour, or on a continuous basis, which is more expensive. Musicians will usually take their breaks, play dinner music, or stroll from table to table when the food courses are served. Bar mitzvah bands play a variety of music and also entertain to promote audience participation. These bands are usually more expensive, especially if they have an excellent reputation.

After the cocktail hour (or sometimes it may be extended to an hour and a half, depending on circumstances) is over, the guests are then asked to go to their respective tables and are seated for the introduction of the bar mitzvah boy into the function room.

Introduction into the Function Room

The headwaiter instructs all the young friends of the bar mitzvah boy, who will be seated at the head table, to line up single file according to height. The bar mitzvah boy, with a parent on each side, is placed after the tallest friend. Any brothers and sisters are positioned after the bar mitzvah boy and parents. They may have the honor of presenting the tallit, a linen prayer shawl worn around the shoulders to symbolize the fringed garments worn in biblical times.

With the lineup completed and the guests seated, the band and master of ceremonies are ready for the introduction. For better organization, it is advisable to place one musician, for example, a trumpet or clarinet player, at the head of the line to lead the children into the room.

The headwaiter signals the master of ceremonies to begin the entry. The children and young adults, led by the musician, are introduced by the master of ceremonies as "the friends and business associates of the bar mitzvah boy." They are led into the function room Pied Piper style by the musician to a rousing tune such as "When the Saints Go Marching In." The line goes completely around the edge of the dance floor. The children are then led to the head table where they are seated.

If there are many children, a double-tiered dais may be used. The guests seated at the upper dais are brought in first, followed by those sitting on the lower dais. The seating arrangements for the dais table are preplanned by the bar mitzvah boy and his parents. Each child has a card with his/her name, seat position, and dais location (upper or lower). The bar mitzvah boy sits at the center of the upper dais, with his closest friends, brothers, and sisters to his immediate right and left. When a less formal seating arrangement is requested by the bar mitzvah boy or his parents, a round or rectangular table may be used and all the friends may be seated together around one table.

The master of ceremonies now has everybody stand as the bar mitzvah boy is introduced and escorted into the room with his parents. They proceed directly to the cake table where they turn around and face the audience. Applause and lively music accompany the introduction. The photographer takes pictures and continues to do so throughout the affair. The tallit is now given by a brother or sister of the bar mitzvah boy to a grandparent or religious elder, who places it around the boy's shoulders. Then the eldest relative on the father's side, usually the grandfather, is given the honor of saying the moitzi (blessing) over the challah (braided bread). This prayer may also be said by an attending rabbi, or in some cases by the bar mitzvah boy himself. In certain instances, it may be requested that the ritual of the washing of hands be performed. In this case, the caterer provides a table near the entrance of the room on which a pitcher of water, an empty basin, and some towels for drying the hands are set. The grandfather takes the bread knife and, cutting into the challah, says the moitzi. He then takes a piece of challah, eats some, and gives some to the bar mitzvah boy, the parents, and brothers and sisters to eat. The headwaiter then requests everybody to be seated and takes the remaining challah into the kitchen to be cut. The challah is then evenly distributed among the guests.

The candle-lighting or flag (performed where candle lighting is not permitted for religious reasons) ceremony is performed at this point or at a later time after the entrée has been served. Most caterers prefer to do it at this point when they already have everyone's attention and also to conclude all the ceremonies, leaving the remainder of the affair free for enjoyment. If done at this point, the headwaiter moves the cake table to the center of the dance floor where he lights and hands a single candle wrapped in a napkin to the bar mitzvah boy. A list of 13 names of honor, composed by the bar mitzvah boy and his parents, is announced by the master of ceremonies. The 13 are called up individually, in pairs, or in groups to light a candle or place a flag on the cake. The list usually starts with the eldest relatives and ends with the brothers, sisters, and parents. The bar mitzvah boy then lights the very last or the 14th candle for everyone else in the room. This is usually done to the accompaniment of lively music. Another effective candle-lighting procedure is to have an individual cake for each table with the appropriate number of candles for each guest at the table. Since many individual cakes are involved, there is usually an extra charge for this service. In the former method, as each honored pair is called upon to light a candle or place a flag, the headwaiter positions them on either side of the bar mitzvah boy. If the honored guests are called individually, they are placed on the left side of the boy so that the photographer can rapidly take pictures of them lighting the candle or placing the flag, after which they return to their seats. The boy hands the lighted candle or flag to the honored guest or guests as they arrive at the cake table. The candles are lit systematically from one side of the cake to the other. When all the candles are lit, the headwaiter takes the lighted candle from the bar mitzvah boy and extinguishes it. The master of ceremonies then has the entire family surround the cake and on the count of three the candles are blown out and everyone joins in singing "Happy Birthday" to the bar mitzvah boy. The cake table is now removed and the master of ceremonies has the bar mitzvah boy, his parents, brothers, and sisters go to the center of the dance floor. He then invites all the guests to form a circle around the family to dance to a lively "hora" or good luck dance.

The Dinner

After the dancing is completed, the guests return to their seats to enjoy the prepared menu, which usually incorporates some Jewish-style foods. Sometimes an intermezzo or sherbet course is given prior to the entrée to refresh the palate. Some caterers offer the guests a selection of two or three entreés for variety, and some extend "seconds" on this course for those who wish it.

After the dinner is completed, the bar mitzvah boy may give a small speech of appreciation to all the guests. Approximately one hour prior to the end of the function, a Viennese table, an elaborate dessert table, is presented on one large, draped buffet table (the buffet table used for the cocktail reception would be ideal) to create a complete, abundant, and effective presentation, or it may be served on individual rolling pastry carts. The general rule is one cart for every three tables. The dessert carts are rolled directly to each table for the convenience of the guests. Usually two or three desserts per person are served and the dollar value is gauged accordingly.

For the sake of presentation, the more variety offered on a Viennese table the more effective it will be. Equipment is also important, for example, silver chafing dishes, samovars serving espresso, silver candelabras, punch bowls, etc., enhance the dessert table.

Along with the Viennese table, a separate coffee or espresso bar can be set up to serve various international coffees. A cordial bar can be set up for various brandies, liqueurs, or after-dinner drinks to be served by the bartenders. Cigarettes may be placed in silver cigarette urns and placed on each table. Cigars may be given to the bar mitzvah boy to pass among his guests. The bar mitzvah cake is usually displayed along with the pastry on the Viennese table.

The following is a list of items that may be used on a Viennese table. Any combination or variety of these desserts will make an effective presentation. The selection should be discussed with your baker for best results. Individual dessert menus may be printed for the Viennese hour. Keep in mind that only kosher products and procedures may be used for glatt kosher functions. Only certified nondairy products can be used when meat items are served on the same menu.

VIENNESE TABLE SELECTIONS

Fruit Tarts or Tartlets

Napoleans

Eclairs (Chocolate, Mocha)

Rum Balls

Assorted French Pastries

Hot Strudels (Apple, Cherry,
   Blueberry)

Assorted Layer Cakes

Assorted Pies

Cream Puffs

Petit Fours

Rugalach

Chocolate Mousse

Jello Molds

Parfaits

Sherbets

Charlotte Russe

Floating Island

Fruit Displays

Watermelon Baskets

Fresh Fruits such as:
   Strawberries
   Raspberries
   Whipped Cream

IN CHAFING DISHES:

Fruit Blintzes with Sour Cream

French Toast

Crêpes

Baked Apples

Waffles

Flaming Cherries Jubilee

Fruit Punch in Decorated Bowls

Assorted Cordial Bar

Demitasse or Espresso Served in
   Samovar

International Coffees such as Irish,
   Jamaican, Mexican & Viennese,
   served and topped with whipped
   cream

After the function comes to a close, the parents may want to have the remaining bar mitzvah cake individually wrapped and boxed for departing guests.

Needless to say, a bar mitzvah is a complete affair. The following is a typical bar mitzvah package plan.

BAR MITZVAH PACKAGE PLAN

Included in your COCKTAIL RECEPTION will be UNLIMITED LIQUOR AND COCKTAILS, a TEEN BAR including FRUIT PUNCH FOUNTAINS, COKE AND 7-UP, plus a delightful selection of ASSORTED HOT HORS D'OEUVRES AND FANCY DECORATED COLD CANAPÉS SERVED BUTLER STYLE ON SILVER SERVICE.

For those who wish AN ELABORATE FULL CONTINENTAL SMORGASBORD prior to dinner, may we recommend the following:

CHAFING DISHES consisting of:

Chinese Pepper Steak

Chicken Cacciatore

Hungarian Stuffed Cabbage

Swedish Meatballs

Fried Rice

DECORATED MOLDS consisting of:

Chopped Chicken Liver

Fruit-Filled Gelatin

FANCY DECORATED PLATTERS consisting of:

Turkey, carved and decorated
Tongue, carved and decorated
Antipasto
Egg Salad a la Russe

Gefilte Fish
Assorted Imported Herrings
Smoked Whitefish
Waldorf Salad

A POLYNESIAN FRUIT DISPLAY consisting of:

An excellent selection of fresh fruits in season attractively presented

PLUS A CARVING TABLE where our chef will carve:

Glazed Hot Corned Brisket of Beef   Lean Hot Romanian Pastrami
Iced Hearts of Celery, Red Radish Rosettes, Green and Ripe Queen Olives

YOUR CHOICE OF APPETIZER:

Fresh Florida Fruit Cocktail "Supreme"   Fresh Chopped Chicken Livers
Chilled Ripe Melon in Season   Fresh Pineapple or Melon Basket Filled
                                     with Assorted Fresh Fruit

YOUR CHOICE OF SOUP:

Matzo Ball Soup
Fresh Garden Vegetable Soup

Consommé Vermicelli
French Onion Soup

Petite Marmite Henry IV

YOUR CHOICE OF ENTRÉE:

Roast Prime Rib of Blue Ribbon Beef,   Boned Capon with Special House
   au Jus   Stuffing

Fresh Fish in Season Prepared to Your
Taste

YOUR CHOICE OF VEGETABLES:

Fresh String Beans with
   Waterchestnuts
Fresh Broccoli Milanaise
Fresh Cauliflower in Season

New Peas and Mushrooms
Grilled Tomato Provencale
Glazed Belgian Carrots
Fresh Vegetable in Season

YOUR CHOICE OF POTATO:

Stuffed Baked Potato
Potato Croquettes
French Fried Potatoes

Pomme Lyonnaise
Pomme Duchesse
Pomme Rissole

Pomme Allumette

ALL ENTRÉES SERVED WITH STUFFED DERMA*

---

*Stuffed Derma or Kishke is a traditional accompaniment to dinner. It is made from the intestines of steer filled with beef suet, matzo meal, flour, bread crumbs, garlic, onion, paprika, and other spices. It is usually served with the entrée.

SPECIAL SALAD:

Fresh Tossed Mixed Garden Green Salad with Sliced Tomato Wedges and our Chef's Special Dressing

DESSERT:

Rainbow Sherbet Parfait Served with Assorted Fresh Baked Cookies

COFFEE   DEMITASSE   TEA

After Dinner Mints and Mixed Assorted Nuts

BAR MITZVAH CAKE: A beautifully decorated Bar Mitzvah Cake with Scroll and Bar Mitzvah Boy's Name. An impressive Candle Lighting Ceremony will be conducted by the Captain and his Staff.

CHALLAH: A fancy formed fresh baked Challah.

BAND: An excellent name band will be selected to make sure your affair is an entertaining success.

UNLIMITED LIQUOR: Served throughout your entire affair with only the finest assortment of premium brands.

ROLLING BARS WITH BARTENDERS: To serve your guests for 5 hours with the selection of drinks they desire before, during, and after dinner.

COLORED TABLE LINENS AND FINE SPANISH LACE: A wide selection is available for your tables—plus a beautifully decorated Bar Mitzvah Head Table with special lighting effects.

COLORED CANDLES: A wide selection to match the color of your table linens.

SILVER SERVICE: The finest silver service available, from the settings on your tables to our silver service trays and candelabras.

MENUS AND MATCHES: Personalized menus and matches for each guest to have as a souvenir.

CIGARS AND CIGARETTES: Presented to your guests with our compliments.

CHECKROOM AND VALET PARKING: Signs will be displayed to inform guests that gratuities have been taken care of.

A CAPTAIN: To conduct your affair from beginning to end and to be at your service for the entire event.

ALL GRATUITIES for Captain, Staff, Waiters and Bartenders are included in your Package Plan price.

VIENNESE HOUR: An attractive, laced Viennese Table is decorated with Fancy Cakes, Petit Fours, Miniature Pastries, Assorted Tortes, Strudels. Served with International Coffees and Demitasse. An excellent selection of Cordials and Dessert Wines will also be available.

Chapter 13

Showmanship

Most banquet guests come to an affair to have a good time and be entertained. Caterers must strive to give their guests that "something extra" to make a function interesting, appealing, and entertaining. Through flair, showmanship, creativity, and innovation your guests will be assured a once in a lifetime, much talked about affair.

The word-of-mouth advertising generated by the positive reactions of satisfied guests will prove to be the most valuable source of promotion available. Serving champagne from a magnum (52-ounce bottle) or jeroboam (104-ounce bottle); placing a jumbo strawberry into each champagne glass; serving a fancy tropical or mixed drink in a coconut shell; putting on a dramatic theme party such as an Old English feast with authentic foods, costumes, and decorations; and engaging a helicopter to transport a bride and groom from the catering house to the airport are some of the ways a caterer can create excitement and spark comments from the attending guests and give individuality to an affair, all of which helps to promote business and increase sales.

There is a definite place in catering for showmanship and creativity. Many clients will spend additional money willingly provided they can be assured that the end result will impress their guests. Added special effects will make the client confident that the caterer cares and is trying to make the affair truly something special. Many clients will openly seek the caterer's advice and ideas on how to improve an affair and make it entertaining and successful. To satisfy such clients, the operator must be willing to make a special effort to do things *differently*—the key to effective showmanship.

Of course, just because a promotional idea is different and innovative does not guarantee that it will be well received. The element of showmanship does not guarantee a successful affair; yet, by observing certain precautions and adhering to certain guidelines, the chances that it will be are increased.

First, don't overdo it. Only a few items or presentations per function need be highlighted if showmanship is to be effective. Being excessively showy can be tacky. Second, make sure you can handle it. Don't invite disaster by getting in over your head.

In catering, large groups must often be served by inexperienced help. In such cases keep your show simple and make certain that the kitchen and service staff are thoroughly trained to handle the performance. Establish a training program to insure personnel are proficient in their jobs.

Many presentations may need to be scaled down to guarantee an effective final show. For example, it may not be necessary to start the preparation of a caesar salad from step one; that is, rubbing the garlic in the bowl, mashing the anchovy fillets, mixing the oil and lemon juice, etc. Service time can be shortened and a perfectly acceptable presentation offered by having the caesar salad dressing premade. Waiters need only pour and mix it into a large wooden bowl, add romaine lettuce, warm croutons, grated cheese and flourishingly toss the greens, dressing and croutons with a salad spoon and fork.

To simplify procedures, many dishes may be partially or fully prepared in the kitchen and brought into the function room for the final show. For example, if a roast duckling a la bigarade is to be flambéed tableside, the duckling could be roasted and prepared with the orange-based sauce in the kitchen and the exact number of needed portions brought hot to tableside on a silver serving dish or in a copper pan. The headwaiter or service personnel (depending on experience) would flame the duckling with cognac or Grand Marnier at tableside. Portions would be plated and served to the customer along with the accompaniments and garnish.

Still another example of simplifying showmanship would be in the case of serving cherries jubilee. The chef would be introduced by the master of ceremonies and stand on an elevated platform with a large heated silver bowl of cherries and sauce. The lights would be dimmed and the chef would proceed to ladle heated kirsch or brandy over the cherry mixture and ignite it. After this performance, service personnel would deliver individual frozen vanilla ice cream balls in silver ice cream dishes to the chef, who ladles the sauce on top of the ice cream, which is then served to the guests. Even though the number of steps in preparing the cherries jubilee has been reduced, the end result and show is still dramatic and effective.

Since one of the prime objectives of any form of showmanship is to draw the guests' attention to the food, beverage, or service, it is imperative that cleanliness and safety are not overlooked. Make sure that all personnel and equipment are spotless. Take steps to avoid accidents, especially when heating elements are needed, flambéing is attempted, or carving techniques are employed.

Stay away from using common approaches. Even the most showy and innovative techniques will, over time, become passé. Use only procedures that will dramatize your presentation and make it exciting.

Since equipment may often be the key element of a presentation, be sure all equipment is appropriate for the presentation. For example, colorful skewered meats, fish, vegetables, and fruits presented on a large flaming shaslik sword becomes an impressive show, whereas without the decorative sword perhaps the presentation would be considered ordinary.

If you have decided to incorporate showmanship into your functions, do not be reluctant to promote it. Have your salesmen display menus, photographs, and brochures that will exhibit and explain your special services.

Do not hesitate to use such outside services as decorators, lighting technicians, florists, party supply shops, novelty shops, entertainers, and trade magazines as a source of ideas. Often the suggestions supplied by such outside services will prove to be interesting and sometimes surprisingly inexpensive.

Obtain feedback and seek comments about your presentations. Note the reactions of guests after a function has been completed. Since employees are directly involved in carrying out your ideas on showmanship, welcome their suggestions and comments. If the feedback is negative from the employees and especially the customers, eliminate or change the show and try something else until an idea is accepted.

Above all, be sure your client wants showmanship in the affair. For some functions, showmanship may be a deterrent, since the customer may feel it is unnecessary or may not be willing to pay an extra tariff for it. Showmanship can take many forms, and with a little thought a variety of ideas, some of them quite simple, will arise to elevate your function a step above the ordinary. Here are some examples of showmanship that can be employed with food, beverage, service, and decor that will give your function that "something extra" it needs to be successful.

Showmanship with Food

Place butter roses in a silver bowl filled with shaved ice. Decorate the border with mint or lemon leaves and place on each table like a bouquet of flowers. To reduce preparation time, butter curls can be presented in the same way.

Display rolls or fruit in cornucopias or baskets made from braided bread dough. These centerpieces can be shellacked for reuse or raffled off after each function, compliments of the caterer.

Present assorted hot breads on a carving board for guests to slice.

Present oversized popovers or brioche either plain or with different mixtures.

Use a whole pineapple as the center of a fruit display. Cut the top off; remove the outside skin; cut into wedges; remove the center core. Put wedges back together; replace top; stick toothpick frills into each wedge.

Put the pineapple on a silver stand; place other fruit around it and position it in the center of each table.

Carve edible vegetable decorations such as radish, tomato, and turnip roses; potato lillies; carrot curls; pickle fans; and scored mushrooms.

Use fresh herbs and flowers to garnish food.

Make edible animal decorations such as apple birds and penquin eggs.

Stuff raw fruits and vegetables with different mixtures, e.g., celery filled with brandied roquefort cheese.

Make and freeze small individual ice-carved supreme cups to hold appetizers or desserts, e.g., fruit, shrimp, or sherbet.

Make baskets from fruit to display food. Use lemon baskets to hold items such as hollandaise sauce, cocktail sauce, tartar sauce, drawn butter, or lemon sherbet. Use orange baskets to hold fresh fruit, chicken or shrimp salad, maltaise sauce, orange sherbet, or marmelades. Use grapefruit baskets for items such as grapefruit sections, cold salads, and a variety of hot dishes.

Use pastry shells, tarts or croustades to hold and contain different types of vegetables and sauces.

Use carved-out raw vegetables and fruit, e.g., slice the top and stem of an apple acorn squash or green pepper; remove the insides and seeds; wash out; and fill with a variety of items such as sauces, condiments, and dressings. Replace tops with stems. Carve out cucumbers, tomatoes, and avocados to serve relishes, sauces, and salads.

Cook and stuff vegetables in combinations for taste and eye appeal, e.g., zucchini, cucumbers, or tomatoes stuffed with purée of assorted vegetables.

Serve cold appetizers and salads and hot appetizers and entrées in such carved-out fruits and vegetables as coconuts, pineapples, canteloupes, and squash.

Use small carved-out pumpkins and watermelons as soup tureens. Use the top for a lid. Shave off bottoms for stability.

Introduce different garnishes on items. Float a fresh slice of tomato sprinkled with basil on top of a cream soup. Put a dollop of sour cream, whipped cream, or yogurt on top of clear or cream soup.

Garnish soups with the soup's main ingredient, e.g., shredded raw beets on top of borscht; shredded carrots on carrot soup; paper-thin sliced cucumber or avocado on respective soups.

Wrap and secure cheesecloth around lemon halves to strain out pits when used for items such as seafood platters.

Make various shapes of croutons for soups and salads.

Obtain a super-sized vegetable or fruit for food presentations. For example, obtain a whole red cabbage, cut a hole in the top and hide a can of Sterno inside; stick hors d'oeuvres on skewers around cabbage; light Sterno. For stability, cut bottom of cabbage off.

Cut a hole in the top of a melon (honeydew or canteloupe). Remove the seeds and rinse under water. Pour various colors of gelatin inside for rainbow effect. Let each flavor jell before adding new color. Slice and serve.

Use skewers or mini-swords for food presentations. When serving a steak, place a small skewered sword into the steak with assorted grilled vegetables to add dimension and color.

Use shells for presentation, e.g., cocktail sauce or a seafood dish served in a scalloped shell.

Use rolling carts for individual food presentations. Arrange assorted hors d'oeuvres, appetizers, salads, soups, desserts, cheeses, or fruits on the carts and roll the cart to each table for the guest's selection.

For children's parties, supply candy carts containing assorted sweets; stock ice cream carts with all the trimmings so guests can make their own sundae. Hot dog wagons and cotton candy, popcorn, and peanut machines are also popular.

Use lighted butter sculptures, tallow work, ice carvings, and other artistic displays as centerpieces.

Carve various items from fruit, i.e., make a boat, car, whale, baby carriage, or basket from a watermelon and fill it with fruit.

Roast a suckling pig on a rotating spit or grill items over a charcoal pit.

Get customers involved by serving them fun foods, e.g., chocolate fondue with chunks of fruits to be dipped into the chocolate sauce.

Have plain ten-inch cakes available so that inscriptions can be added for any unexpected last-minute announcements of special occasions such as a birthday or anniversary.

Serve individual cakes as dessert. Put an inscription or friendly message on them, dim the lights, and enter the room with lit candles and fanfare.

Make specialty cakes for particular functions, e.g., baseball diamond, football field, or tennis court for sport functions.

Flame desserts. To serve baked Alaska, put a cotton ball in half an egg shell; place on top of baked Alaska; pour brandy or rum into the egg and ignite before entering dining room.

Pour cordials or liqueurs on ice cream scooped into edible chocolate cups.

Serve fortune cookies with a pleasant saying and a "thank you" from the caterer.

Serve mints and nuts after dinner.

Serve chocolate-covered strawberries in wrappers with caterer's name.

Put fruit display at exit for guests on way home.

Box party cakes (wedding, anniversary) for guests to take home, compliments of the caterer.

Showmanship with Beverages

Served iced mineral or carbonated water in place of regular water. Garnish with a slice of lemon or lime.

Serve fresh vegetables such as celery stalks and carrot sticks in alcoholic beverages such as Bloody Marys.

Serve a variety of fruits (melon balls, strawberries, pineapple chunks, cherries) on wooden skewers placed in fruited beverages.

Give a complimentary glass of wine or champagne at dinner.

Serve drinks in frosted mugs and glassware.

Put sugar or salt on rims of glasses for specialty drinks.

Hollow out fruit for specialty drinks, e.g., serve a piña colada in a coconut shell or a mai tai in a hollow pineapple.

Use lighted electric fountains for punch or champagne.

Carve out a block of ice and fill with punch or champagne. Place in a vessel to catch dripping water.

Stick toothpicks into sides of thick slices of orange, lemon, or lime and skewer fruit such as cherries, pineapple chunks, and strawberries. Float in punch.

Float fruit sherbet in punch bowl.

Freeze fresh mint leaves, rose petals, or flower buds into ice cubes for summer drinks, punches, and champagne.

Freeze fresh fruit in ice block or ring and float in punch bowl.

Place champagne glasses in pyramid form. Pour champagne into the top glass and let it run down on sides. (The glasses must be stacked flush to catch flowing champagne.)

Put a bottle of liquor (aquavit, kirsch) into a No. 10 can; fill with water, freeze; defrost by pouring hot water around the outside of the can for a few seconds. Serve with ice jacket around bottle.

Employ a costumed sommelier (wine steward) with tasting cup around his neck to serve wine from a wine cart.

Place the name of your operation on the house wine label.

Serve flaming coffees such as café brulot and café diablo from flaming coffee sets.

Serve ethnic coffees such as Irish, Mexican, Greek, or Jamaican with the cordials of each country in the coffee. Use special glassware or coffee service where applicable.

Serve cordials or liqueurs in chocolate cordial cups.

Have cordial carts come to tables after dinner for a complimentary drink.

Showmanship with Service

Dress up doorman in uniform and cap.

Have the service personnel dress in different topical outfits; e.g., top hat and tails for formal dinners; chef uniforms for gourmet dinners; hula skirts for waitresses and gay-colored sport shirts for waiters at luaus; western attire for barbecues.

Issue nametags to service personnel. Make it house policy that each server help seat the customers and politely introduce themselves.

Offer choices at different courses, e.g., a choice of soup or entrée.

Offer second helpings on all foods, especially soup, entrée, and coffee.

Wrap vegetables such as asparagus and broccoli in hot steamed napkins for service.

Set tables with napkins neatly folded in one of numerous possible forms—rose, fan, lotus, swan.

Give patrons a change of napkin after the entrée course.

Have service personnel offer guests a large pepper mill for seasoning.

Serve iced forks for salad.

Serve the bride and groom champagne in a glass slipper.

Serve chopsticks along with silverware for Oriental foods.

Present scented, steamed towels to guests after entrée.

Present finger bowls after serving finger foods. Float a lemon slice or rose petals in warm water. Present hand towel on side to dry fingers.

Decorative and Promotional Ideas

Give a single rose, carnation, or orchid lei to each female guest.

Order floral centerpieces for each table with individual corsages for each guest.

Have the master of ceremonies raffle off the floral centerpieces on each table at the end of the function.

Decorate cocktail tables with stemmed flowers in bud vases on flat fern.

Use ribbons as table decorations.

Use tapers in floral centerpieces.

Use empty wine bottles or birch logs for candle holders.

Offer a free cigar to gentlemen smokers after dinner. Print "compliments of the caterer" on the wrapper.

Have a cigarette girl hand out free cigarettes at coffee time.

Name a menu item or dish after the honored guest or group.

Present miniature menus to guests as souvenirs.

Shape menus in interesting forms—scrolls, maps, or scorecards.

Handwrite menus.

Handprint or print place cards.

Print recipes of the entrée or special items on cards for guests to take home. Recipes can also be placed on the back of business cards.

Provide matchbooks, drink stirrers, fans, pens, or other novelty items printed with your name.

Supply suggestion booklets for various functions, e.g., "What You Should Know About Planning Your Wedding."

Present a free guest book to the host for the signatures of his guests.

Use items or decorations appropriate to the theme of the function, e.g., at a firemen's function, place dinner rolls in miniature fire trucks or firemen's hats. At political functions, decorate tables with American flags, red, white and blue linens and napkins, and paper donkeys for Democrats and elephants for Republicans. For baby showers, make napkins in the shape of diapers with safety pins; put baby shoes on top of the cake; have a baby carriage for gifts. At weddings, put the invitation in a picture frame or inscribe it on an ashtray as a gift; give an engraved knife, compliments of the caterer, with name and date of function. Present the champagne glasses used for the toast to the bride and groom.

Send anniversary and birthday cards to all past customers.

Pass out daily newspapers at breakfast banquets and Sunday papers at late Saturday night functions.

Offer breakfast service (full or continental) after late night functions, or have a bag of bagels prepared for each departing guest.

Present food exhibits or displays in main lobby. Let the gardemanger give demonstrations, for example, how to make vegetable flowers.

Put small candles on appetizers such as a half fruit-filled pineapple. Dim the lights and light candles as guests enter the function room.

Hire musicians dressed as gypsies or troubadours to stroll among the tables.

Use local talent schools as a source of entertainers, musicians, and dancers.

Have a dance instructor give a free group lesson on current popular dances.

Get decorative travel posters for ethnic groups.

Get party kits for such functions as luaus from party supply or novelty distributors.

Give miniature liquor or cordial bottles as favors.

For children's parties, incorporate fun items such as helium balloons, streamers, noisemakers, party hats, Disney characters, and gifts from a grab bag.

Give children T-shirts, baseball caps, bats, yo-yos, and other promotional items with the caterer's name or child's name on them.

Use small tables and chairs for children.

Put lights under head, bridal, and cake tables for effect.

Put pin lights on the cake table.

Decorate cakes with real flowers.

Use mirrors to reflect food displays.

Have caricature artist do sketches of guests.

Employ a skywriter to inscribe a message, like "Congratulations Sue and John," as the guests are leaving the affair.

Post announcements of functions on an outside marquee—"Welcome Rotary" or "Happy Anniversary Mary and Jim."

Set up a hotline telephone number for party information or questions.

Send a bouquet of flowers to the client's home after the function to show appreciation.

SECTION IV

Execution

We've come to the nitty-gritty of catering: executing functions. This section focuses on the intricacies of organizing, supervising, and servicing functions, running the gamut from planning to cleanup. This section also specifies the requirements for running an efficient kitchen operation and discusses the various types of serviceware and furniture needed. Since purchasing is one of the activities leading to execution, the section concludes with a discussion of ordering and receiving practices.

Chapter 14

Banquet Organization and Supervision

Whether or not a banquet is a success depends on a number of factors, most notably the effectiveness of the planning, organization, and supervision devoted to it. Although details vary from function to function, the procedures for meeting the requirements of all affairs should be standardized. As in any business, a simple and sensible system for performing all functions must be developed and then adhered to.

The director of catering or banquet manager coordinates his staff to insure that the food, beverages, service, equipment, supplies, outside services, and physical plant are ready for each function. Then, along with the department heads, he supervises the function to its conclusion. Yet, as important as his role is in the organization, supervision, and, consequently, success of the function, the banquet manager must realize that he cannot do everything alone. He needs the cooperation of his entire staff. Thus, the banquet manager must be an individual who can instill in his staff the need for teamwork in the execution of a function.

The execution of a function usually begins at the weekly meeting when the affair appears on the weekly function sheet and is discussed in detail for the first time. You will recall from Chapter 7 that it is ascertained at this time whether the contract has been completed and signed, whether a minimum guarantee for the number of guests attending has been obtained, what the arrangements are for the submission of the final guarantee, whether any leeway has been allowed regarding the final guarantee, whether a floor plan has been drawn up, and whether any rehearsals need to be scheduled. Since the banquet manager needs this information to proceed, the client should be contacted immediately if any of these details have not as yet been taken care of.

The next step in organizing a function is the preparation of the work order form (Fig. 14-1), which duplicates all of the arrangements detailed in the contract. A copy of this form is sent to each department head or

ABC Catering   Copy to: _____

Date: _____   Room: _____

Name of organization: _____

Name of engager: _____

Type of function: _____

Set: _____   Guarantee: _____   Time: _____

Details of function: _____ _____

_____

_____

_____

_____

_____

_____

_____

_____

_____

Fig. 14-1. Work order form.

person in charge of ordering or requisitioning supplies. The following is a sample list of those personnel who might be given a copy:

    Banquet manager
    Food and beverage manager
    Chef
    Steward
    Head bartender
    Headwaiter
    Housekeeper (in charge of linens)
    Houseman (in charge of setting tables, chairs, etc.)

A copy of the work order form also goes into the customer file and to the accounting department.

A copy of the floor plan should be attached to the work order form and distributed to those employees who will need to refer to it. Floor plans indicate how the required number of tables for a function will be positioned and numbered. (See Fig. 14-2.) Floor plans can also contain such information as room length and width, ceiling height, door width

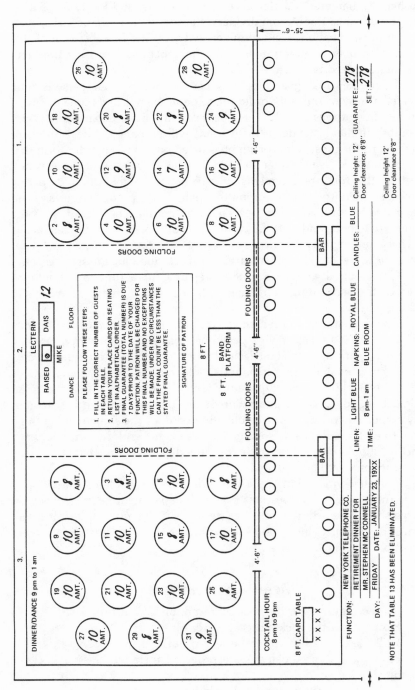

Fig. 14-2. Completed floor plan indicating distribution of guests.

and height, diameter and clearance of chandeliers, and locations of dais, bandstand, dance floor, room dividers, stairways, microphone jacks, electrical outlets, telephone jacks, dimmer switches, etc. Of course, all of this information may be preprinted on the floor plan so that only the table arrangement need be added.

Once the final guarantee has been submitted, all persons who received a copy of the work order form should be notified immediately in writing. Inventories should then be taken in each department. With inventory in hand, the department heads will prepare purchase orders or requisitions for those items or supplies listed on the work order form that are not in stock (see Chapter 19 for a detailed discussion of purchasing). Meeting the food requirements of a function might entail preparing purchase orders for the meat, poultry, fish, dairy, produce, grocery, and baked goods purveyors. For beverages, orders may be placed with the liquor, wine, beer, and soda and water distributors. Finally, miscellaneous purchase orders may be needed such as for equipment rental, paper goods, cleaning supplies, linens, ice, transportation, outside services, etc.

Copies of all purchase orders prepared for a function should be given to the accounting department, the person in charge of receiving, and the purchasing agent.

The next step is to prepare work schedules. All employees, including kitchen personnel, service personnel, bartenders, busboys, porters, housemen, parking attendants, checkroom and lounge attendants, etc., should be estimated. All personnel should receive their assignments as soon as feasible, and backup help should be planned in the event an assigned employee is out due to illness or other reason. Work schedules may be posted on the employee bulletin board, or the assignments can be given to each employee personally. Copies of the work schedule for each function should be given to the accounting department so that labor costs of a function may be calculated.

The elements making up a function will be considered individually in the form of a list of questions that each department head or person in charge should be asking himself as he reviews the work order form and begins to organize his group's contribution to the function's overall execution.

Menu Arrangements

Is food required for the cocktail reception? What types?

How long is the cocktail reception?

Will the cocktail reception be served butler or buffet style?

How many hors d'oeuvres are provided for a butler-style cocktail reception?

Is there a selection of hot and cold hors d'oeuvres?

What is the ratio of hot to cold?

Is there an extra charge for a carving station on a buffet?
Will a separate room be available for the cocktail reception?
Will the dinner be sit-down or buffet?
What type of food is required for the dinner or buffet?
Will the buffet be both hot and cold?
How many feeding zones will there be on the buffet?
May guests have as much as they want from the buffet?
How long will the buffet be open?
Does a sit-down dinner include the following?

    Relishes
    Appetizers
    Soups
    Salads
    Dressings
    Entrée
    Sauces
    Starch
    Vegetables
    Sauces for vegetables
    Desserts
    Coffee, tea, decaffeinated coffee
    Demitasse
    Rolls, breads
    Butter
    Mints, nuts

Are there any additional menu requirements?
Are any of the above subject to extra charges, e.g., flaming desserts or special sauces?
Will any extra dinners need to be planned?
Will there be any children's dinners?
How long will it take to serve the menu?
What time does the meal start?
What time will the entrée be served?
Will there be any interruptions during the food service, e.g., speeches, shows, entertainment, presentations, etc.?
May any outside food be brought in?
Whose responsibility is it to feed the employees? Band? Photographers? Others?

Beverage Arrangements

What types of beverages are required? Liquor? Wine? Beer? Soda?
Which of the above is needed for the cocktail hour? Before dinner? After dinner?
What is the amount to be served?

Is there a limit to the amount to be served?

What are the time requirements or limitations?

How is it to be served?

Has it been sold on an unlimited, consumption, or cash basis?

Are stationary bars to be used? Rolling bars?

Are additional bars needed?

Is wine and beer included within the unlimited liquor? Is extra to be charged for these? If so, how much extra?

Are brand names to be used? If not, is there an extra charge for brand names?

May the customer select the brands?

Are premium deluxe brands extra? How much extra?

Are fifths or quarts to be used?

Is there an extra charge for quarts? How much extra?

Are soda setups and mixes included in the price?

Are they supplied in unlimited quantities? If not, what is the extra charge?

May outside liquor be brought in? If so, is there a corkage fee?

Will an inventory be taken?

Will the client be shown what his party has consumed?

Will there be a refund on any unused liquor?

What is the cost per drink on a cash basis?

Will a liquor and wine list be available?

Will a cashier be needed?

Is there a charge for a cashier?

Will a cash drawer (bank) be needed?

How much of a bank will be needed?

Has the bartender filled out a liquor requisition and consumption sheet for each function?

Service Arrangements

What type of service will be provided? American service? Russian service (also referred to as French service)?

How many waiters are needed?

How many bartenders are needed?

Is there an extra charge for Russian (French) service?

Will the waiters wear white gloves?

Will guests be offered seconds on food?

For small groups or low-income parties, are there extra charges for waiters or bartenders?

Is there an extra service charge for the headwaiter? How much is it? Are his services needed? What will he do?

Are bartenders included in the price?

Most caterers will use the following general rules for good service:

1 waiter per 20 guests for American service

1 waiter per 10 to 15 guests or, working as a team, 2 waiters per 20 or 30 guests for Russian (French) service

1 waiter per 30 guests for buffet service

The above services usually run seven to eight hours per full job depending on the operation. This includes setup, service, and cleanup.

1 waiter per 50 guests for butler style hors d'oeuvres

This service usually runs on a four-hour basis.

1 bartender per 75 to 100 guests for bar service

If the above service is on a full-time basis, the job will run for seven to eight hours. If on a part-time basis, a cocktail hour for example, then the job will run for four hours.

Linen Requirements

How many color selections of table linens and napkins are available? What are they?

Is there an extra charge for colored linens?

Can linen and napkin colors be mixed or alternated?

Is there an extra charge for lace overlay cloths?

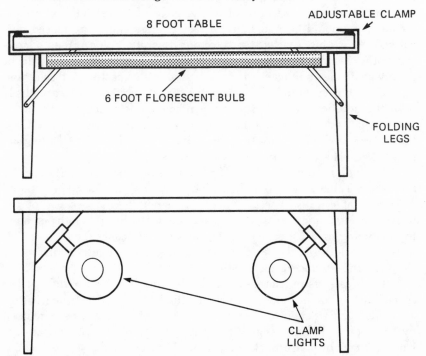

Fig. 14-3. Two ways to add lighting to bridal, buffet, or cake table.

How are the bridal, dais, or buffet tables to be decorated? Can they be lighted? (See Fig. 14-3.)

What tables require skirting?

Are special uniforms needed for kitchen personnel? Service personnel? Parking attendants? Checking attendants? Lounge attendants? Others?

Are kitchen and bar towels needed?

Are service towels needed?

Caterers usually supply their customers with a selection of approximately ten to fifteen colors of linens and napkins. The colors most often offered are: white, yellow, red, gold, light blue, dark blue, light green, dark green, beige, brown, pink, orange, black, lilac, and purple. There is usually no extra charge for colored linens and customers have the option to mix and match their colors. There are many new and interesting prints and easy care fabrics that are available ready-made or that can be custom made to a caterer's specifications. These linens give stunning results, especially to rooms that are simply decorated. Most linens today are made from permanent-press, machine-washable, drip-dry, shrink-proof, color-fast materials.

Lace overlay cloths in most cases are offered at an additional charge, for example, 50 cents per person or $5.00 per lace cloth or table. If the function is sold as a package plan, the price of these cloths is usually included. It should be noted that if lace overlay cloths are placed over colored cloths, this coverage tends to tone down the color of the underlying cloths. Sample swatches of linen colors and lace samples should be readily available on linen charts for a customer's inspection and selection.

Dais, buffet, bridal, and cake tables are decorated more attractively with the addition of table skirting, smilax, candelabras, and floral arrangements. For a special effect, lighting may be placed under these tables (as shown in Fig. 14-3). Other tables that will require skirting are gift, ticket, place card, and registration tables.

You will need various sizes of tablecloths for the many different size tables (see Table 14-1). Some linen suppliers will provide custom round and oval tablecloths. These cloths run higher in cost because of the wasted material and special cutting requirements. Round cloths come in the following sizes: 51, 60, 66, 72, 90, 108, and 120 inches. The 90- or 108-inch round cloth fits the 48- or 60-inch round table. The 120-inch round cloth fits the 60- and 72-inch round table.

Most caterers purchase prepleated skirting because it reduces labor costs. Skirting comes in 29-inch heights, that is, one inch off the floor for an average table height of 30 inches. Premade skirting can be purchased by the foot with sizes ranging from 10, 12, 14, 16, 20, 22, and 24-foot lengths. Stage or platform skirting comes in 8, 12, 24, 32, 40, 48, and 56-inch heights with 4, 8, 12, 16, 20, and 24-foot lengths.

Table 14-1. Linen Sizes and Seating Capacities for Common Banquet Table Sizes

Table sizes	Seating capacity	Linen size
Round tables		
36 in. diameter	4	54 × 54 in.
42 in. diameter (also square)	6	60 × 60 in.
48 in. diameter (also square)	8	64 × 64 in.
54 in. diameter (also square)	8	72 × 72 in.
60 in. diameter[1]	10	72 × 72 in.
72 in. diameter[1]	12	90 × 90 in.
Oval tables		
72 × 36 in.[1]	10	72 × 108 in.
72 × 48 in.[1]	12	72 × 108 in.
84 × 48 in.	12	72 × 108 in.
96 × 48 in.	14	72 × 120 in.
Rectangular tables		
48 × 30 in. (4 ft.)	4–6	54 × 72 in.
60 × 30 in. (5 ft.)	6	54 × 84 in.
72 × 30 in. (6 ft.)[1,2]	6–8	54 × 108 in.
96 × 30 in. (8 ft.)[1,2]	8–10	54 × 120 in.

[1]Most common sizes used.
[2]Also comes in 36 in. widths.
Lace overlay cloth sizes: 90 × 90 in. fits 60 or 72-in. round table; 72 × 108 in. fits 72 × 36 or 72 × 48-in. oval table.
Napkin sizes: luncheon, 20 × 20 in.; dinner, 22 × 22 in.

The length requirements for table skirting for round and rectangular tables are as follows:

Round
    48-inch diameter needs 13 feet of skirting
    60-inch diameter needs 16 feet of skirting
    72-inch diameter needs 19 feet of skirting
Rectangular
    72 × 30 inches needs 12 feet of skirting (one open end)
    96 × 30 inches needs 14 feet of skirting (one open end)

Uniforms add a great deal of prestige to an operation. It is management's responsibility to provide and service uniforms for its personnel. Service towels and cleaning cloths should be supplied in adequate amounts because, if not, costly napkins and linens will be used as substitutes.

How many tables are needed? Chairs?
How many guests will be seated at each table?
What type of serviceware is to be used? Silver? Gold?

Equipment Requirements

Is everything needed for the function ready?

Is room service needed?

Are platforms needed to raise tables, bands, displays, ramps, etc.?

Are all the functions properly posted on the bulletin board or directory?

Are all the needed rooms ready, properly equipped, and clean?

Have the following rooms been checked:

    Men's lounge

    Ladies' lounge

    Checkroom

    Reception area

    Function room

    Meeting/conference room

    Dressing/bridal room

    Overnight accommodations

    Special rooms

    Suites

    Chapel

Are cigarette urns clean?

Has the air-conditioning/heating been checked?

Are exhaust fans working?

Has the dance floor been polished?

Is carpeting needed?

Is carpeting clean?

Are podiums or lecterns needed?

Are microphones needed?

Are lavalier mikes needed?

Has the amplification system been tested? If needed, is the amplification system on?

Are microphone wires hidden and covered?

Is special lighting required?

Have spotlights been focused and tested?

Is a spotlight operator needed?

Is room lighting at correct brightness?

Are flags needed and positioned?

Is the American flag behind and to the speaker's right?

Are banners hung?

Are signs or posters needed?

Are decorations out?

Are blackboards and pointers needed?

Are easels and flip charts needed?

Are pads and pencils needed?

Are projectors and screens needed?

Are raffle drums needed?
Is a piano or organ needed?
Are tape recorders needed?
Is closed-circuit television needed?
Are regular televisions or radios needed?
Are telephones needed?
Is storage space needed?
Is security needed?
Is transportation needed?
Are sanitation equipment and supplies ready?
Are warewashing equipment and supplies ready?
Are exit lights on?
Are emergency lights working?
Are safety and fire equipment available and inspected?
Is first aid equipment available?
Is seating capacity within occupancy limits?

Seating Arrangements

Has a floor plan been drawn up? If not, when must it be completed?
Will place cards be furnished to the client?
Have the table assignments been furnished by the client?
Are place cards needed for the dais table? Bridal table? Each table?
Are cards or lists in alphabetical order?
Are the tables numbered on the floor plan?
Are the correct number of guests placed at each table?
Has a commitment been obtained for the total number of guests?
Did the customer sign the floor plan to verify the number he must guarantee?
Are table numbers and stands on each table?
Has a copy of the floor plan been given to the client and all the responsible individuals in the operation?
Are dinner tickets to be collected?
Have the waiters and headwaiter been informed to request them from each attending guest?

Parking, Checking, and Lounge Requirements

Is valet parking required?
Is coat checking required?
Are lounge attendants required?
Is there an extra charge for these services? How much is it?
May guests park their own cars?
May guests check their own coats?

How will guests know whether or not there are charges for these services?

While the number of attendants needed for these services is determined by the speed of the employee, the following may be used as a general rule:

1 checkroom person per 100 guests
1 parking attendant per 30 cars
1 lounge attendant per lounge

Conducting Rehearsals

Has a rehearsal been requested?
Has a date and time been set for the rehearsal?
Is a facility ready and available for the rehearsal?
Is any food or beverage required before or after the rehearsal?
Is a clergyman or judge needed to conduct the rehearsal or service?
Is there a fee required for their services?
Are all the needed materials ready for the rehearsals?
Have all the key people been notified of the rehearsal?

Chapter 15

The Catering Kitchen and Related Areas

Since no two kitchens are identical and no magic formula exists to solve all kitchen problems, it takes a great deal of knowledge and experience to design an efficient layout for a commercial catering kitchen. The largest and most costly error the inexperienced operator will make is in the selection and placement of equipment. Not only will this result in a capital loss so far as the purchase is concerned, but it will also create losses arising from inefficient working conditions, low production, poor employee morale, and high labor turnover.

To avoid these problems, it is advisable to hire a professional designer, food facility engineer, or architect who specializes in kitchen design for the foodservice industry. These experts are trained to obtain the best results at the lowest cost. They will help solve your layout problems by assessing specific equipment requirements, recommending the best labor-saving equipment available on the market, drafting the necessary specifications, and determining total construction costs including labor, materials, and electrical, heating, and ventilation connections.

Hiring a professional facilities planner does not mean others should not become active in planning and organizing the kitchen. Quite the contrary; anyone who is currently or potentially involved with the kitchen's operation, such as the operator or chef, should be actively involved in solving the problems and planning the practical applications of the kitchen. With this added information, the expert will design a layout and place the equipment to produce everyone's ultimate goal—maximum efficiency and reasonable labor costs.

Important factors to consider in the layout of the kitchen will be the various catering menus offered, the present or anticipated volume of business, the amount of time required to produce the catered meals, the type of service offered, the food-purchasing and storing requirements, and other directly related considerations of the operation affecting the placement and use of equipment such as the amount of fresh, frozen, or convenience foods used.

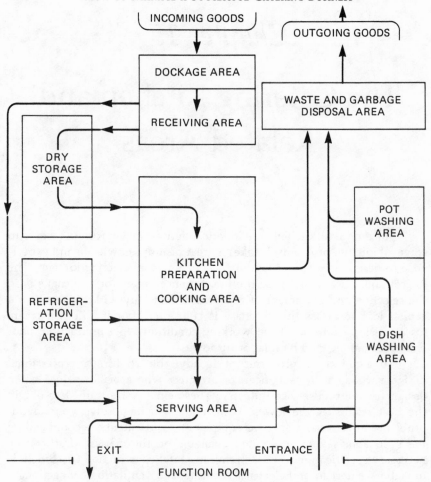

Fig. 15-1. Flowchart indicating sequence of incoming goods from receiving to storage areas.

Construct a flowchart (Fig. 15-1) to show the path of all incoming goods from the point of entry to the following areas in this sequence: storage, refrigeration, preparation, finishing, service, and finally to the banquet rooms. Include the path of soiled dishes and silverware from the function rooms to the dishwashing area, to the storage area, and then back to the function rooms. Also consider the path of the refuse and garbage containers from the dishtable to the dumpster, garbage bin, or compactor area, to the washing and cleaning area, and finally to the storage area. Each operation will have a different flowchart based on the amount of traffic between any two of these departments.

Then construct a layout or configuration of the total area proper using graph paper. Place the necessary equipment using templates or cutouts from construction paper (see Fig. 15-2). Keep in mind aisle space, work areas, walls, stairs, doors, and other dimensions. The templates and graph paper are usually scaled on a ⅛- or ¼-inch to 1-foot ratio. After all the templates are placed and glued, a final schematic drawing is made. This is now given to a professional designer for review and final drawing.

To achieve maximum labor-saving results and efficiency, consider several factors in placing the templates on the layout:

1. Place equipment strategically so that higher paid or more skilled employees need not move longer distances than less skilled employees.

2. Place most often used equipment close together for best utilization by employees.

3. To consolidate space and get maximum usage, place multipurpose equipment at strategic points accessible to several employees.

4. Place equipment so that no cross-traffic of kitchen and service staff occurs.

5. Place equipment so that excess walking and thus fatigue are reduced.

6. Place portable equipment where mobility, reduced workloads, and easy cleaning are necessary.

7. Place equipment so that adequate work aisles and work areas are established for employees to prepare and transfer food easily.

8. Place heavy equipment near major connections for plumbing, electricity, gas, water, and steam sources.

9. Place equipment where it can be changed or relocated. Keep equipment mobile so in the event of a location change it can be moved.

Sometimes equipment is bought on impulse and no real consideration is given to its usefulness and overall benefits. Ask yourself these simple questions before purchasing equipment.

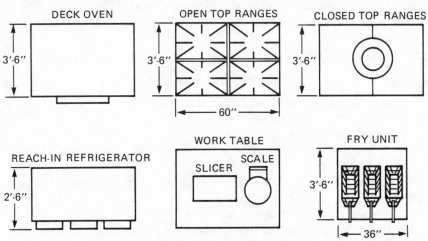

Fig. 15-2. Examples of templates used for positioning appliances when designing a kitchen.

Is it needed?
Will it cut labor costs?
Will it save operating costs?
Will it cut maintenance costs?
Can I do with less?
Can I put my present equipment to better use?

Once a decision to purchase has been made, make sure that your selection is a quality item with the latest features. A good track record for energy efficiency, maintenance, repair, and reliability is important. Be certain that the final price includes transportation and installation.

Exchange and discuss new and innovative ideas with your planning experts. Consider the positive merits of new products. For example, a good grade of commercial indoor–outdoor carpeting covering a kitchen floor may at first seem impractical but may have many advantages over other types of flooring for the following reasons:

1. It increases employee morale.
2. It is easier on the feet and more comfortable for employees.
3. It lowers breakage costs.
4. It reduces accidents.
5. It lowers insurance rates.
6. It can be easily cleaned on a daily basis with the new steam-cleaning machines.
7. It creates positive customer reaction.

Where carpeting is obviously impractical as in greasy and damp areas, such as dishwashing and potwashing sections or behind ranges, it can be cut out and duckboards or rubber mats installed.

It is impossible to list all the features one might find in a catering kitchen, but consider the following suggestions to avoid some of the more common pitfalls.

Receiving and Dock Areas

Locate the receiving area near the point of delivery. Furnish the receiving and dock areas with:

Sufficient dock space

A receiving platform of sufficient height to directly unload goods from delivery trucks

A ramp leading from the dock platform to the street level for portable trucks and handcarts

A scale at the receiving dock

Hand rails on steps leading to dock area for safety purposes

Roofing of proper height over receiving dock to protect against inclement weather conditions

Hot and cold water or steam hose connections and proper drainage facilities for cleaning dock and receiving areas

Adequate receiving area to conduct proper receiving procedures

Sufficient view from receiving office to supervise the flow of goods and the movement of employees

Sufficient desk space and filing cabinets to conduct business and file invoices

A sink for employees to wash hands after handling goods

Storeroom

When designing a storeroom for a catering operation, be sure to furnish:

Sufficient door heights and width for easy accessibility and transportation of goods by carts

Adequate storeroom space with proper ventilation to avoid warm and damp conditions not conducive to keeping goods dry and cool

Sufficient shelving

Sufficient space between and under shelves to store goods, trucks, or mobile bins

Sufficient portable trucks, cans, and bins to move and store items

Raised platforms to keep goods and materials dry and off the floor

A work table in storeroom to organize small orders and parcels

Counter scales in storeroom to check weights of outgoing goods

An area to properly check items leaving storeroom area

Proper security or locking devices for the entire storeroom and especially for storage cabinets where expensive items such as canned caviar, pâtés, lobster, and crabmeat are kept

Adequate provisions and equipment for proper sanitation and upkeep of storeroom

Refrigerator and Freezer Storage Area

When planning a catering kitchen, be sure to locate the refrigerator and freezer storage area near the receiving, preparation, and main cooking areas. In addition, be careful to supply:

Adequate storage space for refrigerators and freezers to avoid a high food spoilage rate and the inconvenience of frequent deliveries

Proper temperature control of refrigerated and frozen foods to avoid damage or spoilage due to conditions being too warm or too cold

An alarm system to alert management of abnormally high or low temperatures, which will prevent spoilage and loss of expensive merchandise

A thermometer for accurate temperature readings

Interconnected doors between refrigerator and freezer units to consolidate and eliminate the loss of temperature

An automatic defrosting device to eliminate the problem of ice accumulating around cooling equipment

Sufficient amount of shelving of adequate width to assure maximum storage capacity of refrigerators and freezers

Sufficient space between shelving areas to permit easy access and passage of workers and carts

Separate areas within the refrigerator to avoid the transference of strong odors between such foods as fish or cheese

Heavy plastic stripping between refrigerator doors and refrigerated area to prevent cold air from escaping when doors are opened

Easy entry into walk-in refrigerators and freezers by constructing sufficiently wide doors

Glass see-through windows on refrigerator doors to avoid accidents

Sufficient and properly located light switches on both the interior and exterior of refrigerators and freezers

Adequate ice cream freezer storage space, service area, and dispensing equipment

Compressors of sufficient capacity to hold temperatures at proper levels, thus holding spoilage to a minimum

Sufficient ventilation for air-cooled compressors, thus avoiding overheating

An auxiliary or emergency compressor system in the event of mechanical or electrical failure

Meat-Preparation Area

With prefabricated and portion-control meats readily available today, many catering operations are reducing the size of the meat-preparation area. This decision will depend on the feasibility of purchasing and preparing whole cuts of meat for your operation. Once your needs have been defined, design a meat-preparation area with:

Adequate area to handle your butchering needs including cutting, trimming, and boning of poultry and fish

A sufficient number of suitably located work tables, meat blocks, benches, saws, grinders, tenderizers, and tendon pullers

Meat racks or rails in the meat refrigerator

Sufficient shelving in the meat refrigerator to hold and store meats, poultry, and fish

Adequate sink and drainboard facilities

Breading table

Sufficient racks to hold butchering tools

Portion scales

Main Cooking Area

The main cooking area is the heart of the catering kitchen. Poor design here will result in inefficiency rippling throughout the operation. Be extra careful to design a main cooking area that is arranged and equipped to prepare and produce the volume of food you will have to handle at one time.

To assure efficiency in the main kitchen, provide:

Sufficient roasting and deck ovens for large quantities or roasted and baked items customarily sold at banquet functions

An adequate broiling section for large amounts of broiled and grilled items such as steaks, chops, and poultry

Broilers located at the end of the cooking line away from the main cooking area to avoid interference between broiling and cooking stations

Broiler grating that is easy to remove and clean

Grease-dripping containers under broiler that are easy to remove and large enough to hold all the fat removed from broiled items

Ranges, ovens, and fry kettles that are sufficiently spaced for easy access

A clear-cut separation between roast oven station and other cooking stations, thus avoiding interference

Easy access into and out of ovens by locating ovens at suitable height from ground level

The cooking area close to the serving area to minimize delay, fatigue, cooling of food, and traffic problems

Solid ranges and ovens for high-volume, heavy-duty cooking demands

Traffic and work aisles that are not too wide, thus avoiding extra steps and lost time and energy, and not too narrow, permitting workers or mobile trucks to pass each other without interference

A separation of work and traffic aisles, easing congestion between cooking and service personnel

Sufficient and strategically arranged work tables to eliminate steps for food-preparation workers

A through access by breaking up long lines of equipment and work tables

Work tables and chairs at the proper height, making it easy for workers to perform their duties comfortably

Work stations and storage areas arranged so employees need not reach for items

Tilted shelving over work tables

Adequate work area when oven doors are open

Sufficient frying capacity

Proper filter, draining, and temperature control systems for deep fat fryers

Sufficient large compartment steamers for large amounts of vegetables

Automatic timers on steam-cooking equipment to indicate when product is finished

An automatic steam shutoff or release valve on steam cookers to assure safety when doors are opened

Sufficient tilting steam-jacketed kettles for large amounts of soup and stock production

Properly installed and maintained steam kettles to guard against loss of steam pressure when kettle is in operation

Faucets over steam kettle for easy filling, rinsing, and cleaning

Gutter drainage facilities in steam-cooking areas to avoid damp and slippery conditions

Sufficient griddle space, waffle bakers, conveyor toaster, and egg production equipment to adequately supply the needs of banquet breakfasts

An adequate garde manger area for elaborate cold food preparation with sufficient work areas, cold storage, serving areas, and preparation and serving equipment

Periodic checking, cleaning, and adjusting of thermostats and timers on equipment

Heavy-duty controls and gauges that are sufficiently heat and moisture proof

Controls on equipment that are within easy reach of employees

Gauges and dials on equipment that are easy to read and understand

Pilot lights that have an automatic safety and are within easy reach

Burners that are cleared of food and carbon deposits, thus avoiding partial or inefficient use of gas

Cool oven door handles for employee safety

Properly spaced interior oven shelving and racks

Sufficient amount and sizes of pots, pans, and other portable cooking equipment needed to perform daily cooking loads, thus reducing lost time, waste, low morale, and friction between kitchen personnel

Sufficient amounts and sizes of roasting pans to permit maximum oven usage

Sufficient and properly located drawers and shelves to store utensils and cooking ingredients

Conveniently located spice racks and cabinets

Sufficient and properly located electrical outlets

Sufficient and properly located automated labor-saving machinery such as slicers, choppers, mixers, grinders, and graters

Sufficient and properly located can openers

Sufficient and properly located sinks and water supply so cooks and kitchen personnel wash their hands and obtain water for job-related functions

Sufficient hot water outlets and hose connections throughout the kitchen for proper cleaning of kitchen area

Steam-cleaning equipment to remove heavy grease and dirt deposits

Sufficiently recessed floor drains and adequately sloped floors to assure proper water drainage

Floor drains located out of worker's way

Ranges, ovens, and other heavy permanent cooking equipment that are two or three inches off the floor with space behind for easy cleaning and maintenance

Space between equipment for easy cleaning

Mobile equipment whenever possible for easy cleaning

Portable dry ingredient bins for staples used in large quantities such as flour, rice, sugar, and salt

Grease traps on equipment where heavy grease deposits accumulate such as in dishwashing, potwashing, meat, and cooking areas

Properly designed ventilation system with adequate fans and blowers to circulate air and remove heat and steam over cooking, dishwashing, and preparation areas

Effective air ducts not too long, too narrow, or having too many turns and curves

Adequately sized and properly designed exhaust hoods and ventilation ducts

Easy-to-reach and clean exhaust hoods and ventilation ducts

Easy-to-remove grease filters to promote proper cleaning, better ventilation, and fire prevention

A system to close ducts to prevent the spread of a fire

A fire-prevention system under hoods, such as a heat-sensitive carbon dioxide system, to function when temperatures reach abnormally high levels

Sufficient lighting and properly positioned lighting fixtures for easy bulb replacement and maintenance

Adequate lighting under hoods of kitchen equipment

Kitchen surfaces that minimize glare, thus avoiding discomfort

Protective glass or plastic shields to cover light bulbs especially where breakage or explosion may occur in areas of high heat, steam, or cold

Vegetable- and Salad-Preparation Area

For maximum efficiency, design your vegetable- and salad-preparation area with these considerations in mind:

Vegetable- and salad-preparation area near receiving area

Adequate amount of work tables to cut and prepare vegetables and salads

Adequate refrigeration and storage for vegetables and salads

Adequate sinks, wire baskets, and drainboards to wash, rinse, and dry produce

Sufficient portable racks to hold and transfer goods

Adequate cutting, dicing, and peeling machinery for efficient vegetable and salad preparation

Adequate drainage, peel trappings, and waste disposal to handle waste materials

Bake Shop Area

Many catering operations eliminate the on-premise bake shop because they find it less expensive to buy their baked products from outside bakers. When a large volume of baked goods is required, the expense of operating a bake shop becomes feasible, and especially when a high level of quality control is desired, a caterer should consider installing a bake shop facility. In planning a bake shop, allot an entire area to it, away from the main cooking area to avoid conflict and dual usage of equipment. Also, locate the bake shop near or accessible to a potwashing area. Be sure to furnish the bake shop with:

Sufficient baking ovens, pastry stoves, steam boilers, batch warmers, tilting kettles, and confectioner's stoves

Adequate space in front of ovens to clear and remove baked goods with ease

Sufficient racks for proofing and cooling baked products

Sufficient mobile racks to transfer baked goods to needed areas

Adequate marble, wood, or stainless-steel work tables

Bakers' tables and proof boxes near ovens

Sufficient number of mixers near bakers' tables

Sufficient dough dividers, retarders, formers, rollers, and troughs

Sufficient refrigerator and freezer storage space to store baked goods

Pastry scales

Apple-paring or coring equipment

Sufficient portable bins

Adequate flour-sifting and storage space

A mixing-bowl truck

Bread slicer

Spice bins

Adequate sink and drainboard facilities

Serving Areas

Plan serving areas large enough to house entire service staff comfortably and as close to the banquet rooms as possible. Be sure that they are supplied with:

Reach-in refrigerators for storing cold appetizers, salads, meats, and other pantry items

Sufficient portable hot and cold food-holding equipment to transfer and store foods at proper temperatures from ovens to service areas

Sufficient china, glassware, silverware, serviceware, and linen

Sufficient and properly located dispensers

Adequate coffee and hot water urns located near kitchen exit for quick service to banquet areas

Drains or drip trays under coffee and hot water spigots

Sufficient and properly located ice-making and storage facilities

Serviceware-Washing Area

Furnish this area with equipment large enough to handle the total volume of dishwashing, sterilization, and drying that will be demanded of it. Locate the area so that everything can be efficiently returned to the appropriate service areas or storage facilities. Be sure to also furnish the area with:

Sufficient automated or conveyor-type equipment to increase speed and reduce labor costs

A rack return fast enough to handle high-volume loads

Adequate stacking area, rack carts, and shelving to store soiled serviceware to await later washing

Properly placed dishtable shelving at convenient height

Overhead shelving and drainage above the dishtable tilted at proper angle for easy placement, sorting, and drainage of soiled serviceware

Adequate hot water booster heaters and storage area to supply an adequate amount of water at the temperature needed to perform proper washing and sterilization and to save on toweling and polishing

Properly maintained heating coils in dish tanks to avoid inadequate temperature for sterilization

A facility for pre-rinsing and scraping dishes to remove food particles before dishes enter machine

Garbage disposal or grinder units near main sources of waste material

Motors on garbage disposals large enough to handle heavy workloads

Properly maintained cutting edges on wheel of disposal unit

A reset button to start motor of jammed disposal unit

Drainage pipes leading from disposal units free from blockage due to poorly ground waste materials, poor plumbing, or water flow

Automatic timing devices for wash, rinse, and drying cycles to insure proper control of cleaning stages

Thermometers to check the water temperature

Sufficient shelving and storage space for lightweight plastic dishes, glasses, and silverware racks

Adequate hoods, ducts, vents, and exhaust system to remove heat and steam from dish, glass, and silver machines

Proper lighting under exhaust hoods and surrounding dishwashing area

Splash guards to stop the spread of water from machines

Sufficient area to sort and divide china, glassware, and silverware

Sufficient space to unload, dry, cool, and store dishes after they leave dish machine

A storage area near dishwashing area

Sufficient mobile dish storage carts to transfer dishes to storage, service, or banquet setup areas

Proper plumbing to avoid water leakage or condensation creating hazardous conditions

Proper drainage to avoid clogged or backup of water system

Soft water treatment or lime removal system to cut down lime deposits and buildup in water supply

Automatic detergent control and alarm system for dishwashing machines

Automatic injected dry agent system to prevent the formation of water drops on wet dishes in the final drying stage and to eliminate the hand drying of serviceware

Sufficient storage space for cleaning materials near dishwashing area

A separate glass-washing and soiled glass table to eliminate the strain on the dishwashing area, reduce breakage, eliminate excessive water change, and produce cleaner glasses

Separate silver-soaking and sorting tank or sink to be used prior to machine washing

Silver dipping or cleaning material for silver soaking tanks

Sufficient silverware separators or boxes to sort, transfer, and store silverware

A burnishing machine or silver polisher to clean large amount of silverware at one time

Vertical or horizontal conveyor belts to alleviate or relocate the excessive flow of soiled dishes to other less congested areas

Potwashing Area

There should be a potwashing area separate from the serviceware-washing station. Locate the potwashing facility near areas of the kitchen where pots are most frequently used. Furnish the potwashing area with:

Sufficient potwashing sinks or three-compartment sinks with grease and skimmer units between first two compartments

An automatic potwasher in high-volume operations

Soiled pot table or storage area of adequate size to hold pots until ready to be cleaned

Enough hot water and steam to remove and clean difficult grease and burnt foods on pots and pans

Sufficient clean pot tables or mobile pot racks to hold and transport a large number of clean pots at one time

Sufficient pot, pan, and utensil racks, storage space, and shelving

Adequate storage facilities for cleaning supplies and materials needed for potwashing area

Adequate facilities for a waste-disposal system to remove large amounts of wasted food and grease

A depressed area around potwashing area for easy positioning of ground level wooden drain boards to relieve fatigue, help keep floor dry, and facilitate cleaning

Sanitation Area

Morale often runs low for workers in the sanitation area. Some of these problems might be eliminated through thoughtful design. Furnish the sanitation area with:

A garbage or waste storage area near areas where the bulk of waste material originates, such as near meat, vegetable, dishwashing, and potwashing areas

Adequate waste storage space and equipment to hold, transport, remove, and condense high-volume waste materials

Adequate waste disposal methods such as incinerators or an adequate sanitation pickup schedule to avoid bad odors, unpleasant sights, and health hazards

Refrigerated garbage storeroom for waste material held over a two-day period

Garbage storage area with easy-to-clean tile and proper drainage

Adequate hot water, steam supply, and equipment to clean sanitation area properly

A steam-cleaning can washer or sterilizing equipment to clean cans properly

Drying racks or storage area to dry cans

A bottle or can crusher to consolidate glass and metal containers

Hand sinks for employees to wash hands after handling waste products and containers

Sufficient storage area so mops, brooms, and other cleaning equipment can be hung and dried after being cleaned

A janitor's closet, storage area, or sink to keep all cleaning supplies and equipment needed for proper maintenance

Walls, Floors, Ceilings, and Doors

Consider the following points when designing a banquet kitchen facility, giving ample consideration to price, durability, easy maintenance, comfort, and safety:

Construct walls that resist water and moisture and have proper sound-absorption properties, especially in vital areas such as between dishwashers and banquet facility

Construct ceilings with proper light-reflecting and sound-absorption qualities

Install unglazed tile floors and walls in areas where heavy grease and dirt accumulate and a high degree of cleanliness and easy maintenance are required

Install ramps for easy transport of mobile equipment where steps or different floor levels prevent easy access

Place rubber or plastic bumpers on trucks and carts to prevent damage to walls and doors

Place metal plates or other protective materials on walls or doors that are constantly being scratched by moving objects such as portable trucks or serving carts

Clearly mark entrances and exits

Construct doors wide enough to permit easy passage of equipment, trucks, large parcels, etc.

Install see-through glass on doors to prevent accidents

Install an electric eye or automatic door opener to free employees' hands

Install safety rails or guards when doors swing into kitchen

Install a double set of doors between kitchen area and banquet facilities to eliminate noise

Install doors of fireproof materials

Install screened doors leading to the outside of the building to keep insects and rodents out during warm months

Install locks on doors where security is required

Chapter 16

Banquet Service

Customers consider many factors when choosing a caterer: the available menus, decor, price, and most important the quality of service. The finest food will go unappreciated if it is carelessly served. All the planning and organization that goes into a function will be worth naught if the guests are thoughtlessly and rudely treated by the service staff. To succeed, it is essential that a catering operation maintain an ongoing service training program in which politeness, neatness, and a comprehensive knowledge of food and beverage are emphasized and the procedures of the banquet service offered are taught.

Unfortunately, no two operations will utilize the same service procedures or setups. All banquet headwaiters interpret for themselves the proper manner of service. Service personnel will be expected to conform to the approach of their supervisor. Whatever the style of service employed, it must be executed consistently and uniformly by all servers if a balanced, well-paced affair is to be achieved. Whether a soup course is served from the right or left side may not be important. However, for an overall effect, it is important that everyone serve it from the same side. This chapter will address itself to the more common and acceptable methods of service. Adjustments will certainly be needed for individual operations.

There are essentially two basic types of banquet service: American and Russian. American service is a simplified, preplated service, whereas Russian service is more elaborate and calls for serving from silver platters. The appropriate choice will depend on the desires of your clientele and what your competitors offer.

Whichever service is used, certain steps must be taken before the banquet room can be set. A logical, organized approach to these preliminary preparations will guarantee that the job is completed efficiently and thoroughly.

1. The rooms to be set must be completely stripped of all furniture and then thoroughly vacuumed. The houseman (or person responsible for setting up tables and chairs) should check to be sure that all posters, banners, masking tape, burnt out bulbs, or other eyesores are removed from the room. Besides the function room, other related rooms should be

checked and cleaned, e.g., restrooms, checkrooms, reception rooms, meeting rooms, dressing rooms, and bridal rooms. Make certain periodically throughout the affair that the men's and ladies' rooms remain neat and serviceable.

2. After the rooms have been cleaned, the houseman should position the lumber work (bare tables, chairs, platforms) according to the arrangement shown on the floor plan. Comfortable spacing (approximately 2½ feet between the backs of the chairs surrounding the tables) should be provided to create adequate service aisles. The legs of the tables should be positioned squarely so that the tablecloths cover the four legs evenly. A drape of at least 12 to 16 inches should extend over the table edges to hide the legs and improve the total appearance.

Some operations place silencer cloths on the bare table tops to act as buffers between the table and tablecloth. Many operations have dispensed with this practice because of the additional time and expense involved. Some manufacturers provide built-in cushioned tops for their banquet tables, which act as the silencer cloth. All creases on the tablecloth should run in the same direction throughout the function room.

3. The chairs may either be stacked (10 high) near each table to expedite setting the table or may be placed uniformly and equidistant around the tables using the exact amount of chairs indicated on the floor plan. In either case, when positioned, the front edge of the chair's seat should barely touch the natural overhang of the tablecloth.

4. The headwaiter then determines the place setting to be used to suit the menu and type of service requested by the customer. The headwaiter composes one sample place setting for all waiters to repeat throughout the entire function room. The average place setting requires approximately 2 feet in width and 1¼ feet in depth.

In some operations, the waiter is responsible for setting up and completing his entire assigned station, while in others each waiter has a specific task to perform for the entire function room, e.g., placing all glassware on all the tables. The latter concept is more of a team effort or mass production method that speeds up setting time. Whatever the system, all the necessary flatware, chinaware, glassware, linens, etc., should be in place prior to the guests arrival into the function room. Sufficient time should be allocated for service personnel to completely set the rooms so the waiters are not rushed and pressured to finish before the guests arrive.

It is very important to have the function room completely set before the guests enter the room. This includes the placement of floral centerpieces, lighting, and candles, the filling of water glasses, and anything else that gives the guest a pleasant feeling and impression of the ambiance of the room. After the room is set, and the guests have started to arrive, the waiters should stand next to their respective stations and direct the guests to their tables, introducing themselves by name. Nametags for all service personnel may be advisable for easy identification by the guests. As soon as the seating is reasonably complete, the headwaiter gives the signal for the waiters to pick up and serve the bread and butter. For uniformity, the service of all food and beverages should start with a key guest at each table, for example, the person closest to the entrance door.

The headwaiter in charge of service is similar to the conductor of an orchestra. The headwaiter must set the pace, supplying all the necessary cues so that the function runs smoothly and efficiently. Properly, all food and beverages are served and cleared in unison. A system of signals is devised to instruct all service personnel of the proper time to serve or clear. This can be either a hand signal, a nod of the head, or in larger operations, a lighting system. For example, a green light may mean that the waiters should pick up from the kitchen and serve; a yellow light, stand by; a red light, clear all the tables. Without some system for controlling timing for both kitchen and service personnel, a function can easily become disorganized. A close liaison between the headwaiter and chef is needed prior to and during the affair so that each party is aware of the proper time for serving each course. This will ensure the food is served promptly from the kitchen in peak condition and at the proper temperature. The chef should be notified well in advance if there are to be any delays or interruptions in service. He must be informed of any speeches, presentations, awards ceremonies, etc., so he can adjust his cooking and serving schedules. It is the responsibility of the headwaiter to reserve a period of time prior to each function to review the service procedures with all personnel so that they are totally familiar with the menu and beverage items, as well as the proper service procedures and sequence.

If functions are fairly standard, then it is advisable to print a service procedure manual that can be posted on the kitchen bulletin board to enable all service personnel to read and review their jobs and responsibilities. Each waiter is responsible for having all the necessary mise en place he needs, e.g., dishes, glassware, silverware, serving utensils, linens, ashtrays, water pitchers, etc., ready to set up or serve, without taking extra time to search for these items during the affair and thus interfere with or slow down the service. Additional items needed for each course, such as condiments, dressings, or spices, should be placed on the tables immediately before serving that course. These items are removed with the dishes immediately after the course has been completed. Waiters should be assigned to pick up their food from the kitchen corresponding to the tables they are to serve. This will lend order to the service. Waiters assigned head tables, bridal tables, or other important tables should be placed at the beginning of the serving line so they can pick up and clear their tables first.

Russian Service

If a caterer desires to upgrade his reputation and increase income, he may adopt Russian service (service a la Russe), which is more elaborate than the conventional American service. Being more elegant, it impresses the guests. The chief characteristic of Russian service is the presentation of beautifully arranged food on platters. Service personnel transfer the food from platters to the guests' plates with the skillful manipulation of silver service spoons and forks.

Kitchen personnel prefer this type of service. The food is prepared, precut, and then neatly and artistically arranged on silver platters, lending eye appeal and speed to the service. Another advantage is the control of waste, since the leftovers from each platter can be returned to the kitchen if they have not been served.

Customers often confuse Russian service with French service. French service is used in luxury restaurants, and food is served from gueridons and often prepared on rechauds (burners) and carved at tableside. Much room and a large professionally trained staff are necessary. French service is expensive and slow, making it impractical for banquets, where large numbers of guests must be served in a short period of time.

General Rules

All empty service plates are placed on the table from the guest's right in a clockwise rotation around the table, starting with the same person (key guest). Always move in a forward direction; never move or step backward.

All food, including soup, is served from the guest's left. Walk in a forward direction, counterclockwise around the table. The serving fork and spoon or ladle are held in the right hand; the service platter or tureen is held in the left. Food is served from the left rather than the right side to insure that the server's sleeve or arm does not rub across the platter.

All beverages are served from the guest's right, in a clockwise rotation around the table.

All serviceware is cleared from the right side with the right hand in a clockwise rotation around the table.

Russian service is usually accomplished best and most efficiently as a team effort with two servers handling two or three tables of eight to ten persons. One server may place the empty hot soup plates in front of the guests, while the other team waiter serves the hot soup from the soup tureen. In some operations, only one waiter is used in Russian service and the entire entrée, starch, and vegetable are served from one large silver platter. Technically, in Russian service, each course should be served individually from a silver platter onto empty service plates. However, because of service, equipment, labor, or timing problems, operations often

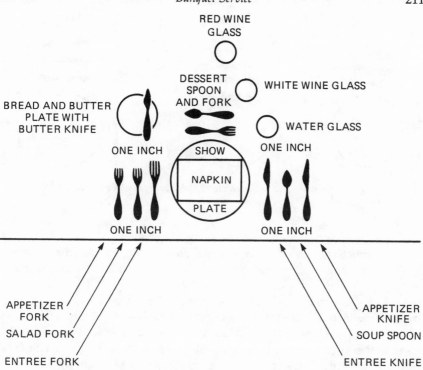

RED WINE
GLASS

DESSERT
SPOON
AND FORK

WHITE WINE GLASS

BREAD AND BUTTER
PLATE WITH
BUTTER KNIFE

WATER GLASS

ONE INCH

SHOW

ONE INCH

NAPKIN

PLATE

ONE INCH

ONE INCH

ONE INCH

APPETIZER
FORK

SALAD FORK

ENTREE FORK

APPETIZER
KNIFE

SOUP SPOON

ENTREE KNIFE

Fig. 16-1. Table place setting for a complete sit-down dinner (Russian service).

will *combine* American service techniques with Russian service for various courses. Preplating one or more courses is sometimes necessary for speed, economy, or practicality.

Whatever type of service is used, all banquet service procedures should be explained clearly to each waiter so that he will know exactly what, when, and how each specific item, course, or service function is to be performed.

Setting the Table

The general rule for the placement of silverware is to position it in menu order from the outside (appetizer) to the inside (dessert). In Russian service, the entrée knife and fork are placed closest to the show plate (also called hors d'oeuvres or service plate) and the dessert setting is placed above the show plate as shown in Fig. 16-1. If an excessive amount of silverware is to be used, or if the table is too congested, some of the silverware can be set immediately prior to the particular course. Whenever possible, set all serviceware before the function. This will save valuable time once the affair is under way.

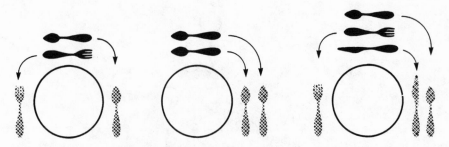

Fig. 16-2. Original (utensils above plate) and final (utensils at sides of plate) placement of dessert silverware.

Let us assume a menu is to be served in the following sequence: hot or cold appetizer served with a white wine, soup, salad, entrée served with a red wine, dessert and coffee. Figure 16-1 shows the proper place setting.

The show plate and silverware should be placed in a line approximately one inch or a thumb's length from the edge of the table. If a show plate has an emblem, picture, or design it should be placed and centered so that the guest can read the inscription or see the design or emblem. Spoons and knives, except the butter knife, go to the right of the show plate and forks to the left. The cutting edges of all knives face left. Dessert spoon and fork are placed directly above the show plate. The dessert spoon and fork will be placed in the proper position by the waiter after the table has been crumbed, just prior to serving dessert and coffee.

If a dessert knife is needed, it is placed directly below and parallel to the dessert spoon and fork with the handle on the right and the cutting edge facing downward. It can also be brought to the table just before the dessert is served. Figure 16-2 shows the original and final placement of dessert silverware.

The bread and butter plate should be centered about one inch above the tines of the forks. The butter knife can be placed either vertically and slightly to the right of the center of the butter plate (as in Fig. 16-1), or horizontally on the top edge of the butter plate with the cutting edge facing downward.

Glassware is placed in the following sequence. If a water glass is used, it is usually placed first, directly above the tip of the entrée knife (refer to Fig. 16-1). The next glass to be used is placed above and to the left of the water glass at approximately the 10 o'clock position. Succeeding glassware follows this pattern. Some headwaiters prefer to have the water glass where the red wine glass is positioned in Fig. 16-1, reasoning that it is more convenient to reach. Glassware can also be positioned in a straight line above the show plate and entrée knife.

A triangular arrangement can be used when placing glassware in a diagonal or straight line seems too congested, interferes with the table setting, or simply looks unattractive. Some examples of triangular patterns are given in Fig. 16-3. After the number 2 glass has been used and removed, the number 3 glass can be moved to the number 2 position before pouring for easy access.

To avoid congestion, usually no more than three glasses are set on the table at one time. Should more be needed, they are placed in the sequence they are needed after the preceding glasses have been cleared.

Sugar bowls should be placed halfway between the center and the edge of the table for easy access. In certain operations, the sugar bowl is not placed on the table until just before the coffee and tea are served. Salt and pepper are placed in front of the sugar bowls, salt to the right of the pepper. Ashtrays are placed equidistant between the sugar and the salt and pepper.

For easy access, three sugar bowls, salt and pepper shakers, and ashtrays should be used for a 60-inch round table, while four sets should be used for a 72-inch round table.

Napkins help decorate a table. Napkins can be the same color as the tablecloth or different to give a contrasting effect. The napkin is usually placed on the center of the show plate. When an appetizer is preplated, the napkin may be placed above or to the left of the show plate. There are many types of napkin folds. The one selected by the headwaiter should be used throughout the entire function room.

There are both simple and fancy napkin folds. The simple folds, usually flat folds, are preferred by professionals because they appear more elegant, require less setup time, are handled less, are more sanitary, and can often be folded by using one hand. The fancy or standup folds,

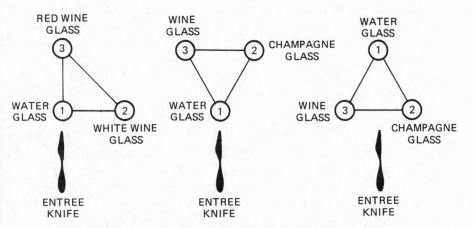

Fig. 16-3. Triangular placement of glassware in order of use.

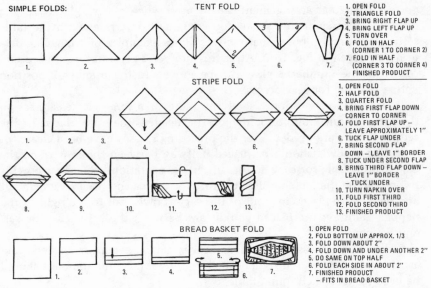

Fig. 16-4. Some simple and fancy napkin folds.

most often preferred by clients, are more decorative. A few sample napkin folds are shown in Fig. 16-4.

Napkin folds can also be used as underliners, e.g., for soup tureens or bread baskets. Some samples are given in Fig. 16-5.

The Serving Fork and Spoon

To professionally transfer food from the silver service platter to the guest's plate, service personnel must become proficient in handling the silver service spoon and fork. The service spoon and fork is used to clamp and serve the food securely with one hand in one easy motion as the service platter is held in the other hand. For certain items, the serving spoon and fork may be held side by side and spread into a "V" shape and used like a spatula. This technique is particularly useful in serving items that are delicate and need support from underneath, e.g., fish fillets or perhaps omelets.

The step-by-step procedure for the standard handling of the serving spoon and fork is given in Fig. 16-6. By using the thumb and index finger to manipulate the fork in a downward motion, and by maneuvering the spoon in an upward movement with the remaining fingers, the utensils become an effective clamp. For ease of handling, the silverware should be held as far back on the handles as possible. When pressed together the tines of the fork should rest comfortably and tightly in the bowl of the spoon.

For certain items, it sometimes is more advantageous to place the tines of the fork inward to get a better grip on the food. An alternative method can be used to achieve a very firm grip. The index finger may be temporarily removed from between the handles of the serving spoon and fork after the item is grasped and placed under the handle of the serving spoon; the thumb presses down on the fork. After the item has been transferred to the desired area, the index finger is placed back into the original position between the handles of the service spoon and fork to release the food.

The professional handling of these service utensils requires some practice before one becomes comfortable and proficient in their use.

Serving the Meal

While each banquet menu will be different, the following is a typical sequence:

Serve bread and butter
Serve first wine
Serve appetizer

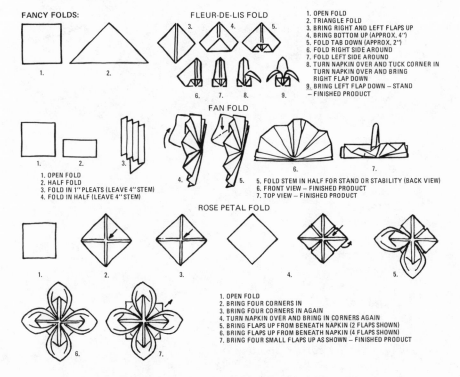

Fig. 16-5. Some ways napkins can be used for decorative purposes.

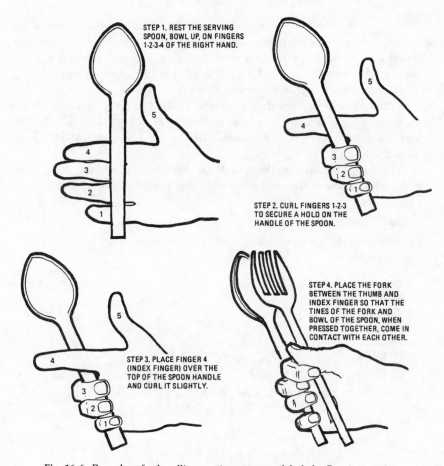

STEP 1. REST THE SERVING SPOON, BOWL UP, ON FINGERS 1-2-3-4 OF THE RIGHT HAND.

STEP 2. CURL FINGERS 1-2-3 TO SECURE A HOLD ON THE HANDLE OF THE SPOON.

STEP 3. PLACE FINGER 4 (INDEX FINGER) OVER THE TOP OF THE SPOON HANDLE AND CURL IT SLIGHTLY.

STEP 4. PLACE THE FORK BETWEEN THE THUMB AND INDEX FINGER SO THAT THE TINES OF THE FORK AND BOWL OF THE SPOON, WHEN PRESSED TOGETHER, COME IN CONTACT WITH EACH OTHER.

Fig. 16-6. Procedure for handling serving spoon and fork for Russian service.

Clear appetizer
Serve soup
Clear soup
Serve salad
Clear salad
Serve second wine
Serve entrée
Clear entrée
Crumb table
Serve dessert
Serve coffee and tea
Clear dessert, coffee, and tea

Serving the Bread and Butter One waiter places a roll onto each bread and butter plate using the serving spoon and fork, while the other waiter positions the iced butter bowls or dishes and service butter knife. Generally, two butter bowls are set at opposite ends of each table of ten guests, e.g., at the northeast and southwest positions. Some operations serve the individual butters directly onto the bread and butter plate.

Serving the First Wine On command from the headwaiter, the first wine, usually white, is served just prior to serving the appetizer. The wine is served by holding the bottle with a folded napkin in the right hand so that the heat of the hand does not come in contact with the chilled wine. The wine label should face the guests so it can be read. Pour from the right side of the guest, starting with the key guest and moving clockwise around the table. Depending on its size, the glass is filled one-third to two-thirds (approximately 3 ounces). Upon completing the pouring of each guest's portion, the bottle should be gently twisted in a circular motion upward and to the right to avoid dripping the wine. At the same time, bring the left hand with the service towel up to the lip of the bottle to wipe the drops that may be starting down the neck of the bottle. After everyone has been served, the wine is returned to the designated area: kitchen, bar, pantry, side station, etc., and placed into an ice bucket or refrigerator for further chilling. The glasses are refilled until the number of bottles ordered have been consumed. Banquet wine service differs from restaurant wine service in that the formality of first allowing the host to taste the wine, then serving the women, and then serving the remaining guests is not required. Some operations do serve the wine first to the women and then to the men seated at the table. Also, the custom of presenting and opening each bottle individually in front of the host and guests is dispensed with, since all bottles are opened at one time prior to service.

In certain instances, especially when more than one wine is being served, there may be a need for wine stewards. This frees the other waiters to serve only food and thus speeds service. A catering operation may offer this convenience to a client at an extra expense to cover the additional labor costs incurred.

Serving the Appetizer On signal from the headwaiter, the appetizers are picked up. The appetizer may either already be preplated or it can be served from silver platters. The service varies with the item being served.

If the item is preplated, each waiter on the team will take a full tray of appetizers for each table and on signal will enter the function room and, starting with the key guest, place the preplated appetizer, with underliner if needed, on the show plate. Service is with the left hand from the left side of the guest. If the appetizer is served from silver platters, the empty hot or chilled appetizer plate is positioned by the first waiter with the right hand from the guest's right, starting with the key guest, and continuing clockwise around the table. After all the empty plates have been placed on the table by the first waiter, the second waiter then serves the appetizer from the silver platter held in the left hand with the serving spoon and fork held in the right hand. Service is from the guest's left in a counterclockwise direction around the table until every guest is served.

Clearing the Appetizer After the appetizer has been served, the waiters should attend to the needs of the guests at their assigned tables and then return to the kitchen with empty trays. On command from the headwaiter, the waiters enter the function room and, starting with the key guest, clear all the soiled appetizer dishes with the right hand from the guest's right, proceeding in a clockwise direction. All leftover food should be scraped toward the waiter from the last plate picked up to the previous plate being held in the left hand. Scrape with a utensil in the right hand and then transfer the utensil from the right hand to the left, and secure it under the stack of soiled plates with the left hand. After the soiled plate has been scraped clean, it is then transferred to the bottom of the stack and another soiled dish is picked up and the same procedure is followed. All scraping of soiled plates should be done with the waiter's back to the customer.

After all the soiled appetizer dishes have been picked up, the silverware is placed on top of the soiled dishes and transferred to nearby trays on stands and then carried to the dishwashing area. For easy handling and as a time-saving procedure, all soiled plates, silverware, and glassware should be sorted on the waiter's tray after each course is completed. If a soiled item such as a supreme dish is to be removed, the waiter should take as many supreme dishes and underliners as can be comfortably carried and take them to the nearest waiter's tray to be sorted and carried to the dishwashing area.

After the appetizer has been cleared, the waiter can collect and organize the table numbers and stands from each table and return them to the headwaiter or storage area for the next function. Dirty ashtrays can be replaced with clean ones at this point. Then the waiter should attend to the other needs of the guests: refilling water glasses, supplying more butter, etc. The waiters should then return to the kitchen to await the signal for the service of the next course.

Serving the Soup The waiters pick up the soup and the soup plate appropriate for the type of soup being served (e.g., hot or cold). The waiters line up at the kitchen door to await the signal from the headwaiter to enter the function room in unison. One team waiter brings in the required number of stacked, empty soup plates carried in the left hand on a clean service cloth and places them (starting with the key guest) directly on the show plate with the right hand from the right side of the guest moving in a clockwise direction around the table. The second waiter brings in the soup tureen with cover and ladle. A damp napkin may be placed between the tureen and underliner to prevent sliding. This is carried in the left hand. The cover is removed and placed aside. Starting with the key guest, the waiter places his left leg forward close to the table's edge to get near the customer, and bends forward to bring the soup tureen approximately one inch over the edge of the empty soup plate. The waiter then ladles the soup into the plate from the left side, moving counterclockwise around the table. To prevent dripping, a double dip motion of the soup ladle should be used. Soup should be ladled gently into the soup plate to prevent accidental splashing. If a soup requires croutons or garnishes, these would be placed on a separate serving plate or bowl with underliner and served with a serving spoon by another waiter directly following the soup. After the waiter finishes serving the soup, he returns the empty soup tureen and excess soup to the kitchen, while his team waiter tends to the needs of the guests, returning afterward to the kitchen to get an empty tray and wait for the signal to clear the soup course.

Clearing the Soup All waiters line up at the kitchen door and, on the signal from the headwaiter, the soup course is cleared. Starting with the key guest, all the empty soiled soup plates are removed from the guests' right in a clockwise rotation around the table. The waiter picks up the first soup plate with the right hand and places it in the left hand holding the soup spoon down with the left thumb. He then moves to the second person and picks up the second soup plate, turns his back to the customer and, if necessary, empties any remaining soup into the first soup plate held in his left hand. He then places the second plate on his lower left forearm, balancing it with a supportive triangle of the forearm, the knuckle of the thumb, and the little and ring fingers of the left hand. The first plate is held by the thumb and index and middle fingers. After proper balance has been established, the soup spoon is taken from the second soup plate and placed into the front soup plate, and the next soup plate is picked up using the same procedure. Any excess soup is poured into the first soup plate. After a comfortable number of soup plates have been removed, they are brought to the waiter's tray on the tray stand and stacked. The silverware is sorted and the tray is brought to the dishwashing area. The other team waiter tends to the guests and the table needs and then returns to the kitchen for the next course.

Serving the Salad In most operations, the salad course is served prior to the entrée, which is an American preference, while the European preference is to serve the salad after the entrée, since roughage eaten after a heavy entrée aids digestion. Also, salad dressings containing vinegar won't conflict with the taste of a wine if the salad is eaten after the entrée.

After the soup course has been cleared, the headwaiter gives the signal to serve the salad course. One waiter carries in the empty chilled salad plates and dressing(s) with underliner, while the other team waiter brings in the salad in a bowl on an underliner. The first waiter starts with the key guest and places the chilled plates from the right with the right hand moving clockwise around the table. He then picks up the dressing(s) with underliner, while the second waiter serves the salad from the left with the right hand using the serving spoon and fork and moving counterclockwise around the table. The first waiter follows directly behind the second waiter to serve the salad dressing(s) from the sauce boat on an underliner from the guests' left going in the same direction as his teammate. The salad dressing is held in the left hand and the serving spoon in the right.

If the salad is preplated, the chilled salad is brought into the room by the first waiter and is served with the left hand from the left moving counterwise. The second team waiter immediately follows, serving the dressings on the underliner from the left, also moving counterclockwise. Some operations mix the dressing directly into the salad. After serving, both waiters tend to the needs of the table and return to the kitchen to await the signal to clear.

Clearing the Salad After the salad course has been finished by a reasonable number of guests, the headwaiter gives the signal to clear. One waiter picks up the salad plate and salad fork with the right hand from the guests' right and moves clockwise to the next guest. The second team waiter picks up the show plate and follows in the same direction. Both waiters place the dishes on the tray. While the first waiter carries the dishes and silverware back to the dishwashing room, the second waiter picks up the dressing(s) and returns it, with the salad bowl, to the salad or pantry area. The waiters tend to the needs of the guests and then return to the kitchen for the signal to serve the next course.

Serving the Second Wine

On command from the headwaiter, the waiters enter the function room in unison, ready to serve the wine before serving the entrée course. One waiter removes the first (white) wine glass with the right hand from the right side, starting with the key guest and moving clockwise around the table. Since guests may object to the removal of a wine glass if some wine remains, the guest should be asked for permission to remove the glass to avoid complaints. The second (red) wine is served at room temperature from the right with the right hand. The key guest is served first, followed by the remaining guests clockwise around the table. The

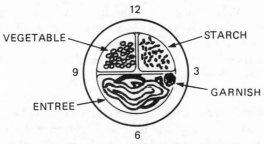

Fig. 16-7. Position of entrée items on a dinner plate.

red wine is poured in the same manner as described for white, filling each glass with approximately 4 to 6 ounces of wine, depending on the size of the glass. The remaining wine is returned to the wine area for additional service at a later time. The waiters return to the kitchen to await the service of the next course.

Serving the Entrée On signal from the headwaiter, both waiters pick up from the kitchen the needed number of hot dinner plates, held with service towels, and return to their tables. Starting with the key guest, these plates are put down with the right hand from the right side in a clockwise direction around the table. Both waiters immediately return to the kitchen and line up for the food platters for each table. One will hold the main item, usually meat, with garnish and sauce; the other the vegetables and starch item. The platters are covered with lids to keep the food hot. Service towels are placed on the waiter's left forearm to prevent burns from the hot platters. When the headwaiter gives the signal, both platters are carried into the function room. Most often the sauce in a gravy boat is placed on the same platter as the meat, but, if served separately, one waiter places the gravy boat with an underliner and serving spoon on the table to be passed around as needed, while the other team waiter removes the lids from the platters and places them on the tray stand. Each waiter picks up his platter, shows it to the guests, and then proceeds to serve. The meat platter is held in the left hand and the serving utensils in the right hand. Starting with the key guest, the food is served from the left. The waiter, keeping the left foot forward close to the table, bends over to position the serving platter close to and slightly above the inside rim of the empty entrée plate. Using the serving fork and spoon, the meat is placed at the 6 o'clock position on the dinner plate. The garnish is placed at the 3 o'clock position, and the waiter proceeds to move counterclockwise around the table. If the item requires sauce or gravy, then the gravy is served over the entrée item unless the entrée is breaded, calling for sauce beneath the item. The second team waiter immediately follows the lead waiter (keeping two seats behind the lead waiter to avoid crowding the guests) and serves the vegetable at the 10/11 o'clock position, and the starch at the 1/2 o'clock position (see Fig. 16-7).

In some operations, for positive public reaction, a second helping of meat, vegetable, and starch is offered to any guest wishing it. Refilling wine glasses and tending to other customer needs may be handled at this point, after which all waiters return to the kitchen to await the signal for the clearing of the entrée course.

Clearing the Entrée   After the guests have finished their entrée, the headwaiter will give the command to clear. The waiter starts with the key guest, removes the soiled dinner plate and silverware with the right hand, and then, turning his back away from the customer, places them in his left hand and scrapes the leftover food into the upper left-hand corner of the plate. He then places the handle of the fork under his left thumb to hold it down securely. The blade of the knife is placed under the bridge of the fork's handle with the sharp edge facing the waiter. The fork and knife will form an "X" on the plate. Moving clockwise, the waiter picks up the second plate from the right and then places it on the left forearm. A triangular balance is achieved by bracing it against the knuckle of the thumb and the little and ring fingers of the left hand. After the soiled plate has been secured, the food is scraped into the first plate. The second fork is placed next to the first, and the second knife is placed under the bridge of the two forks, parallel to the first knife. The remaining soiled plates are placed consecutively on the preceding plates resting on the forearm. All leftover food is scraped onto the first plate and all silverware positioned in an "X" pattern. After a comfortable amount of plates have been cleared, the first plate is placed on top of the last scraped plate with the right hand. Then the waiter takes the tray with all soiled dishes and silverware to the dishwashing area.

Empty sauce boats and other items are cleared from the table before the dessert course. Bread and butter plates and knives, salt and pepper, all condiments used for the entrée, and the empty wine glasses are all returned to the appropriate dishwashing and storage areas.

Crumbing the Table   After the table has been cleared, the waiters crumb the tables starting at the left side of the key guest. The waiter takes a clean folded napkin in hand and scrapes the table toward him, crumbing any debris onto a small flat plate held with the left hand evenly at the edge of the table. After this crumbing procedure is satisfactorily completed, the waiter should move the dessert spoon down to the right and the fork down to the left of each cover, one inch from the edge of the table, leaving sufficient space for the placement of the dessert plates. This procedure is repeated clockwise around the table.

Serving the Dessert   After the tables have been completely crumbed and the dessert silverware set, the waiters should return to the kitchen, pick up their dessert plates and desserts and, on the signal from the headwaiter, serve. One waiter starts with the key guest, positions the empty dessert plates from the right with the right hand, and continues clockwise while the team waiter serves the portioned dessert from the silver tray with the serving spoon and fork from the guests' left moving counterclockwise. If a sauce or dessert topping is requested, then the first waiter, after setting all the plates, will directly follow with a Revere bowl and serving spoon to ladle the sauce or topping on the dessert. If the dessert is preplated, it is served by the waiters from the left side with the left hand and the sauce or topping, if not placed directly on the dessert, is served by the second waiter as above.

Serving the Coffee and Tea The coffee and tea may be served separately after the dessert or together with the dessert. The American public generally prefers coffee to be served with dessert. If served as a separate course after dessert, it goes directly in the center of the place setting. If served with the dessert, the coffee cup and saucer are placed to the right and parallel to the dessert plate. In either case, the empty coffee cups are served heated, and the handle of the cup should be set at the 4 o'clock position for easy handling by the guest. If teaspoons are needed, they are placed around the table. Sugar bowls should already be on the tables. The first waiter picks up the necessary number of heated coffee cups and saucers along with his creamers and places them on a tray. On command from the headwaiter, the creamers, usually two per table, are set at opposite ends of the table. Starting at the right of the key guest, the cups are set clockwise around the table. The team waiter serves the coffee in the same direction. The coffee pot is held on an underliner along with a napkin to be used as a shield to prevent the splattering and dripping of coffee. The cup is normally filled three-quarters full to leave room for cream. If a customer requests black coffee, the cup may be filled closer to the rim. Low-calorie sweeteners should also be available and served separately for those guests who may request them. After the coffee is served, any requests for tea or decaffeinated coffee should be taken care of. Sliced lemon and milk should be available and served separately for those requesting tea. In most operations, the tea is premade and served in tea pitchers or pots. If this is not the case, and individual tea bags are used, they are served to the guest on a plate. Hot water is served separately in both cases for the customer to determine the desired strength of his tea. Second servings of coffee or other beverages should be offered after the first cup has been consumed. Fresh crups and saucers are always appreciated. Ashtrays should be cleaned, water glasses refilled, and other needs of the guests met during the coffee service.

Clearing the Dessert and Coffee After the dessert and coffee service is completed, the dessert plates and silverware are removed with the right hand and placed into the waiter's left hand. Removal is from the guest's right and motion is clockwise around the table. The dishes and silverware are placed on the side tray, while the team waiter removes all the coffee and tea cups, saucers, teaspoons, creamers, sugar bowls, etc., and places and sorts them on another side tray. After the guests leave, the waiters remove the water glasses along with the soiled napkins and linens, which are returned to the laundry.

Placing a Finger Bowl If a finger bowl is needed at the end of a particular course or at the close of a dinner, it should be placed in front of the guest with the left hand. The finger bowl setup consists of a silver or glass bowl half filled with warm water on an underliner with a wedge or slice of lemon or scented flower petals floating in it. An extra cloth napkin should be placed to the right of the bowl for drying the fingers.

Clearing the Linen Napkins are picked up by the waiter after the guests indicate that they are no longer required or when the guest leaves the table or function. Tablecloths should never be removed until the last guest has left. Under no circumstances should a waiter remove a table-cloth to convey to the guests that they should leave. This can nullify any positive reaction the customer may have had about the catering oper-ation. After all the guests have left, the soiled napkins are picked up, laid flat, and counted as are the soiled tablecloths. The napkins are placed in the center of the tablecloth, the corners of which are tied and bundled together to be sent to the laundry as quickly as possible to prevent mildew, stains, and discoloration. If silencer cloths are used, they are checked for cleanliness. If acceptable, they are folded and reused for the next function; if not, they are sent to the laundry with the soiled linen.

Setting Up the Next Function After all the linen has been removed, the waiters are expected to do a general cleanup and to make sure that their stations have been completely cleaned and cleared and any related work has been finished. Any leftover food if used or touched during service should be discarded and those items not used or touched should be returned to the kitchen. Items like salt and pepper shakers and sugar bowls should be cleaned, refilled, separated, and placed on trays for the next function. After the function room and kitchen are completely cleaned to the satisfaction of the headwaiter, the waiters are dismissed from the function. Then the housemen arrive to break down the lumber work, vacuum, and reset for the next function.

American Service

Most caterers prefer American service, a preplated service, because it is a simple, fast, direct, and economical way to serve banquet food.

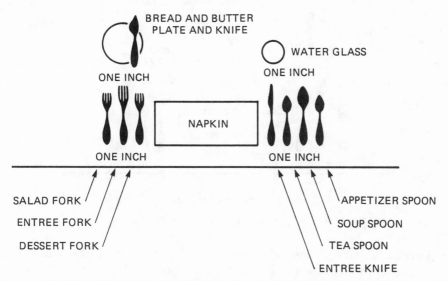

Fig. 16-8. Table place setting for a complete sit-down dinner (American service).

Training for this type of service is easy, even for the inexperienced. No special serving skills are needed to transfer food from platter to plate as in Russian service. After one or two on-the-job situations, the routine is learned quickly. For the owner, no large inventories of serving equipment and utensils are required, and labor costs are lower.

General Rules

In American service, all food or solids (including soup) are served from the guest's left with the left hand. The waiter serves counterclockwise around the table. All beverages are served from the guest's right with the right hand, moving clockwise around the table. All soiled serviceware is cleared from the guest's right with the right hand, moving clockwise. The average rule of thumb for American service is one waiter for two tables or approximately 20 guests.

Moments before the guests' arrival in the function room, the water glasses are iced and filled three-quarters. As the guests enter, the waiters, standing at their respective stations, direct guests to their tables and help them to be seated.

Setting the Table

To illustrate American service, let us assume the following typical menu is served: a cold appetizer, a hot soup, a salad, a hot entrée, dessert, and coffee. The place setting to be used for this menu is shown in Fig. 16-8. Note that no show plate is required, although one may be used for

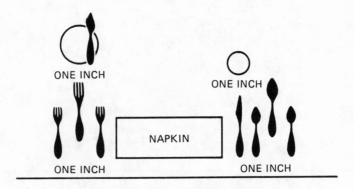

RAISING THE SILVERWARE

Fig. 16-9. Silverware setting variations for American service.

American service. If wine glasses are needed, they can be positioned in the various ways shown earlier for Russian service.

Some headwaiters prefer a variation on the standard silverware setting. An example is shown in Fig. 16-9.

The placement of sugar bowls, salt and pepper shakers, and ashtrays is the same as described for Russian service. Also, any one of the napkin folds shown for Russian service can be used for American service as well.

Serving the Meal

When about ninety percent of the guests are seated, the headwaiter gives the signal for the waiters to pick up the bread and butter and relish trays (if offered) for each table. The relish trays are placed at opposite ends of the table. In most instances, the bread is served in baskets or trays lined with napkins. They are placed at opposite ends of the table. Bread may be served individually on the bread plate by the waiter shortly before or immediately after the guests are seated to keep it fresh and warm. A sufficient number of rolls, usually two per person, should be available and placed on the table within easy reach of the guests. The butter, usually two pats per person, should be served in iced butter bowls with underliners or on the individual bread and butter plates. There should be a butter knife for the guests to transfer butter to their individual butter plates. Periodic checks should be made after the bread has been placed, and more bread and butter should be offered throughout the service. This solid food item should be served from the left side of the guest, the side of the bread plate, to prevent reaching across a customer.

Serving the Appetizer For a total room effect and a fuller table setting, the appetizer may be preset or placed moments prior to the guests' entry into the room. However, it is more correct to serve the appetizer after the majority of guests have been seated. On command from the headwaiter, the appetizers for each table are brought from the kitchen on trays, which are placed on side stands. Starting with the key guest, the waiter serves with the left hand from the left side of the guest, placing the appetizer in the center of the place setting and moving counterclockwise around the table.

Clearing the Appetizer After the appetizer course has been completed, on command from the headwaiter the waiter picks up the appetizer plates and silverware from the right side with the right hand, moving clockwise around the table. All soiled serviceware is neatly placed and separated on the waiter's tray. The waiter returns to his table, collects all the table numbers and stands, and returns them to the headwaiter to be organized and stored. Additional rolls, butter, and water are served where needed. Dirty ashtrays are cleared and replaced with clean ones, and, after all the needs of the customers have been met, the waiters return to the kitchen to await the service of the next course.

Serving the Soup Each waiter prepares his stack of hot soup cups and saucers ready for the soup service. The headwaiter gives the signal for the soup course to begin. The kitchen serves the soup, and the headwaiter gives the command to enter the function room. Saucers are not immediately set under the filled soup cups so that if spills occur the saucers will remain clean. The tray of saucers and soup in cups is placed on the waiter's tray stand near the table to be served. The waiter places the soup cups on the saucers, carries a comfortable number, and, starting with the key guest, serves the soup with the left hand from the left side moving counterclockwise around the table until the table has been completely served. If the soup requires a garnish such as croutons, it is either placed directly in the soup prior to service or placed in a separate serving vessel with underliner and serving spoon and placed prior to the service of the soup so that the guests can pass it around the table. After the soup has been served, the waiter tends to the needs of the table and returns to the kitchen to await the signal from the headwaiter to clear the course.

Clearing the Soup On command from the headwaiter, the waiters enter the function room with their empty trays and start to clear the soup cups and saucers starting with the key guest. All soiled items are picked up from the right with the right hand, clockwise around the table. The soiled soup cups, saucers, and soup spoons are sorted and stacked on the waiter's tray and taken to the dishwashing area. The waiters then prepare for the next course and wait for the signal to serve.

Serving the Salad On command from the headwaiter, the waiters pick up their preplated salads and dressing(s) and place them on their trays and enter the function room in unison. If the dressing is not premixed into the salad and separate salad dressing(s) are served, each waiter goes to his designated table and places the salad dressing(s) with underliner and serving spoon at opposite ends of the table. Starting with the key guest, the chilled preplated salad is then served from the left with the left hand counterclockwise around the table. After the salad has been served, the table is checked for further needs such as additional water, rolls, butter, clean ashtrays, or other customer requests. The waiter then returns to the kitchen to await the clearing of the course.

Clearing the Salad When the salad has been finished by all the guests, the headwaiter gives the signal to pick up the soiled dishes. The waiters enter the function room in unison with their empty trays, place them on the side stands, and proceed to clear, starting with the key guest at each table. First, the salad dressing(s) are removed and placed on the waiter's tray. Then the soiled salad plates and forks are taken from the guest's right with the right hand clockwise around the table. The soiled dishes, silverware, and dressing vessels are sorted and stacked on the waiter's tray and taken to the dishwashing area. The waiters then prepare for the command to serve the next course.

Serving the Entrée On command, the waiters line up in order to pick up the required number of preplated entrées. Plate covers are essential to keep the food hot and stacked neatly. For ease and convenience, the kitchen staff usually places all items, meat/fish/fowl, vegetable, and starch on one serving platter for quick plating and service. Sauce is usually placed directly on the item or may be served separately in a sauce boat. Sauce or gravy is served on top of an entrée item except in the case of breaded items when it is served underneath. On command, the waiters enter the function room and, going to their designated stations, place the tray on the tray stand. If gravy is served separately, the gravy boats with underliners and serving spoons are placed at opposite ends of the table for the customers to pass. The covers are removed from the plates and the food is served. The waiter takes as many plates as he can comfortably carry. Starting with the key guest, the food is served with the left hand from the left, counterclockwise around the table. After the entrée has been completely served, the waiter checks the table for any customer needs or requests. He then returns to the kitchen with the plate covers and awaits the signal to clear the entrée.

Clearing the Entrée On command from the headwaiter, the waiters bring their empty trays into the function room, place them on the tray stand, and proceed to clear the soiled serviceware starting from the right of the key guest, picking up with the right hand, and moving clockwise around the table. The entrée plate, silverware, gravy boat and underliner, bread baskets or trays, bread and butter plate, relish tray, salt and pepper, and condiments are assembled and sorted on the waiter tray. The serviceware is sent to the dishwashing area and the dormants and condiments are neatly organized at the assigned storage or pantry area. After the table has been cleared, it is crumbed, the water replenished, the ashtrays cleaned, and any other needs attended to. Then the waiters return to the kitchen for the next course.

Serving the Dessert On command from the headwaiter, the waiters pick up their preplated desserts, place them on their trays, and await the signal to enter the function room. They proceed to their stations and serve, starting with the key guest, serving with the left hand and moving counterclockwise around the table. Desserts in American service will usually have the sauce and topping preplated, but if it is to be served separately, the sauce is placed in Revere bowls on underliners with serving spoons and placed on the table at opposite ends for the guests to pass. In most cases, the coffee and hot beverages are served with the dessert.

Clearing the Dessert and Coffee After the dessert and coffee have been consumed and second cups of coffee have been offered, the waiters, on command, enter the function room with empty trays and remove the dessert plates, coffee cups and saucers, silverware, creamers, and sugar bowls from the right with the right hand starting with the key guest and moving clockwise around the table. These are returned to the trays, sorted, and brought into the wareroom and pantry or storage area where they are neatly put away. The water glasses and napkins are removed after the guests have left. The linen is taken from the table only when all guests have departed. The linen and napkins are sorted, counted, bundled and brought immediately to the laundry area.

In American service, simplicity and speed are essential. Certain rules may be put aside to make service more convenient; for example, the salad course may be eliminated or served simultaneously with the entrée; the coffee cup and saucer may be preset on the table prior to the start of the function. These practices are not recommended as standard procedure, but there may be times when, for the sake of speed, they are more practical.

Common Service Faults

In banquet service, many problems can occur during a function. The following is a list of informal "rules" that should be enforced. Following these guidelines will eliminate common faults and improper habits of service personnel, thereby improving service and avoiding accidents and crises during a function.

1. Do not come to work without the proper uniform. Always look neat and presentable. Practice good personal hygiene at all times.

2. Do not come to work without the proper service tools. Always carry a pad, pen, or pencil, corkscrew/bottle opener, and matches.

3. Never be rude, impolite, or discourteous to a customer. Always be friendly, helpful, and cheerful and give the service you would expect to receive if you were the guest.

4. Do not smoke, eat, or drink in the function room. Go to a designated area.

5. Never serve an item you would not eat yourself.

6. Never serve hot foods cold or cold foods hot, nor cold plates for hot food or hot plates for cold.

7. Do not serve any item that you cannot explain to a customer. Ask, and get to know, how your menu items are prepared. Know ingredients, accompaniments, garnishes, pronunciation, and preparation of all food on the menu.

8. Never leave your area or station dirty or disorganized. Keeping your area clean is just as important as serving your guests properly.

9. Do not take any equipment from your fellow workers without their permission. This causes tension and resentment.

10. Do not stand or talk in groups during service, especially when guests require your attention.

11. Never be without a service napkin. Never put it in your pocket, belt, or on your shoulders. Always carry it on your arm or wrist.

12. Do not put your service spoon and fork in your pocket. Carry them in your hands or leave them on your side stand.

13. Do not place any soiled or spotted serviceware on the tables. Wipe all silverware and steam all glasses before service.

14. Do not carry silverware in your hands. Use a service plate with napkin. When placing silverware, hold each piece by the handle.

15. Do not touch glasses or cups on the rims, nor place fingers inside glasses or cups when setting, serving, or clearing dishes. Always handle objects by the stem or base and carry them on service trays.

16. Do not place fingers inside the outer rim of any food plate being served.

17. Do not stack coffee cups or soup cups on top of each other.

18. Do not overstack trays. Carry only what you can comfortably manage.

19. Do not pick up or lower any tray without bending knees for proper support.

20. Do not unbalance your tray. Keep heavy dishes in the center to balance the weight.

21. Do not rest your tray on your shoulders.

22. Do not use greasy or wet slippery trays. Dry them completely to avoid accidents.

23. Do not let an item slide on your tray. If a tray does not have slip-resistant materials, a damp napkin or cloth will prevent slipping.

24. Do not bring a tray to the dishwashing area unless all glassware, silverware, and dishes are sorted and all leftovers are on one plate.

25. Do not put hot and cold items next to each other on a tray.

26. Do not put trays on tables. Use tray stands.

27. Do not keep both hands on a tray except for temporary balance. Use your left hand to carry tray and right hand to open doors.

28. Do not remove beverage glasses from the table to refill them. Pour beverages into glasses resting on the table.

29. Do not remove partially filled liquor, wine, beer, or cordial glasses without first asking permission from the guest.

Chapter 17

Banquet Serviceware

Serviceware includes china, silverware, glassware, and serving pieces and accessories. Most on-premise caterers will purchase most of this equipment because its constant use makes it logical to do so, but in the case of some specialty items that may have limited use it may be more practical to rent.

Customers are very interested in the serviceware a caterer offers. A distinctive table setting with quality serviceware will help to sell the customer on your establishment, whereas cracked, chipped, tarnished, or mismatched serviceware indicates to a customer that the operation is careless.

When purchasing serviceware, always consider the following points.

1. The area and type of clientele. Certain areas or clientele will demand a higher grade or quality of serviceware than others.

2. Type of banquet menus. A caterer should first analyze his menus item for item and then consult his key service and kitchen personnel to ascertain the best service items for the various menu offerings.

3. Type of service. Caterers should take into consideration whether they will use American or Russian service. If a caterer decides to use Russian service, he will need more elaborate serviceware, such as soup tureens, serving platters, serving spoons and forks, etc.

4. Seating capacity. The maximum amount of guests the catering operation can accommodate at one time should be determined.

5. Turnover and re-setting of function rooms. The amount of times a room is used during the course of a 24-hour period is an important factor. For example, it may be possible that several different functions, such as a breakfast, lunch, cocktail hour and dinner, may be booked in one room within one day.

6. Dishwashing facilities. If dish- and potwashing areas are efficient, then less items may be needed because of the quick recycling of equipment.

7. Multi-use equipment. If certain items are interchangeable for different uses, for example, an appetizer plate may be recycled as a salad plate and then a dessert plate, then less equipment will be needed, which reduces inventory.

8. Maintenance costs. These should be analyzed when considering the overall cost. For example, stainless-steel equipment may be preferable to silver because it requires less polishing and is more sanitary because it can retard scratching better than silver.

9. Ease of stacking and storage. Is the item conducive to being stacked and stored easily and safely to eliminate breakage, chipping, and theft?

10. Durability. This is one of the most important factors for most serviceware, since the longer serviceware lasts, the less money is spent on replacement.

11. Availability of an unlimited open stock. Can replacements be obtained quickly and conveniently when needed? The item ordered should have good prospects for availability at any time. Some items may not be readily available, since there may be a waiting period, sometimes months, due to seasonal production schedules prior to heavy demand periods. Be careful when buying bargains, since they often become discontinued items.

12. Reliable vendors. Buy from reputable dealers or manufacturers who have various lines of service equipment and who guarantee satisfaction and replacement of unwanted goods. Salesmen should be readily available when needed. Before buying a product, a sample of the item should be used for a trial period to examine its usefulness.

13. Cost. Get the best quality item for the best price. Lowest cost is not always the answer, since often it is more practical to pay a higher price for a better made or more durable product that will pay off in the long run.

Caterers should be careful not to over-order serviceware, which will result in a large inventory and tie up capital. At the same time, they should be careful not to short inventories, since this creates a bad reflection on the service and image of the operation. When determining service equipment requirements or inventories for an operation, a caterer should not only consider multiplying the needed settings by the seating capacity and turnover of function rooms but also factors such as breakage, loss, wear, and pilferage. Most items as a general rule should be multiplied by a factor of approximately $1\frac{1}{2}$ to 2 for adequate coverage. Some items require a higher factor because of their nature, for example, glassware used to serve drinks, especially on an unlimited basis. Certain items may be best figured by the table rather than per person, for example, salt and pepper shakers and sugar bowls.

Chinaware

China or porcelain is made from refined clays and fired at very high temperatures to produce a durable hardness. Chinaware should blend in

Table 17-1. Chinaware

Item	Size	Times seating capacity [1]
Show or service Plates	11½ in.	2½–3
Dinner plates [2]	10½ in.	2½–3
Soup plates (9⅛ oz)	9 in.	2½–3
Bouillon cups (no handle) [3]	7 oz.	2
Salad/dessert plates	7 in.	3
Bread and butter plates	5½ in.	3
Compotes	8 oz.	2
Grapefruit bowls	8 oz.	2
Coffee/teacups	7½ oz.	3
Saucers	5⅞ in.	4
Demitasse cups	4 oz.	1
Demitasse saucers	4⅝ in.	1
Platters	12½ in. oval	½
Casseroles	Round/oval	½

[1]The figures used are for a well-stocked inventory. Reduced amounts may be used for budgetary reasons as long as proper coverage is maintained.
[2]Some operations may also stock a luncheon plate, which is smaller than the dinner plate (e.g., 9 in.). To reduce inventories, some use the dinner plate for all functions.
[3]Unhandled bouillon cups are more practical, since handles chip and break easily.

with the decor, linen, and table setting of the function room. Its appearance should enhance the presentation of food but should never "overpower" it. Dishes should act as a border around the food, and the portion size should coincide with the plate size for maximum eye appeal. Often, simple patterns are the most elegant. For maximum appeal, caterers should consider using a design not easily recognized on the domestic market. Generally, for cost and convenience, one pattern of china is used most often for an entire catering operation. Some caterers prefer to use a different pattern for each function room to blend in with the decor of the individual room and also to help control the use and inventory for each specific room.

Chinaware should be serviceable. A vitreous (glazed finish) and nonporous material is best, since it will protect the design from discoloration, stains, smudges, and fading. It is also easier to wash and holds the temperature of food longer. A medium weight is generally best because it is not too bulky or heavy to carry nor too light or fragile. Grooves and ridges on china should be avoided to prevent the collection of dirt. Rolled-edged dishes are best because they have the advantage of resisting chipping at the edges, help prevent bacteria from accumulating for better sanitation, and make the plate easier to handle with its wide rim. Avoid oversized or unusually shaped plates, since they can cause washing, stacking, and storage problems. Table 17-1 lists the components of a standard chinaware set.

Flatware

Flatware is a term generally used for utensils such as forks, spoons, and knives. The term cutlery is ocasionally used to designate knives or cutting utensils. Most flatware is made of sterling silver, silver or gold plate, or stainless steel. Most caterers use silver-plated or gold substitutes for flatware, since sterling silver and gold have become too expensive. Since there are many thicknesses of silver plating achieved through the electroplating process, the thickness or coat of silver placed on the underlying metal should be examined for wearability. The more coats or the higher the dwt (pennyweight), the better the grade of silver plate. Some caterers promote or sell a "gold setting," which usually includes goldware and gold-rimmed china and glassware at an extra expense, for example, $2.00 per person. Some caterers have converted to using stainless flatware, not only because of the many new and exciting patterns available but also because of the advantage of low maintenance. Like china, flatware patterns should have a track record of availability, good looks, be comfortable to grasp, and easy to maintain. Table 17-2 lists a complete flatware service.

Table 17-2. Flatware	
Item	*Times seating capacity*
Knives[1]	
Dinner	2
Butter	2
Fish	$1\frac{1}{2}$
Steak	1
Fruit[2]	1
Cheese[2]	1
Forks[1]	
Dinner	3
Salad	2
Dessert	2
Fish	$1\frac{1}{2}$
Cocktail	$1\frac{1}{2}$
Snail[3]	1
Spoons	
Tea	4
Dessert	2
Bouillon	2
Soup	2
Iced tea	1
Demitasse	$1\frac{1}{2}$
Serving spoons and forks	$\frac{1}{4}$

[1]Most operations use one size knife and fork for lunch and dinner to reduce inventory.
[2]Fruit and cheese knives should only be ordered when the demand for these items warrants.
[3]Snail forks, holders, and plates are needed only if snails are a common menu item.

Table 17-3. Glassware

Item	Size	Times seating capacity
Water goblet	10 oz.	3
Highball	8 oz.	5
Old-fashioned (rock)	5 oz.	3
Champagne		
Saucer	5½ oz.	2
Tulip	6½ oz.	
Whiskey sour	4 oz.	1
Cocktail	3 oz.	1
Tom Collins	12 oz.	½
Cordial	1 oz.	1
Liqueur	3 oz.	½
Brandy snifter	8 oz.	¼
Sherry	3 oz.	¼
Port	4 oz.	¼
Shot	2 oz. (with 1 oz. line)	⅛
Wine[1]		
White	7 oz.	1½
Red	9 oz.	1½
Beer	10 oz.	2
Iced tea	12 oz.	½
Fruit juice	5 oz.	1½
Sherbet	6 oz.	2
Parfait	5 oz.	2
Punch cups	4 oz.	½
Finger bowls/underliners	6½ oz.	1½

[1]Some caterers use an all-purpose wine glass for both red and white wine.

Glassware

The shape and design of your glassware should blend in with your chinaware and flatware. Higher-quality glassware will be more expensive. Consideration should be given to having standard sizes or using all-purpose glassware to reduce inventories and simplify storage. Clear glassware is most often used, but some caterers prefer using colored glassware for conversational value. Avoid defects such as varied thicknesses and bubbles in the glassware. Rims should be smooth and glassware should be able to withstand a reasonable degree of abuse. Glassware can be processed to give greater strength and durability by heat-treating the upper part of the glass. Fragile or stemmed glassware should be avoided because breakage will be too high. Glass racks will help cut down breakage as well as ease washing, storing, and transportation. Separate glass washers will also help reduce breakage and result in a cleaner product. Table 17-3 lists the kinds of glasses that should be stacked.

Table 17-4. Serving Pieces and Accessories

Item	Size	Times seating capacity
Plate covers	To fit dinner plate	$1\frac{1}{2}$
Supremes/rings/inserts	7 in.	$1\frac{1}{2}$
Vegetable dishes	20 portion (2 compartment)	1 per 2 tables
Gravy/sauce boats/underliner	15 oz.	1 per table
Platters with covers		
Oval	18, 20, 22, 24 in. length	1 per table
Round	12, 14, 16, 18 in. diameter	1 per table
Rectangular	18 x 12 in.	1 per table
Soup tureens/underliners/ladles	10 portion	1 per 2 tables
Bread trays	$10\frac{1}{2}$ in.	2 per table
Relish trays	$10\frac{1}{2}$ in.	2 per table
Champagne coolers		1 per 2 tables
Ice buckets/spoons	7 in.	1 per table
Revere bowls/ladels	4, 7, 10, 12, 15 in.	2 per table
Butter dishes		2 per table
Sugar bowls	7 oz.	4 per table
Creamers	7 oz.	3 per table
Oil and vinegar cruet sets		1 per 5 tables
Ash trays	$4\frac{1}{2}$ in. square	4 per table
Salt and pepper shakers	—	4 per table
Celery dishes	—	3 per table
Ice bowls	—	3 per table
Carafes	—	3 per table
Bud vases	—	1 per table
Water pitchers with ice guard	54 oz.	1 per 2 tables
Coffee pots	54 oz.	1 per table
Teapots	11 oz.	2 per table
Punch bowls/ladles	5 gal.	1 per function room
Electric fountains with colored lights	5 gal.	1 per function room
Chafing dishes (frame, water pan, food insert, cover, fuel holder)[1]		1 per buffet item

[1]Most caterers use the two-gallon capacity for large buffets and order extra inserts for backup demand.

(Continued on next page)

Table 17-4 (Cont'd)

Rectangular	1 gal. (1, 2, or 3 compart- ments) 2 gal.	
Round	2 qt. 3 qt. 4 qt. 6 qt. 7 qt. 8 qt.	
Square	2 qt. 3 qt.	
Oval	6 qt.	
Serving spoons/forks		2 per chafing dish
Candelabras		
Single	—	2 per table
Three-light .	—	1 pair per function room
Five-light	—	1 pair per function room
Samovar		1 per function room
Silver coffee urn	100-cup	1 per function room
Cake or pastry stand		1 per table
Petits four stand		1 per table
Candy/bonbon dishes		1 per table
Nut dishes		1 per table
Mint dishes		1 per table
Cigarette urns		1 per table
Waiter tray stands		1 per 2 tables
Waiter trays		1 per table
Cocktail trays		1 per table
Crumbers		1 per table
Table number stands		2 per table
Plastic table numbers		2 per table
Cake knife and server		1 per function room
Carving board		1 per function room
Carving sets (knives and forks)		1 per function room
Wooden salad bowl/ spoon/fork		1 per table
Bar equipment (cocktail shakers, mixing glasses, strainers, mixing spoons, etc.)		1 per bartender

Table 17-5. Paper and Plastic Goods Commonly Used as Service Equipment

Item	Packaged per box	Use
Doilies[1]		
4 in.	1,000	Underliners for hors d'oeuvres and food
5 in.	1,000	
6 in.	1,000	
10 in.	500	
12 in.	500	
14 in.	250	
16 in.	100	
Cocktail napkins	250 (per bundle)	Bar and hors d'oeuvres
Toothpick frills	1,000	Bar and hors d'oeuvres
Stirrers	1,000	Bar

[1]Doilies also come in silver and gold for special occasions.

Serving Pieces and Accessories

The quality and amount of serving pieces and accessories will help the caterer to upgrade his food and beverage presentation. The more successful caterers attach a great deal of importance to "show" pieces to enhance their image. Usually a variety of sizes, shapes, and forms of quality serving equipment is used to create positive customer comment, which in turn helps sell functions. The term "hollowware" sometimes is used to describe any item other than flatware that is used to carry or transport food and beverages to a customer, for example, tea and coffee pourers, water pitchers, serving platters, vegetable dishes, etc. See Table 17-4 for the serving pieces and accessories considered essential for any catering operation.

Miscellaneous

To complete your serviceware, some plastic and paper goods will be needed (see Table 17-5). It is just as essential to keep adequate amounts of these items in stock, and, since they are relatively inexpensive compared to other serviceware, large inventories are recommended.

Chapter 18

Banquet Room Furniture

Banquet room furniture is the "lumber" needed to set up a function room such as tables, chairs, platforms, bars, speaker's rostrums, dance floors, room dividers (also the means to move the equipment such as hand trucks and dollies). Since you will want to keep this equipment in good condition to make an impression on customers, the following points should be considered when purchasing furniture and the like.

1. Durability. Most banquet room furniture takes a great deal of abuse, since most functions require different physical setups, and furniture that is moved around constantly will deteriorate quickly unless it is properly constructed.

2. Price. Does the price compare to the quality of the item? Is it more feasible to buy new, used, or to construct it yourself? Many items can be easily and economically bought used or constructed, such as platforms or tables. To make in-house construction easier, a lumber yard can precut materials according to your specifications, and you can buy the hardware needed. With the addition of indoor–outdoor carpeting, platforms can be covered inexpensively and attractively.

3. Beauty and comfort. Does the item enhance the overall appearance and add to the atmosphere of the function room? Does the item give maximum comfort to the guest?

4. Easy to maintain. Is the item easy to repair and are service and parts readily available?

5. Easy to transport and set up. Can the item be moved quickly and easily to reduce labor costs and increase productivity through faster turnover?

6. Easy to store. Can the item be placed, folded, or stacked into the smallest amount of space?

7. Multi-purpose items. Can it be used in many different situations?

Estimating Seating Capacity

How much furniture will you need? This depends on the number and sizes of your function rooms, how many rooms you will use simultaneously, and the shape of the table you select. But just to illustrate how to estimate for one room, let's assume we need to know the seating capacity of a function room 40 by 60 feet. The following formula can be used:

$$\text{Seating capacity of room} = \frac{\text{Area of room (length} \times \text{width)}}{\text{Square footage per person}^1}$$

$$= \frac{2,400 \ (40 \times 60)}{12}$$

$$= 200$$

$$\text{Total number of tables} = \frac{\text{Seating capacity of room}}{\text{No. of guests per table}}$$

$$= \frac{200}{10}$$

$$= 20$$

Keep in mind that, to accurately determine the maximum number of guests, any area not used for seating, such as a dance floor, bandstand, buffet table, pillars, posts, etc., must be deducted from the total area before being divided by the square footage per person.

Tables

Banquet tables should be sturdy, lightweight, easy to handle, and mobile. Most banquet tables are made from plywood and some manufacturers provide built-in padding or a silencer cloth made from vinyl-covered foam, which affords quieter service and eliminates the cost of laundering silencer cloths. Caterers should consider purchasing plastic laminated tops for their tables to reduce laundering costs, especially when tables are being used for seminars, business meetings, or conferences. When purchasing tables, make certain that the legs are positioned far enough beneath the table to prevent the guest from bumping his knees into the legs. Wishbone legs (Fig. 18-1) are the best type of banquet table leg to order because they require the least amount of space and give the guest the greatest amount of freedom.

It is also advisable to check that the locking devices on any collapsible leg are easy to work and secure enough to brace the legs securely when set. Since tables are rolled and abused through transportation, metal

[1]As a general rule, use the following per-person square footage for the various sized tables: *round* (60 inches), 12 square feet; *rectangular* (96 × 30 inches), 10 square feet; and *oval* (72 × 36 inches), 8 square feet.

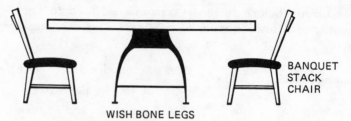

WISH BONE LEGS

BANQUET
STACK
CHAIR

Fig. 18-1. Table with wishbone legs.

edging or molding should be used to cover the rim or edges of the table to prevent chipping or splintering.

There is an unlimited variety of table shapes one can purchase. Some of these are described below.

Round Tables

The round table has long been the most popular type of banquet table used by caterers because it allows guests to converse with all other guests seated at the table without difficulty. It is also the most practical because it can be moved quickly and easily. Round tables come in the following sizes: 36, 42, 48, 54, 60, 66, 72, and 84 inches in diameter. To allow for adequate aisle space, place approximately 5 feet between the tables (1½ feet for chairs that are back to back and 2 feet for a service aisle). To get maximum seating, it would be advisable to stagger rows of round tables as shown in Fig. 18-2.

Half-round tables are best suited to rounding off rectangular or square tables. They can be either 60 or 72 inches in diameter. Figure 18-3 shows some uses of the half-round table.

Quarter-round tables help give a rounded edge to the corners formed by joining two or more rectangular tables (see Fig. 18-4). Quarter-round tables usually measure 30 × 30 inches (sides that form the right angle).

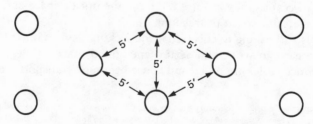

Fig. 18-2. The best placement for round tables in the function room.

Oval Tables

Most caterers prefer to use oval tables rather than round, since, even though they cannot be rolled as easily as round tables, they still promote

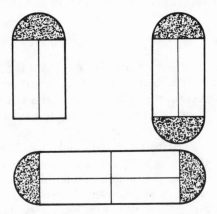

Fig. 18-3. Some uses of the half-round table.

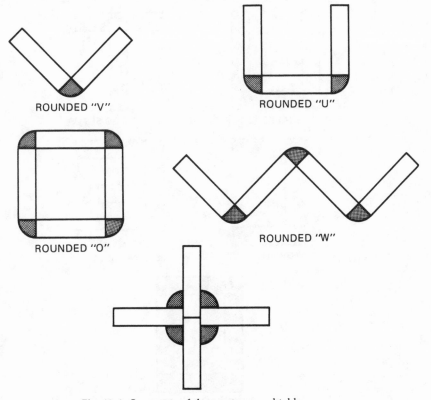

ROUNDED "V"

ROUNDED "U"

ROUNDED "O"

ROUNDED "W"

Fig. 18-4. Some uses of the quarter-round table.

conversation and have the added advantage of creating a larger seating capacity. Oval tables can be placed in such areas as around the dance floor more easily than round tables can. Oval tables most commonly come 72 × 36, 72 × 48, 84 × 48, and 96 × 48 inches.

Rectangular Tables

Rectangular tables have a multitude of uses especially in conjunction with other types of tables. Caterers seldom use rectangular tables for sit-down functions because they do not have the esthetic appearance of round or oval tables, nor are they conducive to conversation among the guests. The sizes most commonly used are 48 × 30 inches (4 feet); 60 × 30 inches (5 feet); 72 × 30 inches (6 feet); and 96 × 30 inches (8 feet). Although caterers prefer to use 30-inch widths, these tables can also be purchased 36 inches wide. Rectangular tables also come 15 or 18 inches wide for classroom style table arrangements used for meetings requiring writing. Some configurations that can be achieved using rectangular tables are shown in Fig. 18-5.

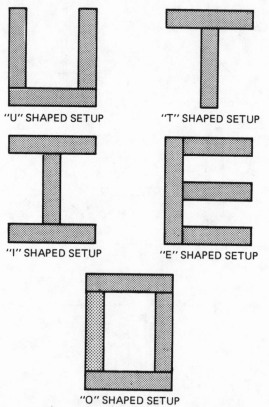

"U" SHAPED SETUP   "T" SHAPED SETUP

"I" SHAPED SETUP   "E" SHAPED SETUP

"O" SHAPED SETUP

Fig. 18-5. Some configurations using rectangular tables.

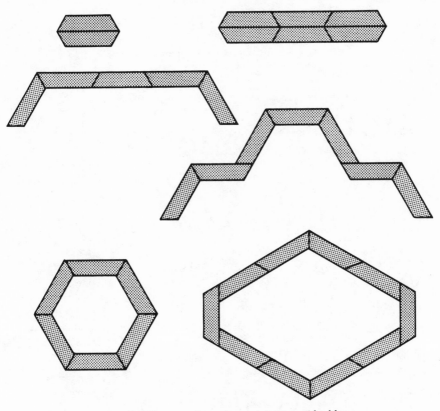

Fig. 18-6. Some configurations using trapezoid tables.

Trapezoid Tables

Trapezoid tables are relatively new and offer fresh and interesting patterns (Fig. 18-6). These tables usually measure 60 × 30 inches.

Serpentine (Crescent) Tables

Serpentine or half "S" tables are perhaps the most versatile of all folding tables. An unlimited number of combinations can be created by using these tables alone or with other types of folding tables. See Fig. 18-7 for some examples. Serpentine tables usually measure 60 and 30 inches on the curves and 30 inches wide.

Chairs

Banquet chairs should also be sturdy and lightweight and should be stackable for ease in handling and transportation. Chairs are usually stacked in units of ten (the number usually needed for one table) at a

Fig. 18-7. Some configurations using serpentine tables.

height of approximately 6 feet. Rubber or plastic nipples should be fixed onto the legs to prevent scratching and damage to the fabric on the seat when the chairs are stacked. Padded foam rubber seats covered with durable and easy-to-clean material are the most practical for banquet use.

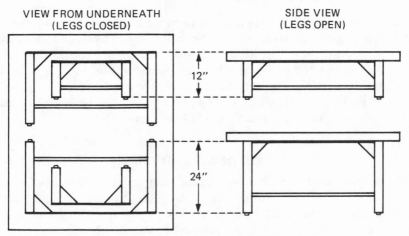

VIEW FROM UNDERNEATH
(LEGS CLOSED)

SIDE VIEW
(LEGS OPEN)

12"

24"

Fig. 18-8. One means of achieving a multi-level platform.

Stackable chairs are a must, since it takes less time to move them from room to room and they allow a room to be cleaned thoroughly between functions.

Platforms

Since platforms and risers are used to support head tables, stages, speaker's rostrums, runways, bandstands, etc., they should be constructed of sturdy materials and contain secure locking devices to withstand the additional weight and stress placed upon them. To prevent accidents, especially due to tripping, the platforms and risers should meet flush. For flexibility, multi-height platforms (to create upper and lower tiers on a dais, for example) may be constructed by simply adding dual sets of legs of different heights in any combination to each platform (see Fig. 18-8), for example, 8- and 12-inch; 12- and 24-inch; etc. Some platforms and stages have the dual advantage of being folded in half and of being mobile by way of wheels that are raised off the ground when locked into position. They also carry the advantages of being dual height and carpeted, which reduces noise and increases safety. Steps, stairs, and guard rails leading to and from elevated areas can also be purchased in a multitude of sizes for convenience and safety.

Portable Equipment

There are many portable items used as function room furniture that can change the appearance of the room and that can also be stored easily and efficiently when not in use.

1. Room dividers and screens can be utilized to divide or decorate rooms and also hide unattractive areas from public view.

2. Dance floors may be used on carpeted areas or where permanent installation may not be feasible. It should be easy to move and assemble, have a good fit and a hard finish (refer to Chapter 3 for further details).

3. Lecterns and podiums with microphone attachments can be added for such functions as meetings and fashion shows.

4. Rolling bars are usually made of stain-resistant, laminated Formica, which is attractive, practical, and easy to clean.

Miscellaneous Equipment

So that function room furniture and equipment can be moved easily and quickly and can be stored when not in use, the use of hand trucks and dollies is recommended. Hand trucks designed to transport stacks of ten chairs at one time can be purchased, and dollies can be custom ordered to transport all sizes and shapes of tables. Remember, though, that you are going to have to store this equipment as well, so before you invest in too many trucks and dollies, consider the overall space you have for storage.

By utilizing the various types and configurations of function room furniture it is possible to change or enhance the entire appearance of a banquet room and accommodate many different types of functions. Since banquet furniture and equipment is a large investment, though, be sure to make your selections carefully.

Chapter 19

Purchasing for Volume Catering

Purchasing procedures vary depending on the size of the catering operation. In small ones, purchasing is generally done by one person or a small group of key personnel, such as the owner, banquet manager, chef, and steward. In high-volume operations, as ordering becomes more complex and frequent, each department head is responsible for ordering for their own segment of the function. In still larger or chain operations, orders are submitted to a central purchasing office or agent, affording tighter control over costs.

Buying skillfully is no easy task. It takes many years of experience and knowledge. Those who handle purchasing have many responsibilities, which are listed below.

1. He must be familiar with the markets he buys from and should learn how they operate by visiting them frequently.

2. He must know how, when, and where to buy the highest quality food, beverages, supplies, equipment, and special items for the lowest possible price.

3. He must know current inventory and storage capabilities.

4. He must be able to detect when too much is being ordered, spent, or budgeted for functions.

5. He must be familiar with all menu items and their ingredients and know their purchase weights or sizes and yields.

6. He must be familiar with how food and beverages are prepared and served and the portion sizes for each type of function.

7. He must inspect all goods delivered and return any product that is not acceptable and does not meet his specifications.

8. He must have a thorough understanding of purchase orders, invoices, service charges, and accounting principles related to buying.

9. He must keep organized records for easy reference and current files, price lists, market quotations, catalogs, and trade publications on all available products.

10. He must keep abreast of new products and ideas.

249

11. He must know how to successfully deal with salesmen.

12. Above all, he must be a trusted individual with good business sense.

Ordering

Purchase orders should be made out for all orders, even though they may have been placed by phone. This is to assure that each purchase for every function is recorded. The original copy of the purchase order is sent to the purveyor and the remaining copies go to the receiving clerk, the accounting department, and the purchasing agent. An example of a purchase order is given in Fig. 19-1.

ABC Catering
120 Main Street
New City, N.Y. 10956

Date: _____

NO. _____

Name of Purveyor:_____

Address:_____

City, State, Zip_____

Copy to:

☐ Purveyor
☐ Accounting Dept.
☐ Receiving Dept.
☐ Purchasing Dept.

Quantity	Unit	Item	Unit price	Extension	Quantity received
			Subtotal	$	
			Less discount	$	
			Total	$	

List Name(s) and Date(s) of functions for above purchases

_____
_____
_____
_____
_____

Ordered by_____
Approved by _____ Date _____
Department _____ Date _____
Received by _____
Department _____ Date _____

Fig. 19-1. Example of a purchase order.

Table 19-1. Canned Goods

Size	Average net wt.	Average fluid oz.	Cups per can	Cans per case
No. 10	6½ lbs.	103.7	12–13	6
No. 5 or No. 3 cylinder	3 lbs., 3 oz.	46	5¾	12
No. 2½	1 lb., 13 oz.	26	3½	24
No. 2	1 lb., 4 oz.	18	2½	24
No. 303	16 to 17 oz.	15	2	24

Table 19-2. Canned Heat (Sterno)

I.D. No.	Can size (inches)	Ounces per can	No. per case
4006LP	2⅝ diam × 1⅞ high	2⅝	144
4008LB	3⁷⁄₁₆ diam × 2⁷⁄₁₆ high	7	72
4028	Gallon	6 lbs., 14 oz.	4

Purchasing units may vary from area to area, but it is important for a buyer to know the local area and how items are packaged and priced individually and in bulk. Pricing and packaging may be by the individual unit (each) or by the carton, case, package, bushel, bunch, block, crate, flat, sack, bag, can, basket, lug, hamper, till, pound, or other container. Knowing counts, sizes, and weights is vital in relating items to price. It is essential to know such information as how many slices of bacon come in a pound, what size and how many shrimp there are in a pound, and a multitude of other details. As an example, Table 19-1 illustrates the packaging specifications for canned goods.

In addition to food products, there are many other related items that are used for catered functions, e.g., canned heat (Sterno) used for chafing dishes. It is important to know the various sizes when ordering canned heat (see Table 19-2).

It should be noted that a savings can be realized by using the smaller can (2⅝ ounces) rather than the 7-ounce size for chafing dish items for cocktail parties, since the can is generally discarded after each function.

To reduce purchasing errors, it is advisable to make out for easy reference a complete detailed purchasing list of all standard goods.

Consistent standards or specifications should be established so that the purveyor and purchaser share an understanding of what is being ordered. If a question arises as to size or counts, weights, volume, shape, color, texture, smell, or other characteristic, several reliable producers, packers, or purveyors should be contacted to obtain the correct information. An example of a standard purchasing specification is given in Table 19-3.

Since catering offers the advantage of knowing before each function the exact number of guests or portions to be served, the amount to be ordered for each function can be closely determined. To reduce waste, buying should only be done for what is needed. One of the most common

Table 19-3. Purchasing and Packing Guide
ICEBERG LETTUCE

Grade used	Condition	Packed	Weight and count to check
U.S. No. 1	Crisp, fresh, outer leaves; pale interior; white and tender; heavy for their size. Avoid excess stem, outer wrapper leaves, rust or decay. Best season: from May to July	Case	Weight: 42–45 lbs. Count: 24 heads per case

problems is overordering, which results in a costly surplus. This is usually done by a purchaser who feels insecure and fears running short of items. It also results from careless inventory-taking or when the purchaser simply does not know how to order. By periodically monitoring purchasing practices, management can pinpoint any problems before they become too costly.

Not all food purchasing can be estimated exactly. To provide a cushion for unforseen incidents, such as unexpected guests, spillage or breakage, and unexpected production or service problems, an overage should be calculated for each function. The percent of overage can be fixed for each function, for example, 8%, or it can be placed on a sliding scale, using the maximum percentage for smaller functions and lower ones for larger functions, e.g., for 100 guests, 10% overage (10 extra orders); for 200 guests, 9% or 18 extra; 300 guests, 8% or 24 extra, etc. The cost of these extra purchases should be built into the menu price, since they constitute an additional food cost.

There are primarily two methods used to determine how much to order. One method is to determine the number of guests guaranteed for a function, add the overage percentage, and then multiply by the amount of each ingredient needed to prepare a single portion for each item on the menu. Assume the following menu was requested for a function of 400 guests:

> Baked Grapefruit au Rum
> Hearts of Lettuce, Vinaigrette Dressing
> Roast Prime Ribs of Beef au Jus
> Baked Idaho Potato, Sour Cream and Chives
> Sautéed String Beans
> Assorted French Pastries
> Coffee, Tea
> Assorted Dinner Rolls and Butter

Let's further assume that we have no inventory for this menu. Here's how we would proceed.

First, we would calculate how many portions we need:

No. of guests + overage percentage = No. of portions
400 + 7% (28 portions) = 428

On the sliding scale mentioned earlier, we would use a 7% overage for 400 guests.

Next, we would determine the portion size for each item on the menu, then multiply it by the number of portions. Finally, we would check our purchasing list to determine how the item is packaged and then order accordingly.

Here's how we would order for the above menu.

Baked Grapefruit au Rum

Portion size: One-half grapefruit with 1 ounce of sauce.

Since one grapefruit will serve two people, divide the number of portions (428) by 2 (214). Grapefruit are packed 36 to a case. Therefore:

$$214 \div 36 = 5.94 \text{ (6 cases, or 216 grapefruit)}^1$$

One quart of sauce serves 32 people, so about $13\frac{1}{2}$ quarts of sauce will be needed ($428 \div 32$). The sauce is made from equal parts honey, brown sugar, and rum with a garnish of fresh mint leaves, and since it is made by the quart, we would multiply all ingredients in the sauce recipe by $13\frac{1}{2}$. *Order:* Six cases seedless grapefruit, 8 lbs. honey, 8 lbs. brown sugar, 4 quarts rum, and 5 bunches mint leaves.

Hearts of Lettuce, Vinaigrette Dressing

Portion size: One-sixth of a head of iceberg lettuce with 2 ounces of dressing.

Since one head will serve six people, divide the number of portions by 6, which equals 71.3 (72) heads of lettuce. There are 24 heads to a crate, so:

$$72 \div 24 = 3 \text{ crates}$$

For the dressing, 2 ounces per person equals 856 ounces (428×2). Since the dressing is made by the gallon, divide 856 by 128 (ounces in a gallon) to get $6\frac{3}{4}$ gallons. Then, checking the dressing recipe, multiply all ingredients by $6\frac{3}{4}$.

---

[1]In many instances, exact ordering becomes impossible, since many purveyors will not split or break case lots due to resale difficulties.

Order: Three crates iceberg lettuce, 5 gallons salad oil, $1\frac{3}{4}$ gallons wine vinegar, 6 bunches of parsley, and 3 bunches of chives.

Roast Prime Ribs of Beef au Jus

Portion size: 16 portions from a roasted, oven-ready, boned, and tied rib weighing 18–20 pounds.

Management determines from yield testing that 16 cuts or portions can be realized from a rib. Therefore:

$$428 \div 16 = 26\frac{3}{4} \ (27) \text{ ribs}$$

Order: 27 prime ribs of beef and 20 bunches watercress as a garnish (5 bunches per 100–110 persons).

Baked Idaho Potato, Sour Cream and Chives

Portion size: One No. 1 Idaho potato with 1 ounce sour cream and a garnish of chopped chives plus 1 pat of butter.

One potato per person equals 428 potatoes. There are 90 to a box:

$$428 \div 90 = 5 \text{ cases } (450 \text{ count})$$

The sour cream is bought by the gallon or the quart. Divide 428 portions by 128 (ounces in a gallon) to get 3.3 gallons. Round off to 3 gallons and 1 quart, 12 ounces or 2 quarts.

Sour cream can also be purchased by the tub, and there are 5 pounds to a tub. In this instance, first determine how many pounds you will need by dividing the number of portions by 16 (ounces in a pound):

$$428 \div 16 = 26\frac{3}{4} \text{ lbs.}$$

Then:

$$26\frac{3}{4} \div 5 \text{ lbs.} = 5.35 \text{ tubs}$$

You will need to order six tubs, which is a lot more than you need. So buying by the gallon and quart is more economical in this case.

For the chives, you will need about 6 bunches per 100 to 110 people. For the butter, you will need 428 pats (one per person). There are 90 pats per pound. Therefore, $428 \div 90 = 4\frac{3}{4}$ (round off to 5 lbs.)

Order: Five cases No. 1 Idaho potatoes; 3 gallons, 2 quarts sour cream; 24 bunches chives; and one 5-lb. block chipped butter.

Sautéed String Beans

Portion size: Three ounces string beans plus approximately 1 ounce of butter per pound of string beans for sautéeing.

$$428 \times 3 \text{ oz.} = 1,284 \text{ oz.}$$
$$1,284 \div 16 = 80\tfrac{1}{4} \text{ lbs.}$$

If frozen string beans are ordered, the following calculation would be used. There are $2\tfrac{1}{2}$ lbs. per box of frozen beans:

$$80 \text{ lbs.} \div 2\tfrac{1}{2} \text{ lbs.} = 32 \text{ boxes}$$

There are 12 packages per case:

$$32 \div 12 = 2 \text{ cases plus 8 boxes (or 3 cases).}$$

If fresh string beans are ordered, the following calculation would be used: Need 80 lbs. of string beans plus 10 lbs. due to waste (10–12%) for a total of 90 lbs. There are 30 lb. to a bushel: $90 \div 30 = 3$ bushels.

Butter for sautéeing: Approximately 1 oz. of butter is needed to sautée 1 lbs. of string beans, so 80 oz. of butter will be needed: $80 \div 16 = 5$ lbs.

Order: Three cases of frozen or 3 bushels of fresh string beans and 5 lbs. of butter.

Assorted French Pastries

Portion size: One pastry per person.
You need 428 pastries, which are sold by the dozen:

$$428 \div 12 = 35.7 \text{ dozen (round off to 36 dozen)}$$

Order: 36 dozen assorted French pastry.

Coffee and Tea

Portion size: $1\tfrac{1}{2}$ cups coffee, 1 cup tea, $\tfrac{1}{2}$ ounce cream, one wedge of lemon, 2 packets of sugar.

It is estimated from past affairs that approximately 85% of the guests will want coffee, 10% tea, and 5% decaffeinated coffee.

For coffee: 85% of total $428 = 364 \times 1\tfrac{1}{2} = 546$ cups. There are 50 cups to be made from a pound: $546 \div 50 = 10.9$ lbs. (round off to 11 lbs.)

For tea: 10% of total $428 = 43$ tea bags. $43 \div 12$ (per dozen) $= 3.6$ dozen (round off to 4 dozen tea bags).

For decaffeinated coffee: 5% of total $428 = 21$ packets. $21 \div 12 = 1\tfrac{3}{4}$ dozen (round off to 2 dozen packets).

For cream: $428 \times \tfrac{1}{2}$ oz. $= 214$ ozs. $\div 32$ ozs. (per quart) $= 6.7$ qts. (round off to 7 qts.).

For lemon: approximately 43 wedges are needed for the number of cups of tea anticipated. So, $43 \div 6$ (wedges per lemon) $= 7$ lemons (42 wedges)

For sugar: $428 \times 2 = 856$ packets (round off to 1 case, 1,000 packets).

Item: __VEGETABLE SOUP__

Portion size: _6 ounces_

Ingredients	Number of portions		
	25	50	100
1. Beef bones	5 lbs.	10 lbs.	20 lbs.
2. Water	1½ gal.	3 gal.	6 gal.
3. Chopped celery	1/2 lb.	1 lb.	2 lbs.
4. Chopped onions	1 lb.	2 lbs.	4 lbs.
5. Chopped carrots	3/4 lb.	1½ lbs.	3 lbs.
6. Diced potatoes	3/4 lb.	1½ lbs.	3 lbs.
7. Chopped fresh tomatoes	2½ lbs.	5 lbs.	10 lbs.
8. Cooked peas	1/2 lb.	1 lb.	2 lbs.
9. Cooked string beans	1/2 lb.	1 lb.	2 lbs.
10. Salt	1 oz.	2 ozs.	4 ozs.
11. Pepper	1/2 teas.	1 teas.	2 teas.
12. Chopped parsley	1/4 oz.	1/2 oz.	1 oz.

Recipe: Cook stock (beef bones and water) for approximately
4 hours on low heat. Add celery, onions, carrots, potatoes and
cook 1½ hours. Add fresh tomatoes. Cook additional 1/2 hour and
then add cooked peas and string beans for another 1/2 hour.
Season to taste. Add parsley before serving.

Fig. 19-2. Example of a standard purchasing guide and recipe.

Order: 11 lbs. coffee, 4 dozen tea bags, 2 dozen decaffeinated coffee
packets, 7 quarts cream, 7 lemons, and 1 case sugar packets.

Assorted Dinner Rolls and Butter

Portion size: Two rolls and two pats of butter.

428 × 2   = 856 portions
856 ÷ 12 (per dozen) = 71.3 dozen (round off to 72 dozen)

For the butter, you will need 856 pats (two per person), which is double what was needed for the baked potatoes (10 lbs.).

Order: 72 dozen assorted dinner rolls and two 5-lb. blocks of chipped butter.

Seasonings for Meat and Vegetables

Order: 1 lb. salt and $\frac{1}{2}$ lb. pepper (as determined from recipes).

Another method used to accurately determine how much to order is to establish predetermined purchasing guides for standard recipes yielding 25, 50, and 100 portions. The actual amounts ordered can be increased or decreased according to the number of portions needed. An example of a standard recipe and purchasing guide is given in Fig. 19-2.

Receiving

It is very important that the receiving clerk set aside a certain time of day to receive deliveries. He should closely compare all incoming goods with the purchase orders and invoices as to the quantity, weight, measure, quality, and price of each item as ordered. This will insure that the purveyor has delivered and charged for the merchandise ordered. If this procedure is not thoroughly followed, purveyors may take advantage of the operation. For example, if scales are not present at the receiving site, the receiving clerk may be short-changed on merchandise bought by weight and not know it. If the quality or quantity is not checked, inferior low-grade products and short counts may be accepted. If anything is wrong with the order, the receiving clerk or purchasing agent must bring the matter to the immediate attention of the purveyor. The goods should be returned as soon as possible. Receiving clerks should be instructed to only accept orders that concur with purchase orders and specifications. All other orders should be refused.

If goods are returned, it should be recorded and copies should go to the purveyor, accounting department, the receiving clerk, and the purchasing agent. When goods are accepted, then the invoices should be forwarded to the accounting department so the cost of merchandise used for each function can be calculated.

SECTION V

Options

Sooner or later, every caterer considers broadening the scope of his operation and looks for ways to make his business more profitable. This section explores the options available to the caterer who wants to expand his operation to attract a larger clientele. The choices include off-premise catering, kosher catering, and offering related services, such as music and photography, to his customers.

Chapter 20

Off-Premise Catering

Off-premise catering refers to any function that is serviced by a caterer outside his establishment or commissary. The food is partially or fully prepared at the caterer's full-time location and then transported, finished if necessary, and served at the designated location. In addition to food and beverages, all the necessary equipment and labor must be transported. A client's off-premise request may range from the delivery of a simple hor d'oeurves platter to perhaps the execution of a full-scale function requiring a tent, dance floor, decorations, music, and food and beverages served on silver service by a full staff.

Many successful on-premise caterers have histories of starting out as off-premise operations primarily due to limited capital. Many started from their homes[1] or commissaries, renting equipment as it was needed. Some caterers, to reduce their cash outlay, required large advance deposits from their clients. By arranging, preparing, and serving these functions by themselves or with a minimum of labor, they managed to keep expenses low. Many of these caterers, through hard work and talent, managed to serve attractive food and beverages at reasonable prices and thus developed a solid business with repeat clientele. As volume increased, additional personnel, most often part-time employees, were hired to work and supervise functions especially in instances when several affairs were being held simultaneously at various locations. After accumulating sufficient capital, many started to buy or lease their own on-premise operations, often continuing with their off-premise catering.

Caterers have varying views about contracting off-premise work. Some welcome it for the additional revenue, especially during slower periods, and for the opportunity to more fully utilize staff and equipment for both types of catering. Others avoid it, pointing out that it interferes with the effectiveness of the on-premise operation in that, especially during busy periods, staff and equipment may be spread too thin. Caterers who wish to discourage clients from holding their functions off premise usually point out the following advantages of holding it on premise.

---

[1] In certain states, depending on current board of health regulations, it may be illegal to prepare food in the home.

1. It's less expensive. There are no transportation costs involved.

2. It eliminates the wear and tear and possible damage to the client's facilities.

3. It utilizes the built-in features of the catering operation, such as dance floors, dressing rooms, air-conditioning, etc.

Of course, caterers wishing to encourage off-premise catering will point out the advantages of having a more personal or unique affair at the client's home or location. If off-premise work is offered, brochures, menus, handouts, and other forms of advertising should be used to promote and develop this facet of the business.

Equipment

Some off-premise caterers rent their equipment to avoid purchasing, storing, and transporting it to the client's location. When renting equipment, it is advisable to do comparative shopping and to reserve equipment well in advance of the function date, particularly in areas and seasons of high demand. Of course, to reduce high rental fees, off-premise caterers should consider buying those items that are used most often, such as dishes, silverware, glassware, and chafing dishes, and renting those items that are seldom requested or that require high transportation costs. Also, if an inventory of cooking and service equipment can be built, the caterer can become the renter. Equipment rental can become an additional source of revenue, when properly checked and supervised. At today's rental prices, the caterer can realize a return on his investment quickly.

When a caterer decides to rent out his own equipment, he should check the prices of several local rental firms and, to induce business, charge slightly less. Just as the caterer is held responsible to the rental firm for any loss or breakage of rented equipment, clients should be held financially responsible to the caterer for damage or loss. This is best stated in the conditions of contract. An entry should be placed on the final bill for any breakage that might occur. Of course, where minimal breakage occurs, it may be overlooked by a caterer especially for functions from which high revenues were obtained. As a tax benefit, it may be advisable to consider establishing a separate equipment rental business to handle this aspect of his operation.

Off-premise caterers should transport their equipment in marked, covered wooden or plastic boxes, containers, or racks for protective purposes. Equipment should be sanitized, separated, and packed tightly to avoid breakage in shipment. Each item sent should be clearly marked so that it can be readily identified and inventoried quickly before leaving and returning to the establishment. This systematic checking is vital to maintain proper inventory control and to record both broken and misplaced items. Needless to say, it will not take long for the inventory to become depleted if at each function a certain number of items is lost, broken, or stolen, the major problems when dealing with the transportation of equipment. To best prevent and control losses, a responsible person should be assigned to count, pack, and record each shipped item on an equipment list and to check that each item is returned.

To cover all situations, it is advisable to pack additional items, for example, a 10% overage, for emergency situations that may arise such as breakage during transportation, handling, or service or perhaps last-minute guests. Caterers should consider packing additional commonly used equipment such as worktables, card or gift tables, chairs, linens, canned heat, coat racks, hangers, folding screens, and sanitation items. A "catering bag" should be brought to each function containing small nuisance items that are commonly forgotten such as thumb tacks, straight pins, cello tape, masking tape, string, cord, bow ties, corkscrews, bottle openers, knives, staple gun, extension cords, tools, nails, screws, etc. Having these items handy often helps solve problem situations and saves a great deal of valuable time.

More often than not, tents, gazebos, canopies, or overhangs will be requested as protective coverings. You will want to rent this equipment, since it is hard to store, and should reserve it early. Make certain that the tent is large enough (see Table 20-1) to cover the entire function area including the tables, dance floors, etc., for protection against inclement weather. Flaps to cover the exposed area around the tent should be requested for the protection of the guests. Tents, linens, flowers, candles, and decorations should be color coordinated for overall effect.

Level ground is a prime requirement for best results for placing tents, dance floors, and other equipment, such as platforms for head tables, the band, and food displays. Air conditioners, heating units, sound systems, carpeting to cover grass, and special lighting are also available for tents. To avoid last-minute confusion, request that your tent or equipment supplier deliver and set up his tent and equipment as early as possible, preferably a day in advance. This will give you sufficient time to lay out the tables and chairs and check the equipment for shortages well in advance of the arrival of the service personnel.

Food Preparation

Keep food preparation out of sight by using folding screens to hide the kitchen areas. Usually the best food-preparation area for outside functions is a garage or an area where water and electrical outlets are available.

Because of the handicaps involved in many off-premise locations, for example, inadequate heating or oven space, refrigeration space, and

Table 20-1. Tent Sizes and Capacities

Size	Seating capacity	Center poles
14 × 14	25	1
16 × 16	30	1
12 × 25	35	2
20 × 20	40	1
20 × 25	50	2
20 × 30	60	2
20 × 40	80	3
30 × 30	90	1
30 × 45	135	2
30 × 60	180	3
30 × 75	225	4
32 × 32	90	1
32 × 48	150	2
32 × 64	200	3
40 × 40	160	1
40 × 60	240	2
40 × 80	320	3
40 × 100	400	4
50 × 50	250	1
50 × 75	375	2
50 × 100	500	3
50 × 125	625	4
50 × 150	750	5

storage facilities, it is important to keep menus simple for easy preparation, transportation, and service. In most instances, the food is usually prepared at the establishment or commissary, transported by truck, and then held or, if needed, finished, reheated, or cooled at the job location by use of portable (propane or canned heat) stoves, warming or refrigerated cabinets, or insulated holding units before service. Wherever the affair is held, food must be served at the proper temperature. It may be feasible for a high-volume caterer to design or customize a delivery truck or trailer with heavy duty shocks containing commercial kitchen equipment, such as propane stoves with vents, refrigerators operated through generators, worktables, etc., to act as a self-contained food-preparation unit. This will also prevent any damage being done to the client's equipment or facility by careless employees or by use of heavy-duty commercial equipment.

Taking along additional food should be considered to prevent shortages, especially when buffets are served and the food consumption may be difficult to figure. This supply of additional food should be brought to the attention of the host so that no misunderstanding arises as to its ownership and also to point out to your client your concern that a sufficient amount of food is being provided for his guests. Caterers should be wary of taking any food that has been purchased by the host back to their establishment after the job is completed. It creates bad feelings on the part of the client, who feels he has legitimately purchased it. Caterers will find that offering any leftover food to the client will create good will. Besides, such food is of little use to the caterer, since it cannot be suitably reused for other functions because delayed use or temperature changes may possibly create health hazards.

Emergencies or shortages cannot always be predicted so petty cash (approximately $50.00) should be available at each job in the event you may have to send a runner for items that have been forgotten or you're short of. To do a complete and professional job, cleaning up after the function has been completed is extremely important. The client should never have the chore of clearing the caterer's debris. Removing all garbage and cleaning the host's facility as thoroughly as possible will show the host that you care about his property. The facility should be left as clean as when you arrived on the job. This practice often leads to repeat or referred business. For maximum impact, even consider mowing a client's lawn after a lawn party if feasible.

Estimating the Cost

Because off-premise affairs vary in size and scope, it is often necessary to take more time to estimate the cost of each function than for on-premise affairs. Caterers should not be hasty in giving estimates, but rather should wait until all costs have been properly analyzed. Keep in mind that off-premise caterers must transport their goods and equipment to the client's destination. This involves considerable additional costs. Some clients may find it difficult to understand why it is more expensive to have a function at their home or place of business, ignoring the fact that the caterer must move his operation, i.e., food, equipment, and service personnel, to the client's location.

The preliminary details may either be discussed at the client's location or at the caterer's operation. However, at least one visit to the client's location is essential to examine the facility for adequate space, bathroom and dishwashing facilities, electrical and gas hookups, heating, refrigeration, and water supply. After inspecting the premise, the menu and other details concerning the arrangement can be planned and estimated.

Off-premise caterers should print menus and brochures offering a client a variety of food, beverages, equipment, and service. A "helpful-hint" type of booklet to tell a client what he should have available to best facilitate his function will assist the host as well as serve as an advertising aid.

Since each affair will differ in its requirements, giving estimates and final bills requires an off-premise caterer to analyze each affair separately.

Table 20-2. Breakdown of Costs

Item	Per-person cost	× No. of guests	= Total cost
Food	$10.00	× 200	= $2,000.00
Beverage	5.00	× 200	= 1,000.00
Total food and beverage	15.00	× 200	= 3,000.00
Tax (5%)	.75	× 200	= 150.00
Labor	10.00	× 200	= 2,000.00
Equipment	10.00	× 200	= 2,000.00
Additional/outside costs	2.50		500.00
Total cost	$38.25		$7,650.00

Some caterers prefer to quote a per-person charge, combining all the various items and costs requested into one lump sum per guest, while others prefer an individual breakdown of the entire function into various categories. The former method will, of course, require less time but often is not as accurate as the latter method. The final determination should be made by the caterer by observing which most of his clients prefer. Most important, all costs should be considered when quoting prices. Keep in mind that many hidden or less obvious costs may be part of a function such as employee meals, secretaries, lawyers, accountants, bookkeepers, etc., which can be easily overlooked, since they are not visably present at a function. Table 20-2 shows a sample breakdown of the key items on an estimate.

Caterers estimate and bill customers in different manners. Some charge an additional fee for their labor to cover extra costs such as payroll taxes, benefits, etc., then add a profit to their labor costs. Kitchen and maintenance labor can be itemized and charged for separately, e.g., chef, $100.00; cook, $60.00; dishwasher, $35.00. Overhead and transportation costs can be itemized separately on a bill but are generally figured into the food, beverage, and equipment charges. Therefore, when costing each component of a function, determine the selling price with the profit margin built in as for on-premise catering, then add in all additional costs to be incurred by moving the function to an off-premise location.

Planning the Function

In addition to the usual planning that goes into the execution of a function, there are other details to attend to relative to each off-premise location you have to work with. For example, for each location, you have to consider how traffic is going to be directed to avoid congestion or blocked driveways, and whether you will have to keep your vehicles to a minimum because of limited space.

Your standard setting-up practices will have to be adjusted according to the requirements or limitations of the location. Also, there might be extra duties not usually performed at your establishment that will have to be distributed among the staff. It is advisable to draw up the duties for all personnel and distribute them so that each knows what he is responsible for. Finally, to avoid confusion, draw up a schedule for the function listing the times each segment of the function will be executed. This is also important at locations where, due to space limitations, advance preparation or setting up is not possible and employees have to be informed when certain things can be done.

Chapter 21

Kosher and Kosher-Style Catering

Should your operation become kosher or kosher-style? What steps, procedures, and basic rules should you follow to operate a kosher establishment properly? These are the questions to be considered in this chapter.

An operation should consider becoming kosher when the amount of inquiries and potential sales warrant such a move, for example, when there is a marked demand from a large Jewish population or when few kosher facilities exist in your area and competition is thus at a minimum. Jewish patrons will seek either a strictly kosher (*glatt kosher*) or a kosher-style (nonkosher) affair depending on their interpretation and observance of religious and dietary laws and beliefs. Strict observers of the Orthodox or Conservative branches of the Jewish faith will require their affairs to be conducted in a glatt kosher manner. Reform Jews may believe that modern sanitary measures make rigid adherence to the dietary laws less significant and may thus feel at home with a kosher-style affair not governed by any requirements or regulations. Under no circumstances may a nonkosher operation advertise itself as being kosher or conduct its affairs as if it were kosher. To mislead the public in this way is a violation of the law and runs the risk of a fine or other serious penalty.

If an operation decides to offer kosher service, it should first consult a rabbi to discuss the procedures that must be followed to meet the rigid requirements of the kosher food business. Only operators with a thorough knowledge of kosher laws will be acceptable to both the rabbi and the Jewish community to be served. After approval from a rabbi has been granted, the operator must hire a *mashgiach,* an inspector who has been trained to supervise the preparation of all food and beverages served at kosher functions. The mashgiach, who can be a rabbi or a religiously responsible person appointed by a rabbi, is usually a salaried employee of the caterer. He is hired for the sole purpose of making sure that all foods offered as kosher conform to the dietary laws of the Torah (segment of the Old Testament) as dictated by God in biblical times, and also to those laws initiated by rabbis for sanitary reasons and handed down through the centuries to protect the health and hygiene of the Jewish people. Observance of these dietary laws (*kashruth*) guarantees that all foods are kosher; that is, proper and fit to be eaten. The mashgiach is responsible for the entire food-handling operation including the supervision of all kitchen personnel. Should any product, food, utensil, or procedure not be handled according to the dietary rules, the mashgiach must intervene at once to correct the infraction. A violation of the kashruth would result in the product being discarded, and the utensils used in making the product would need to be cleansed before reuse.

The word used to describe any forbidden food or procedure is *trephah*. This term also refers to any animal that has been imperfectly slaughtered. Such animals cannot be sold for use as kosher meat, but, after further inspection and approval, may be sold on the open, non-kosher market. In certain localities, additional supervision by kosher inspectors is mandated as a double-check on catering operations. These inspectors are similar in function to municipal health inspectors, having the authority to issue a violation notice if unacceptable foods, products, or procedures are used on an inspected premise. If the violation is not corrected, the establishment will lose its kosher privileges.

The intricacy of kashruth regulations makes reputable kashruth supervision mandatory, but the caterer, too, should make himself familiar with the working rules of a kosher operation. The following are some of the major dietary laws.

1. All meats must be purchased from authorized kosher butchers or purveyors. Only animals that chew their cud and have split hooves are acceptable for consumption. Since pigs do not chew their cud, all pork products are forbidden. Any animal that dies a natural death, has not been properly slaughtered, or has been mutilated by wild animals is considered impure and thus cannot be eaten. To be kosher, all meat must be slaughtered under strict rabinnical supervision. This involves the skills of a *shocket*, a butcher or trained man authorized by the kashruth (*rabbinical supervisory*) division. The shocket must slaughter the animal with a sharp razor applied to the jugular vein to cause a quick and painless death. The animal is then cut open and inspected internally for any disease, lesion, or other imperfection with particularly close examination given to the lung area. If for any reason the shocket finds the animal imperfect, he will declare it to be *trephah* or forbidden. If, on the other hand, the animal passes the inspection, it is labeled with stamps and tags indicating that it has been approved and giving the date of slaughter. Since the rigid inspection process of the kosher meat and poultry calls for a second set of inspectors, known as *bodkim*, and supervisors, known as *mashgiachim*, kosher meat and poultry products are more expensive than nonkosher ones.

2. All blood must be removed from meat and fowl before cooking. Only the forequarters of animals such as cattle, deer, goats, and sheep are

used for kosher meat because the veins in the hindquarters are so intimately conjoined with nerves, sinews, and fatty tissue that a great amount of costly skill and time is required to excise them. For this reason, hindquarters are usually sold on the nonkosher market where they will return a higher profit. Even the hearts and lungs of animals must be cut open and all veins removed.

3. To be kosher, fowl must be of a domestic breed such as chicken, capon, turkey, duck, goose or cornish hen that has been raised, slaughtered, and inspected under kashruth supervision. The head of the fowl is cut to drain the blood, and the vein that runs along the neck between the tendons is removed. The tops of the wings and the talons must also be cut off. A metal identification tag, called a *plumba*, is attached to a wing to assure the purchaser of the kosher origins of the bird. A fowl without a plumba should never be used by a kosher caterer. Wild birds, birds of prey, and scavengers are forbidden for use as kosher foods.

4. All meat and fowl must be soaked and salted (*kashered*) after slaughter and before being cooked to ensure that all blood has been removed. Soaking must take place in vessels solely reserved for this purpose under running cold tap water for one-half hour. The meat or fowl is then rinsed and placed on a tilted drainboard, usually made of wood or plastic, to allow the remaining blood to run freely. It is then rubbed with a coarse salt, called *kosher salt*, so that all parts of the damp surface are covered. Fowl must also be rubbed inside its cavity. Thereafter, the meat or fowl must be placed on the drainboard for one hour and then rewashed for use.

Considerable care must be exercised during koshering. Should the product accidentally fall back into the soaking water, or come into contact with blood, it would automatically become trephah. Should any uncertainty arise, a competent rabbinical authority should be consulted immediately.

Broiling can be used in place of salting for the koshering process. For example, liver is first cut and then broiled so that its blood can run freely. After being broiled, it must be washed before further handling. Care must be exercised during broiling so that drippings of blood do not splatter back onto the liver, since it would then become trephah.

5. The use of both meat (*fleishig*) and milk (*milchig*) products at the same meal is forbidden. A distinct interval must be observed before dairy products can be consumed after meat has been eaten. Kosher operations offering both products must keep them completely separated so that they do not come into contact with each other, even in refrigerators or freezers. Separate sets of dishes, silverware, kitchen utensils, crockery, containers, and cooking equipment must be maintained for each. Different patterns of silverware, china, platters, etc. should be used so that any employee can easily identify the difference between the meat and dairy equipment to be used. This equipment should be marked in some readily identifiable

way in different areas so that the two sets cannot be carelessly inter-changed. The cooking process requires extreme precautions to prevent contact between the two products. For example, if cooking pots are placed too close to one another on top of the stove or both meat and dairy dishes are placed in the same oven, the danger of mixing exists. All precautions should be exercised to the extent of using separate cleaning or cooking towels or cloths, dishwashers, dishracks, sinks, or wash pans. Only kosher soaps, detergents, and scouring pads may be used, and any clean-ing agent containing animal fat is strictly forbidden.

Most kosher catering menus offer meat as their main item or entrée. Dairy foods must be scrupulously avoided with such meals. Cream sauces may not accompany meat dishes, nor may butter be served, nor milk nor cream be offered for coffee or dessert. Any chocolate used must be free from milk products if served at the same meal with meat.

Many nondairy products on the market can be used as substitutes for milk or milk products, provided they carry the proper certification. These items are called *pareve,* a term denoting that they contain no milk or meat products and that they can be used either independently or com-bined with meat or dairy products without restriction. Such products are made solely from vegetable or chemical components that are free of meat or dairy properties. If the word *pareve* appears on the label of a product, the label should also carry the proper kashruth endorsement. All fruits, vegetables, cereals, and eggs are considered pareve. Although eggs can be used with milk or meat dishes, there are certain exceptions to the rule. For example, eggs found in slaughtered fowl cannot be eaten with milk or meat products; an egg found to contain a blood spot must be discarded because kosher foods must be free of blood.

6. To be kosher, fish must possess both fins and scales and does not require any special koshering ritual, since it is permissible to eat blood from fish. To be assured the fish purchased is kosher, obtain it from a kosher fish purveyor to eliminate the possibility of its having become trephah through contact with nonkosher fish. Only fish with scales that can be scraped off easily without mutilating or removing the skin or flesh are kosher, for example, herring, halibut, bluefish, salmon, whitefish, and tuna. Fish with scales that cannot be removed without damaging the skin are nonkosher, for example, eels, sharks, catfish, and puffers. All mam-mals, such as dolphins or whales, are nonkosher. To be kosher, caviar must come from a kosher fish, for example, salmon. All crustaceans (shellfish), such as lobsters, shrimp, mussels, clams, oysters, crabs, and scallops are nonkosher.

7. Only cheeses that are properly certified and labeled as kosher may be consumed.

8. The basic rule for alcohol is that wine or wine products such as champagne, vermouth, cordials, and fruit liqueurs that are made from a grape base must be prepared under kasruth supervision and certification.

Grape brandy may be produced only from kosher wine. Kosher wine must be made under the direct supervision of a mashgiach from the grape in the vineyard through all processes of distillation and pasteurization until the final product is bottled and labeled with the proper identification, endorsement, and signatures. Liquor distilled from grain and cereals is kosher except during special religious holidays, such as Passover, when it is strictly forbidden. These liquors do not require rabbinical supervision.

9. No foods may be cooked or even heated on the sabbath (*shabbat*), which commences at dusk on Friday and ends after sundown on Saturday, at which time a mashgiach must be present before any heating can begin. Cold foods may be laid out and decorated, however, provided no cooking is involved in the preparation.

10. All manufacturers who sell kosher products to kosher caterers must carry the necessary kosher certification or symbols to indicate their products are free from nonkosher ingredients and have been supervised and certified by a recognized rabbinate. The most stringent and reliable endorsement of a kosher product is the one given by an organization called the Union of Orthodox Jewish Congregations of America, which issues a Ⓤ symbol on those products that have passed its scrutiny. Another acceptable symbol commonly seen on kosher products is the Ⓚ endorsement issued by a recognized rabbinical authority.

Many nonkosher caterers who may want to offer their facilities to kosher clients to increase revenues do not feel able to meet the rigid requirements of kosher dietary laws. Such caterers often affiliate themselves with a reliable kosher caterer, in essence forming a partnership. Both caterers benefit, especially if the nonkosher facilities are attractive. The nonkosher caterer is able to offer strictly kosher affairs under the supervision of a responsible kosher caterer, and each caterer can refer business to the other. The kosher caterer benefits not only from the additional business referred to him but from the ability to offer his clientele an attractive off-premise facility not previously available.

Each caterer must make certain that the reputation of the other is trustworthy and that the two of them are compatible if customer satisfaction and mutual profit are to ensue. In this type of partnership, both parties must enter into a prior agreement on the extent to which each will share in the services provided to the client and the costs of food, beverages, and other provisions. Arrangements will differ according to the nature of the partnership, but the following breakdown of responsibilities may be given as an example.

Responsibilities of the Kosher Caterer

1. To supply and pay for all the required food and soft beverages: hors d'oeuvres, buffet spreads, dinner courses, cakes, challah, rolls, soda,

coffee, tea, nondairy creamers, Viennese tables, and so forth. To insure all food and beverage are kosher and have been handled properly.

2. To supply and pay for the labor involved in the preparation and service of the food, that is, for cooks, waiters, dishwashers, drivers, and so forth. At times, the on-premise caterer may supply the help listed here for reasons of convenience or accessibility, but the kosher caterer will remain responsible for paying them.

3. To supply and pay for all equipment needed to make the affair kosher, for example, dishes, pots, pans, work tools, and silverware. These items must be cleaned under kashruth supervision. For convenience, this is generally done on the premises of the kosher operation because dishwashers on non-kosher premises must be properly sanitized before it can be used for kosher use.

4. To supply and pay for outside services needed to complete the affair, for example, flowers, menus, matches, yamulkas, and the like.

Responsibilities of the Nonkosher Caterer

1. To supply and pay for all costs relating to the use, cleaning, and maintenance of the whole premises, that is, the kitchen, dining areas, reception areas, and so on.

2. To supply and pay for all equipment needed to set up the function, such as tables, chairs, platforms, podiums, lecterns, and microphones.

3. To supply and pay for the following labor and outside services: bartenders, checking and lounge attendants, parking attendants, musicians, and the like.

4. To supply and pay for all the liquor and kosher wines needed. Since liquor laws may stipulate that no liquor be brought in from the outside, the on-premise caterer must supply all liquor.

Since more time and expenses are involved, some on-premise caterers charge an additional fee for kosher affairs, say, $5.00 to $10.00 per person. This charge is retained by the on-premise caterer. The kosher clientele is made aware of this extra charge when the estimate is given. Some kosher caterers also charge an additional fee, for example, $100.00 for the services rendered by the mashgiach.

Most kosher caterers partially prepare or cook most of their menu items at their own commissaries, truck them to the nonkosher premises with all necessary equipment, unload, and finish off the preparation and cooking at the site of the affair. Before beginning this last step, however, the kosher caterer must undertake a thorough cleansing of the nonkosher premises to make certain that they are acceptable for use. This job includes a thorough scrubbing with hot water, detergent, steel wool, and brushes of the interiors and exteriors of the relevant stoves, including the racks, which must be scorched with intense heat, usually with a propane blow torch. To prevent the use of nonkosher products or equipment, every step should be taken to keep them out of reach. For example, cabinets, refrigerators, and freezers should be kept locked; pots, dishes, silverware, etc., should be stored away. All working surfaces where nonkosher foods were previously prepared must be covered with paper, plastic, aluminum foil, linen, or the like so that the kosher food does not come in contact with nonkosher tables or work areas. The mashgiach may require that grates be placed on the cooking surfaces so that kosher pots do not come in contact with the nonkosher surfaces of stoves and burners. After all areas have been approved by the mashgiach, the final stages of the cooking may take place under his direct supervision. He should always be available to any patron who has any question or problem about the food being served or its supervision. Special care must always be exercised when both kosher and nonkosher kitchens are involved. A separation or partition should be erected to make certain that they are maintained as two distinct work areas. For equipment, materials, or food from one kitchen to come in contact or mix with that of the other is to violate the kashruth and creates serious problems for all concerned. Should a difficulty arise for any reason, a rabbinical authority should always be consulted immediately.

In order to schedule affairs properly, it is advisable to obtain a Jewish religious calendar, since there are certain periods and special dates, for example, Passover, when functions should not be held. The dates should be reviewed with a rabbi and noted on the calendar so that an inquiring client can be made aware of them.

Chapter 22

Outside Services

In years past, caterers assisted clients with such services as music, photography, flowers, printing, limosine, and bridal services by referring them to outside firms without thought of compensation. Today, caterers either receive commissions for their referrals or supply these services themselves, charging separate fees or building them into their package plans. Some outside services often find it profitable to rent facilities or storefronts directly on the caterer's premises. These photography studios, floral shops, formal wear shops, etc., have the twofold advantage of a visible street location and convenient referrals from the caterer's clients. The store rental charges obtained from these facilities will often assist in offsetting the caterer's operating expenses.

Clients many times realize that caterers have continual dealings with many of these outside services and thus value their opinions and seek their advice. In certain instances, clients neither know where to find these services nor have the time to sort out or investigate them. Proprietors of outside services will seek out caterers because they realize how many valuable inquiries or potential clients a caterer receives daily for their goods and services. Since caterers have this constant and often voluminous source of lucrative business leads, they can obtain commissions from outside proprietors for referrals, for example, 10% of the selling price quoted to a customer. The outside proprietors will preset their prices beforehand to include the caterer's commission in the price quoted to the client. Some caterers with volume referrals may even require a set sum of money from an outside proprietor for the privilege of being the only service recommended by the caterer for a specific period of time. The service that has the privilege of being the sole representative of the caterer is referred to as the "house" service, for example, the house band, house photographer, or house florist. These house services aid the caterer in executing a professional and successful affair while proving to be a source of additional revenues.

Some caterers may hire more than one house service of the same type, for example, two house bands, to keep them competitive and offer better service to the client. Other caterers do not follow this practice because friction arises between the competing services and may create confusion for the customer trying to select the better service.

If for any reason an outside proprietor does not provide a client with satisfactory goods or services or sell a sufficient number of jobs, a new proprietor should be sought. Since most proprietors realize that a caterer offers them a great source of potential clients and they would be foolish to jeopardize this business relationship, this problem seldom occurs.

Because most caterers have neither the time nor the technical knowledge required to directly handle contractual arrangements for outside services, these details are generally left to be worked out between the client and the outside proprietor. This practice also releases the caterer from any legal responsibilities. Some services such as supplying favors that do not require a great deal of time or knowledge are often handled directly by the caterer.

The house service usually collects leads on a weekly basis of those clients that have booked with the caterer. The client is then contacted by phone, and the proprietor introduces himself as the official house service recommended by the caterer. If the client shows interest in the offered service, the proprietor then tries to sell his service over the phone or he may invite the client to see or hear his service or product at the caterer's operation, at the off-premise business, or, in some instances, at the client's home. The signing of a contract is generally in order, if and when an agreement on goods and services has been made between the proprietor and the client. A down payment or deposit is usually required as a binder.

At times, customers may wish to furnish their own outside services. Although this practice is not usually recommended by caterers, it is usually permitted, since caterers cannot legally force outside services on a client. On package plans where the outside service has been incorporated into the pricing formula, a fair allowance should be made to those clients who choose to use their own outside services. Caterers prefer to recommend their house services not only because it will generate a commission, but also because they know that through past experience the services will be performed professionally and in conjunction with the caterer's timing. At times, customers will select inferior, inexperienced services because of a low price. Since most attending guests will assume that the caterer has supplied or recommended these outside services, the caterer's reputation will be tarnished by any poor goods or performances. Thus, to increase selling house services it may be advisable for the caterer to offer incentives to clients if they book these services, for example, free dinners for the band or photographer.

Caterers should submit all the names of potential clients to the outside proprietor even though the client may choose to hold his function elsewhere. Sometimes even though they do not book the caterer, the client may decide to book the outside service and a commission can be made on this referral.

All outside services should supply the caterer with brochures and printed materials detailing the services performed and the prices charged. These brochures should be placed into the caterer's presentation folder or given to the client upon inquiry. If outside services require extra or overtime rates, this information should be explained to a customer prior to their function.

Music and Entertainment

Caterers realize the importance of good bands and entertainment to the success of a function, and how bad music can ruin an otherwise good affair. Caterers prefer to hire professional musicians and entertainers who can take charge of an affair and make a party lively by inviting guest participation and playing all types of requested music. Working in conjunction with the headwaiter, professional musicians know how and when to coordinate their playing time with to the serving of the various courses, speeches, and presentations. Every band should provide a leader or master of ceremonies who knows how to conduct and direct all entertainment, announcements, and procedures that may be needed or requested. Sometimes a vocalist may also be requested by a client to sing with a band. If a vocalist is hired, he/she may or may not play an instrument with the band. In either case, the vocalist is considered and charged as a member of the band. Bands should be able to play for a floor show if needed, that is, be able to read sheet music for the talent requesting it. In general, a professional band should be able to handle any entertainment situation or request that might arise during the course of a function.

Prices for music are based on the number of musicians hired and the length of their playing, which in most cases is a four-hour period per affair. The number of musicians is usually determined by the guest or caterer, unless union musicians are hired. Unions will determine the number of musicians required by the size or seating capacity of each room. Each function room is classified in a handbook issued by the musician's union listing the name of the function room and the number of musicians required for that room. In union houses, it is the responsibility of the band's owner or leader, prior to each function, to file each job with the union as to the date, name of the operation, name of room, and number of musicians required for the job. The union will periodically send a delegate, unannounced, to a catering operation to check that the proper number of musicians was hired for each room and that each job has been properly registered by the band owner or leader. Should any violation occur, the band owner or leader is reprimanded and fined for breach of the contract that had been drawn up between the owner or leader and the union. Since most musicians in union areas depend heavily on union jobs for a livelihood, they find it an advantage to join the union, pay their dues, and become card-carrying members. Whether a band is union or nonunion, it is important that clients do not skimp on their musical requirements, since small bands in large rooms usually do not produce effective results.

Music is usually sold in one of two manners: on a *regular* basis, that is, 20 minutes of playing and 10 minutes of break time, or 40 minutes per hour of music; or on a *continuous* basis, that is, 50 minutes of playing and 10 minutes of break time.

Continuous music is more expensive than regular music and is generally requested by clients who want a lively affair with plenty of music. This becomes an advantage for the caterer in that it makes the affair more entertaining at the client's expense. Regular and overtime rates for the above types of music are determined by the band owner or leader. Some bands will ask higher rates than others depending on their talent and demand. Some talented bandleaders or singers may ask for additional money if they are requested to be part of the band. Prices quoted by house bands include the commission paid to the caterer as with any other outside service. For union musicians, a minimum pay scale is set in the union contract for each musician. This scale must be adhered to by the owner or leader of the band.

The term "preheat" refers to cocktail hour music. A client may request any number of muscians to play, most commonly one, two, or three musicians, who usually play for a one-hour period prior to the scheduled function at an additional fee, for example $100.00 per musician per hour. A client may request a preheat because he desires music to be played immediately as his guests arrive for the cocktail hour. Band salesmen will recommend preheats and continuous music to not only increase sales, but to make the band more effective and entertaining for the guests, who may be considering music for their future event. Most clients will not take a preheat because they feel that music is not necessary for a cocktail hour, especially since their guests will be mingling and introducing themselves on arrival.

Musicians may also be needed to play for ceremonies or chapel arrangements. A suitable charge is made to the client, for example, $100.00 per organist, who on the average plays for approximately one-half hour.

Customers will often inquire as to what instruments will be used by the band or may insist on certain instruments, players, vocalists, or entertainers to be part of the band. Some may even request to have these conditions stipulated in the music contract to assure their presence for their function.

If name or headline entertainment is required, it would be advisable to deal with a talent agent, who usually charges 15% of the total cost of the act. This is a recommended practice because, if an act cancels for some reason, an agent will be able to furnish a replacement or substitute equal in talent and cost to the cancelled act. Agents also can book acts at better prices because they use them frequently or may book them into other nearby locations.

Bands usually charge additional fees for rehearsing or playing for acts that require sheet music. This is particularly true of union bands.

Good bands are usually booked well ahead, and it is thus important for a caterer or client to make certain to reserve them with sufficient advance notice, especially for prime dates or times. A music or entertainment contract should always be signed by the band owner or leader and the client. The contract will serve as a confirmation of the booked date and should clearly state all agreed upon stipulations, including overtime rates. Deposits are usually required by the band owner or leader with the balance due at the conclusion of the affair.

The following is an example of how music rates can be set up by the band owner or leader so the caterer can easily quote prices to a client.

Number of musicians	Number of hours	Regular music	Saturday night
1	4	$100	$125
2	4	200	250
3	4	300	375
4	4	400	500
5	4	500	625
6	4	600	750

All overtime will be computed at $30.00 per man per hour. Continuous music will be computed at $50.00 per man per function (four hours).

Feeding of the band, as well as any other outside service personnel, should be discussed between the caterer and the client before the affair, since this means additional costs for the caterer.

Florist

Nothing enhances the appearance of a room or table setting more than an arrangement of fresh flowers. Table flowers may be ordered and charged separately or, in the case of a package plan, may be included by the caterer. In either event, caterers, due to volume purchasing power, get their flowers at reduced rates and then mark up the price for a profit. Some caterers will recommend a direct visit to the florist by their clients when a request for specialized floral arrangements or personal flowers needs the expertise of a florist. This procedure gives the florist the opportunity of explaining or showing the client the floral arrangements. If the floral arrangements requested are more expensive than usual, then the client must pay for this difference. This visit also affords the florist the opportunity to sell additional floral work.

Caterers usually include a floral centerpiece per ten persons in their package plans based on the average number of guests (10) seated at a table, for example, $15.00 per centerpiece or $1.50 per person. Some caterers will make a floral adjustment on the final bill if a client has more than ten guests eated at a table. For example, if there are twelve guests seated at a table, technically the caterer owes the client for two guests, that is, $3.00 (2 X $1.50). However, if there are eight guests seated at a table, the client owes the caterer $3.00. Some caterers will not make this adjustment, but will simply state on their package plan that one center-piece will be provided per table regardless of the number of guests seated at that table. Of course, it is important to note that if a client requests reduced seating overall, that is, less than ten persons at each table, the expense to the caterer becomes higher due to the increased costs for flowers, linen, and service personnel needed to cover the extra tables. Caterers will usually charge additionally for these increased costs, al-though this situation does not occur frequently.

Most florists and caterers will permit a client to select two or three color selections for their floral arrangements to be coordinated with the color selection of their linens. For example, if blue cloths were selected, the floral selection might be dark blue, light blue, and white. White is a color commonly used to offset many color combinations. If a client should request a certain type of flower, care should be taken to make certain that the special flower requested is in season or that it does not require additional charges.

Regular centerpieces are usually placed in round, square, or oval bases and the flowers will be visible from all sides, since they are placed directly in the center of the table. Long, larger centerpieces can also be ordered to be placed on the dais and bridal or buffet tables. These centerpieces, usually rectangular, have most of the flowers placed on one side, that is, the side facing the guest, for best results. These long centerpieces are usually higher priced because of the additional size and amount of flowers needed. Some florists will supply or rent bud vases to be used with such flowers as single stem roses for cocktail or small tables. Flat table ferns should be considered by caterers for placement under-neath floral arrangements or along buffet tables to enhance the appear-ance of the floral pieces as a way to decorate a table inexpensively.

Florists offer various products to the caterer to enhance an occasion, such as floral canopies, aisle baskets and runners, floral sprays, smilax, garlands, potted plants, trees, palms, lemon leaves, and other floral aids. All these decorative aids are charged for separately. Flowers that are used for a ceremony may also be moved to the function room later for maximum use and effect.

A house florist should provide the caterer with either a sample centerpiece or photographs of their arrangements so that his work can be shown to a potential customer. A visit to the floral shop should be suggested to a client if the client wishes to see more samples of the florist's work.

Some clients may wish additional floral arrangements, such as individual corsages for each guest or a floral centerpiece placed in a five-pronged candelabra. These special requests are at an extra cost. Most caterers will provide candles for the tables upon request or include them in their package plans. Tapers or thin candles may be used in place of the more expensive table candles. Tapers may be included in the floral arrangements at no extra charge, or be added onto the bill. All candles should be color coordinated with the table linens as well as the floral arrangements. Caterers should have color samples available for customer inspection and selection. Some florists provide candles to caterers for a fee, but most caterers provide for their own needs through candle-manufacturing companies.

It is important to note that flowers that have been paid for by the client belong to them and should never be taken by the caterer or his staff after the function is completed. To avoid this embarrassment, a caterer may recommend that the host permit the master of ceremonies to raffle off or select one person at each table to be the lucky winner of the centerpiece.

Although most caterers permit their clients to use their own florist, it is not a recommended practice, since the workmanship of these florists cannot be guaranteed. Most caterers who allow outside florists on their premises will give a floral credit or allowance to a client who has booked a package plan that had already included the floral arrangements.

Photography

Photography is an important and often requested service by clients to help them remember their catered affair for years to come. Professional photographers should be reserved several months in advance of the function to assure their services, especially during peak seasons. House photographers should supply the caterer with a multitude of photographs and albums to be shown to a prospective client as well as to assist the caterer in showing and selling other outside services such as flowers, cakes, and decorations.

Most photographs for common functions such as weddings, bar mitzvahs, and anniversaries usually have their own package plan that includes a variety of pictures and albums. Prices are determined by the final number of prints a client selects, but some photographers may require a minimum order or guarantee for an affair. Portrait sittings at the photographer's studio may be included as part of the package plan. Black and white pictures for newspaper announcements is another service many photographers perform. Some studios even offer slide presentations, motion pictures, or video cassettes of the affair at higher prices. Most of the work done is usually in color, although black and white may also be selected at lower costs.

Some caterers will include photography in their package plans, but most sell it as a separate service to keep their package plan price structure low. House photographers will arrange the details either at their studios or on the caterer's premises. If volume warrants it, a photography studio may be set up at the caterer's establishment for the client's convenience.

Photographers will usually take pictures at the client's home, church, or temple, and at the catering establishment. Weather permitting, outdoor pictures are also usually taken. Photographers usually include a mix of formal and informal or candid pictures in their selection. Silhouette views, candlelit moods, soft focus, and interesting superimposed photos are often incorporated into their styling. Parents' albums are always appreciated, and custom finished, framed enlargements can be made to decorate the home.

Photographers usually take one or two months from the date of the function to finish the prints. The proofs are usually kept by the photographer, but the client is permitted to order any number of additional prints after the initial order. Caterers should find out what recourse their clients have should the house photographer produce bad results, although most house photographers make every effort to give professional results. Photographers should not be overbearing on the day of the function, but rather should plan their photographs around the function so that the celebrants can enjoy the festivities. Since the photographer generally spends many hours with his clients on the day of the function, provision for his meal should be discussed between the client and the caterer.

Limousine Service

Prices for limousines are based on the number of hours and the type and number of cars and chauffeurs needed. Limousine services usually have a minimum time requirement of between two and three hours for the use of each limousine. Most limousine services use luxury cars equipped with the newest and most modern conveniences. Clients are usually quoted hourly rates, for example $50.00 per hour per limousine. The client is usually driven from the home to the ceremony and to the reception hall if needed. Better services will provide uniformed chauffeurs. Caterers or clients should inquire whether the price quoted by the limousine service includes the gratuity for the chauffeur or whether a separate tip is expected.

A few caterers will incorporate limousine service as a selling feature into their package plans, but most sell this service separately or refer it elsewhere. One caterer whose hobby is collecting antique cars provides them as a service to any client who books a function at his operation; another promotes his operation through use of a horse and buggy; and still another provides a double-decker London bus.

Printing

There are many types of printed materials a caterer might furnish a customer directly. Samples of available printed materials should be exhibited through attractive displays and catalogues. Some of these items are menus, matchbooks, cocktail stirrers and napkins, novelty items, favors, and souvenirs. These items are purchased by the caterer and marked up to insure a profit. Most caterers do not have the time nor technical knowledge for some printed items and leave it up to the client and the printer to work out the arrangements. Items such as invitations, announcements, response cards, thank you cards, journals, programs, tickets, business correspondence, forms, etc. require a knowledge as to format, proper wording, typeface, paper quality, layout, and design needed. Most printers will require clients to come to their shops, but some will go or send representatives to the client's home if sufficient income can be made.

Caterers too need printers for their own use to supply such items as place cards and direction cards, which are furnished automatically to the client for each function. Various types of tickets and checks will also be needed such as hatcheck, parking, and raffle tickets, waiter and bartender checks, as well as the necessary correspondence, menus, advertising and promotional materials, and business forms needed for day-to-day use.

Caterers are often called upon to order menus and matchbooks that are color coordinated with the table linens and flowers. Printers supplying these items for caterers will usually give the caterer several samples of the different colors and typefaces available. The caterer will usually phone or send in the requested menu in advance. Once printed, these items are mailed back to the caterer. It is important to note that for any printed item, orders should be placed in sufficient time, often a month in advance, to insure prompt delivery.

Printed menus may vary as to the format designated by the printer, but usually carry the name, initial, or logo of the honored guests or organization on the outside cover. On the inside left-hand page, the name of the occasion along with the day and date is usually listed. On the bottom of this page, caterers usually print their own name as advertising. On the inside right-hand page, the menu and beverage arrangements are listed. If wine is to be served with the dinner, it may be listed in one of several ways: to the left of the food item it is being served with; after or below the course it is being served with; or listed separately at the bottom of the menu. Most clients may prefer to have their menus written in English or French. Those preferring English may not want to intimidate

FRONT

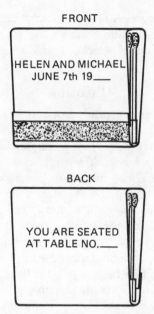

BACK

Fig. 22-1. Example of a combination matchbook/place card.

their friends or relatives with a foreign language. Caterers should always check their menus before sending and after receiving them from the printer to make certain that no errors have been made.

Some clients or caterers may request or provide a menu and matchbook for each guest, while others may request one set per couple or an alternating match and menu per guest. Caterers may also print their own matchbooks to advertise their catering services. Some may supply combination matchbook/place cards at an extra charge. See Fig. 22-1 for a sample matchbook/place card.

Specially printed items, such as stirrers, ashtrays, etched champagne toast glasses, bridal knives, printed cigar wrappers, printed menus or linen napkins, printed yamulkas, prayer books, guest books, etc., must be ordered by the caterer from either a printer or novelty shop. These special items may be included in the package plan or charged for separately.

Formal Wear

Every bride and groom will determine the type and color scheme of their attire and also that of the members of their wedding party. The choice will depend on the personal taste of the participants as well as the type of wedding. To insure that the color scheme of the male and female attendants matches, a formal wear specialist's advice is often sought. Most brides will purchase their own wedding dress, but the groom and most of the other male attendants will often rent their attire through a formal wear shop. Caterers will often refer clients to an outside formal wear shop if there is not one on the premises.

Clients will either have a semi-formal, formal, or strictly formal affair. The semi-formal affair is usually held during the day with the bride and her attendants wearing short or informal dresses, and the groom and his attendants wearing matching or color-coordinated fashions. The formal affair usually dictates that the bride wear a long dress with a short train and medium-length veil and the men be dressed in formal black or color-coordinated fashions. For the strictly formal affair, the bride will wear a long gown with a long train and veil, and the men will be dressed in formal tails or cutaway fashions. Whatever the style of the function or selection of attire, the entire wedding party should make certain that all arrangements are made in sufficient time to assure proper fittings and color selections.

Audio-Visual Equipment Rentals

Caterers will provide clients with a certain amount of basic audio-visual equipment for each function room, for example, one or two microphones, a movie screen, a podium, or lectern. When clients need additional or more sophisticated audio-visual equipment, the services of an outside audio-visual rental firm may be necessary. When such rentals are handled by the caterer, an additional fee is charged and added to the final bill. When these rentals are handled by the client, billing is done directly by the outside rental firm.

The following is a sample list of the equipment that may be rented.

16mm sound projector (manual)
16mm self-threading sound projector
16mm silent projector
Extra speakers
$1\frac{1}{2}$, 3, or zoom lens
Carousel with zoom and remote
$3\frac{1}{2} \times 4$ slide projector
Opaque projector
Overhead vuegraph projector
Tape recorder
Microphone (lapel or on stand complete)
Mixer (4 inputs)
Mixer (8 inputs)
Portable PA system
Mobile PA system
Mobile PA with tape player
Floor lectern with mike and light

Heavy duty floor lectern with mike and light
Table lectern with mike and light
8mm projector
Super 8mm projector
Dual 8mm with stop motion
Bull horn
Heavy duty bull horn
6 ft. screen
$7\frac{1}{2}$ ft. screen
5 × 7 screen
9 × 9 screen
$10\frac{1}{2}$ × 14 screen
Easel
Pad/paper
Magic marker
Blackboard
Spotlights
Projection table
Filmstrip projector with phono
Filmstrip projector with tape
Strobe light
Trumpets and tripods
Sound column and tripod

Other Outside Services

Tobacco companies—provide cigars and cigarettes needed for a catered function. The client is charged directly or the price is included in the package plan. Some companies supply printed cigar wrappers with names requested by the host.

Travel agencies—supply travel needs or arrangements for clients, for example, honeymoon trips.

Insurance agencies—supply insurance needs and coverage for newly-weds.

Jewelry stores—supply wedding rings and jewelry requirements for a bride and groom.

Furniture stores—supply the furniture needs of the apartment or home of the newlyweds.

All outside service enterprises must be professional and have impeccable reputations. They must furnish reliable and prompt results and offer quality work and products, since the reputation of the caterer is often directly linked to the performance of these outside services. To insure that outside services can furnish consistently high-quality results, the caterer must allow sufficient time between orders or referrals and delivery.

Index